The Ideal and the Community

By the Same Author

THEORIES OF AMERICANIZATION

PREFACE TO AN EDUCATIONAL PHILOSOPHY

EDUCATION FACES THE FUTURE

The Ideal
and the Community

A Philosophy of Education

by I. B. BERKSON

Professor of Education
The City College of New York

HARPER & BROTHERS PUBLISHERS NEW YORK

Library of Congress catalog card number: LC 57-13200

To *the Memory*

of

My Mother

Contents

Part Three
Profile of an Educational Policy

Part Four
Conclusion

Preface

In this book I continue an endeavor, begun some years ago, to outline an educational philosophy related to contemporary necessities and possibilities. My position denies the validity of basing education on a metaphysical principle or on an abstract social conception. A philosophy of education involves the correlation of an ethics with a politics: it must be formulated on the basis of a definite pattern of values conjoined with a specific system of social and economic institutions. In my view the pattern of values which provides the ground and the goal of the educational process is found in the historically developed culture of the Western world. The philosophy proposed reflects a high regard for the social heritage as the reservoir of our values. It is at the same time pervaded by the consciousness that we are entering a new epoch in civilization—one pregnant with opportunities for humane achievements as well as fraught with the possibility of irremediable catastrophe.

Although it shuns utopianism, the viewpoint may be called "future-centered": it is motivated by the concern that during the emerging era the age-long ideals be more consistently and more fully embodied in the institutional life than they have been in the past. The hope is that the sharp contrast between the spiritual vision and the spotted actuality of social life which has hitherto been the mark of Christendom should be diminished—should be converted from a stark contradiction to an impelling tension.

This emphasis on the social aspects of education as reflecting the needs and ideals of definite communities does not imply any depreciation of the liberal conception of education as the cultivation of the mind and the spirit of man. But it is opposed to any definition of education solely in terms of personal development—whether conceived in terms of salvation, self-transcendence, self-realization, or, as John Dewey thought of it, a process of growth with no end beyond itself. A statement of educational purposes must include the formulation of definite social aims. Education is never merely in the service of the good life in general. It must be related to a definite conception of a way of life in a particular society. Agreeing that the word "democracy" is a fitting designation for the way of social life we cherish, it still remains necessary to make clear what we mean by it, both as an ethical conception and as a body of social, political, and economic institutions related to the conditions and imperatives of the present era.

I take the philosophy of education propounded by John Dewey and by W. H. Kilpatrick as a point of departure. Much in the confrontation of the educational problem as outlined above is in consonance with their views, but my emphasis on the importance of clear definition of the ends of education indicates a basic difference of orientation. The present proposal is an attempt at a revision of the experimentalist philosophy—not a rejection, but a reconstruction which aims to incorporate its invaluable contributions to modern educational thought and practice.

The discussion is introduced by a review of the major educational ideas of Dewey and of Kilpatrick. Besides serving as a basis of criticism, this exposition, it is hoped, will clarify the experimentalist viewpoint and justify it against misinterpretations by opponents who misrepresent it, and by the uncritical devotees—its worst enemies—who reduce it to absurdity by superficial statements and extravagant applications.

The writings of Dewey as well as of his followers are properly open to some of the major criticisms that have been directed against the experimentalist educational philosophy—e.g., that it lays excessive emphasis on the role of individual experience, on the function of action in validating thought, on the principle of change in social life—to the exclusion of countervailing factors. Among the elements that weaken the experimentalist philosophy is its failure to realize the significance of formulation, its underestimation of the part that clear ideas, definite principles, firm convictions, play in the intellectual and moral life. Another is the underemphasis on history and the cultural heritage as the source of values.

This deficiency is characteristic of experimentalist doctrine despite the fact that Dewey's writings contain fine passages on the debt we owe the past. The experimentalists' diffidence toward formulation creates a reluctance also to envisage definite solutions of social problems even when these would seem to be in harmony with democratic principles and with observable trends. The experimentalist philosophy is better adapted for criticism of existing conditions than for positive programs of action. It is open to the charge that it fails to induce the decisiveness needed in periods of crisis and more generally that it fails to offer adequate guidance in the sphere of personal life.

My deviation from the usual experimentalist position involves a change from a biological-social interpretation which emphasizes the process of personal development to an historical-cultural approach which places institutional achievements and the enduring ideals of civilization at the center of consideration. This difference in orientation will have significant effects on the educational program and on the method and content of the curriculum. However, my proposed position is not irreconcilable with the Dewey philosophy. In its emphasis on the political and economic involvements of education, my own view may be regarded as an extension—necessitated by the contemporary situation—of the experimentalist concern with the social aspects of education.

Other differences are personal. I confess to a leaning toward the notion that man possesses a sixth sense—I would call it the power of imagination rather than the power of reason—by means of which we form and apprehend ideas but little related to personal overt experience. Ideas may be initially stimulated by, or subsequently chastened by, experience—but are not necessarily derived from individual experience. Ideas have a constructive creative power; they change the quality of experience; they serve to direct conduct against the dictates of habitual experience.

Another difference concerns the significance of the inner life. The experimentalist interpets self-realization wholly or mainly in terms of active participation in the works of society. We cannot fully realize ourselves in the activities of the social life. As soon as we step into the public view we curtail our true selves—tend to conceal the best part as well as the worst part of the self. The full self needs an invitation to the soul—through loafing, through contemplation, through prayer even though this be occasional; through listening to music and the quiet enjoyment of works of art; and most of all, through continuous study and re-study of the great masterpieces of literature. To cultivate the garden of mind and spirit to the exclusion of one's obligations to one's kindred and fellowmen is rightly regarded as culpable self-indulgence. But granted that we have responsibly fulfilled our duties, it is essential to the restoration and ascent of the soul that it be led beside the still waters.

Something of the body-mind dualism of the sense of struggle between spirit and matter, characteristic of traditional philosophy and of religion, adheres to my conception of man's condition. But I do not think of the struggle as due to man's original sinfulness. Rather it is due to his superiority in being endowed with the power to see visions and conceive ideals—a power at odds with a recalcitrant nature, with that part of his own nature inevitably rooted in animal background, and with the nature of the material world in which he lives. Faith remains in the ultimate victory of the Power of Light over the forces of darkness, but any complacent belief in an inevitable evolutionary progress is a delusion.

The better world we hope for can be achieved only through devotion to a clearly conceived ideal and through the persevering effort to embody it in the institutions of society.

* * *

I am greatly indebted to Ordway Tead for his painstaking reading of the manuscript. I gained much from our exchange of thought as we discussed our agreements and disagreements. His penetrating criticisms—always friendly—led me to do considerable rewriting. He was hard on me, and I am grateful.

I. B. BERKSON

New York City
March 3, 1957

INTRODUCTION

THE NEED OF A POSITIVE EDUCATIONAL PHILOSOPHY

It was natural and inevitable that in an age of great individualism there should have been an unparalleled demand for education, and that talented educators should have arisen to fulfil it. But it was inevitable also that that generation should have come to see that, more than any other, it lacked the greatest of all educational forces; rich as it was in talents, it had not the most precious and most necessary gift, an ideal toward which to direct them.

—WERNER JAEGER on the Sophists
Paideia: The Ideals of Greek Culture

THE NEED OF A POSITIVE
EDUCATIONAL PHILOSOPHY

An outstanding change in current American educational thought is the reaction against neutralism. Underlying the contemporary conflict of educational theory is a recognition of the need of a definite philosophical basis for education, of clearly formulated aims resting on accepted or acceptable principles.

Educational theory was dominated for a considerable period by the conception that education is a continuous process of growth "with no end beyond itself." The conception found its ultimate support in the instrumentalist pragmatism of John Dewey, better known as the philosophy of experimentalism. More directly, however, the version of experimentalism which came to prevail in the field of education derived its pattern and owed its widespread acceptance to the teaching of William H. Kilpatrick. For a score of years between the two world wars, Teachers College of Columbia University became the educational mecca of America. From all parts of the United States— indeed, from all parts of the world where there were stirrings of new forces—students flocked to learn of the educational ideas of America's leading philosopher as creatively interpreted and concretely applied to the work of the school by America's celebrated teacher of education.

Sharing with experimentalism the position of leadership on the educational frontier was the "progressive school" movement with which Professor Kilpatrick became closely identified. Progressive education, of course, antedates both Dewey and Kilpatrick, although both have contributed greatly to its development. As generally understood, it traces back to the romantic naturalism of Jean Jacques Rousseau. The immediate European forerunner was Friedrich Froe-

3

4 THE IDEAL AND THE COMMUNITYTHE IDEAL AND THE COMMUNITY

bel, a mystic who united a great affection for children with a profound love of nature, seeing in all things and persons a revelation of divinity. In the United States, the initiation of progressive education may be attributed to Francis Wayland Parker. He, too, was inspired by confidence in man and in nature, by faith in the potentialities of the child and in the developmental possibilities of education. A democrat and individualist in the good old American sense he was a non-conformist, opposed to all that was fixed and finished. Progressive education still preserves the influence of trust in nature, the child-centered outlook, and the humanitarian sentiment of the earlier period. In recent years, as it absorbed the Dewey-Kilpatrick educational philosophy, progressive education has placed main emphasis on critical intelligence, on group cooperation and on concern with concrete social problems.

1

As a result of the fusion of the older forms of progressive education and the experimentalist philosophy, a conception has emerged which deprecates the formulation of objective aims which do not arise directly out of the educative process. In accordance with the experimentalist-progressivist view, every educative activity must at each moment of learning be based on the needs and interests of the learners themselves. Education is to be related as closely as possible to actual life activities; it must be "life itself," not a preparation for life. Initiative, creativity, and independent thinking are to be fostered along with a spirit of cooperation and a sense of responsibility to others. Permeating the whole view are the concepts of process and change: life is a "constantly growing, changing, developing affair." An education related to life will thus require a continuous readjustment to a changing situation. Consideration of the factor of change, it is held, is specially important today in our era of transition and crisis. In fine, the aim of education is stated in terms of a never-ending development of the personality within an ever-changing social scene.

These positive concepts involve negations. The exaltation of process and change leads to a rejection of anything that savors of "fixed ends," "*a priori* judgments," and "metaphysical absolutes." To the emphasis on independence of thought is joined a severe opposition to authoritarianism, to any "imposition from above," as the phrase goes. A major tenet in the progressive pedagogic creed is "non-indoctrination," accentuated by the admonition, "teach how to think but not what to think." The children and youth are to be stimulated to think for themselves, to inquire and to discuss, and to arrive at their own conclusions. In some versions of the conception, everyone but the teacher is to be allowed to express an opinion; he is to remain neutral. The teacher ceases to be an instructor conveying accurate knowledge or transmitting great ideas; he becomes an intellectual midwife in the alleged manner of Socrates, or at best a guide—not a guide in the sense of a leader or inspirer, but one who helps the children and youth toward self-understanding and self-realization.

There have been misinterpretations of the progressivist philosophy by both expounders and opponents—exaggerations both in statement and in putting the new ideas into effect. To what degree the introduction of the novel practices has contributed to poor learning of fundamentals is far from established. The newer educational practices are more difficult to use and undoubtedly their ill-considered introduction may have led to inferior results in some cases. However, the studies that have been made, although perhaps not decisive, point the other way—to the pedagogical superiority of the modern methods when properly applied. In any case, the wholesale attacks in recent years against progressive education as responsible for ineffective teaching in our schools, for looseness of contemporary morals, or for radical political tendencies are without warrant. Too often, such attacks reflect an ideological antagonism on the part of groups opposed to the liberal implications of modern education.

Taking the movement as a whole, wherever it has been introduced in genuine form with commonsense consideration of limiting circumstances, progressive education has been a major force in guiding our schools toward a better type of education, particularly at the elementary levels. It has done much to eliminate mechanical learning, has brought teaching procedures into greater accord with contemporary knowledge of human nature, has stimulated the desire to think seriously, has directed school work strongly to social concerns. As important as the pedagogical advance has been the influence of progressivism on the spirit of education. It has served as a primary factor in imbuing our schools with a cooperative and democratic outlook on life, leading teachers and parents, too, toward a humane,

socially-minded view of the educational process. Educators of various
shades of opinion, even some strongly opposed to the experimentalist
philosophy, have testified to the salutary effect of the fresh breeze that
has emanated from the progressive schools. They have praised the
new procedures—the activity program, the project method, and the
core curriculum—as valuable supplementary techniques of teaching.

It is not on pedagogical issues that contemporary progressivism is
properly open to challenge, but on its broader—educational, cultural,
and philosophic—implications. Recent books intended for use in
teacher education institutions seem to have gone off balance in their
interpretation of the experimentalist ideas—in exalting process and
change as paramount principles and in repudiating the formulation of
educational purposes by the adult generation. Organized subject
matter is condemned as authoritarian and undemocratic on the
ground that it represents primarily the "fixed ends" of the teacher
and not the "pupil needs."

An influential book on the democratic process in education advises
letting the children have the major share in making their own curricula; it urges the teacher to substitute "directional process goals"
for the "fixed end goals" of traditional education.[1] The primary object
of the professional education of the teacher, in Professor Hopkins'
view, should be directed toward promoting the understanding and
use of "the democratic process of cooperative action" and not toward
learning of definite subject matter in designated areas. A text in
Secondary Education to which outstanding names are attached includes a brief discussion of "Changes in Ethics and Religion."[2] The
authors make an appeal for the cultivation of self-reliance. To this
we would all agree, no doubt, but they go on to contrast self-reliance
with authority which they say "means reliance upon the judgment
and the mandates of others and as such is an unsafe and undesirable
basis for intelligent, democratic living." And further: "The forces of
social institutions, of laws made by and for older people, are turned
loose to restrain youth and to direct their every step." Somehow,
they conclude, education must find a way to liberate the powers of
youth to give them freedom for expression without "the constant
dictation . . . of "those principles which have stood the test of time."

Leaders in the experimentalist school have severely criticized the
superficial statements and loose practices of so-called progressives. In
the Kappa Delta Pi lecture published in 1938 under the title *Experi-*

ence and Education, John Dewey attempted to correct some of the misunderstandings. Much of what is objectionable in the progressive school movement is no doubt due to the distortion of valid conceptions. But this is not the whole story. In its one-sided emphasis on process and change and in its overevaluation of individual experience, the experimentalist doctrine must itself bear a large measure of responsibility. The extravagances of latter-day progressivism are the result of the widening of a fault, so to speak, in the foundation of experimentalism.

The new emphasis in American educational literature on the need for philosophy as a basis for educational policy reflects a dissatisfaction with the unqualified relativism of experimentalism which places this stress on process and avoids definition of the ends of education. The main body of American educators have never accepted the experimentalist philosophy underlying the progressive movement even when adopting its pedagogical devices. There has been, also, explicit opposition. Philosophies of education influenced by religious viewpoints have opposed the guiding attitudes of experimentalism—its diffidence toward tradition and institutional authority, its overconcern with present-day social problems as against inner development and abiding values. In allegiance to the philosophy of absolute idealism, the late Herman Harrell Horne subjected the Dewey educational ideas to persevering criticism.[3] The most effective opposition has come from the scientific-sociological school represented by Charles H. Judd and Henry C. Morrison which reflects a neo-realistic and institutional approach.[4] Until the nineteen-thirties, however, differences of viewpoint among American educators—with the notable exception of the Catholic position—did not constitute distinct philosophies of education.

In the decade of the nineteen-thirties—with the unsettlement of opinion, the rise of the New Deal social philosophy, and the upsurge of the ideologies of fascism and communism—alliances became sharper, and "radical" as well as "reactionary" trends appeared. Particularly significant was the fact that the educators from the experimentalist wing joined with those of other schools to the abandonment of philosophic neutrality, long considered the guiding idea of American educational theory. The positions differ widely, and within each point of view there are important variations in metaphysical assumptions, in social orientations, and in pedagogical applications. Three viewpoints, the essentialist, the absolutist or perennialist, and the reconstructionist—are sufficiently distinct to be considered divergent educational philosophies. A brief review of a number of representative positions will serve to illustrate the issues involved in the growing opposition to the progressivist-experimentalist educational philosophy.[5]

2

The "essentialist" represents the viewpoint of schoolmen concerned with the work of elementary and secondary education. In this conception, education is defined in terms of the transmission of the cultural heritage and the reproduction of the social type. It is conceived as having a twofold purpose: to equip the younger generation with the habits, skills, and knowledge that will enable each one to take his proper place in society; to conserve the valuable elements in the cultural heritage as means to the perpetuation and stabilization of the social order. Most essentialist formulations include a reference to further social evolution, provide for consideration of contemporary contributions to the cultural heritage, and encourage the development of critical-mindedness based on knowledge. But the major emphasis is laid on the conservationist function of education, on its responsibility for developing respect for tradition and for institutional authority. On the philosophical side, the essentialist position includes idealistic and realistic orientations. The former would emphasize literature, art, and the aspirational aspects of religion; the latter would lay the stress on the natural and social sciences, and on the mores and the accepted institutional forms of religion.

The essentialist educator recognizes the value of the new types of teaching method when used as supplementary devices. But he objects to the substitution of these informal activity procedures for the "systematic and sequential learnings" embodied in the logically organized subject matter of the traditional curriculum. He opposes making individual experience the basis of the learning process, dislikes the emphasis on creativity as against mastery, condemns diminishing the responsibility of the teacher as instructor and inspirer. On the secondary level, he blames progressive education for dropping the "exact and exacting studies" of classical languages and mathematics and for enlarging the study of contemporary affairs, particularly when the object is to promote programs for social reform. The heaviest attack is directed against the progressivist conception of discipline which, the essentialist believes, in its lack of respect for tradition and authority, intensifies a crude individualism and "enthrones a glorified hedonism." In writings published before the Second World War, William C. Bagley, an outstanding representative, pointed approvingly to the European practices—especially in Germany— where universal education based on a conception of thorough learning and strict discipline had, so he thought, ensured freedom from disorder and furthered social evolution.[6]

Essentialism is averse to the emphasis on the metaphysics of change, and to the relativistic conception of truth. But its philosophic criticism is auxiliary to its major pedagogical and social objections. A direct philosophic critique of the experimentalist-progressivist educational position comes from the side of "perennialism," to use the apt designation suggested by Professor Brameld for the absolutist point of view. In the form espoused by Robert M. Hutchins and Mortimer J. Adler, perennialism proposes to base education on a groundwork of metaphysics conceived as the "science of the highest principles and first causes."[7] It repudiates the modernistic emphasis on the natural, psychological, and sociological sciences as basic to education and looks to a reinstitution of the classics, of logic, and of mathematics as the true means of cultivating the intellect and drawing out the essential, rational, and moral components in human nature.

The perennialist asserts, in the spirit of medieval scholasticism, that education must be based on ultimate ends, on absolute, universal, and eternal truths. Hence, the perennialist maintains that the ends of education should be essentially the same for all men, always and everywhere, irrespective of cultural and individual differences. If education is rightly understood, it will be conceived in terms of the cultivation of the intellect and the development of good habits of thought and action. The contention rests on two pillars—the absoluteness and unchangeableness of truth which is the task of education to transmit, and the uniformity and constancy of human nature which is the responsibility of education to draw out. In the application of these basic principles some adaptation to particular situations may be necessary, but, essentially, education, implying as it does the transmission of truth and the drawing out of the human capacity for reason and rectitude, will be the same under all types of political, social, and economic organization.

In the writings of Jacques Maritain, we have an authentic expression of the significant elements in the medieval synthesis of classic thought and Christian feeling. Like Hutchins, he holds the perennialist view that the task of education is to shape universal man. But unlike other perennialists he does not think in terms of the "Platonist man in himself." The task is "to shape a particular child belonging to a given nation, a given social environment, a given historical age."[8] Against the limited view of man as a creature of intellect, Maritain regards him as a spiritual being, endowed with a soul as well as with a mind. Intuition and love, not logically perfect reason, are regarded as the source of knowledge and understanding. Although he sees truth as absolute, as revealed to the insight of the man of faith, he does not regard it as static. Truth is an infinite realm, revealing itself progressively in the active consciousness of man although its fullness ever transcends our powers of perception.

In his educational views, Maritain, idealistically orientated, evinces sympathy for many of the conceptions associated with progressive education in its best sense. He is concerned with the development of the young child as well as with the college student. Learning, he believes, requires both intellectual guidance on the part of the teacher and the inner propelling force that comes from the vital principle active in the one to be educated. He has good things to say about the achievement of modern education in reducing the element of "abstract and bookish individualism" and in bringing instruction close to life experience and to social concerns. Although he condemns as a major fallacy the failure to define the ends of education, he sees an important element of truth in the idea of growth as a continuous self-realization of personality.

Despite important differences of outlook, Maritain stands with Hutchins and Adler against Dewey. He praises Hutchins for his insistence on the need of a hierarchy of values and on the indispensability of "intellectual order." He condemns severely, as reducing mind to an animal level, the biologically rooted experimentalist view that thinking is an instrument of survival and satisfaction of creaturely wants. Human thought, Maritain asserts, is spiritual intuition; it begins in insight, not in a problematic situation, and ends in deeper insight, verified not by the pragmatic test of consequences but by its power to further man's aspiration to self-perfection. Pragmatism's lack of trust in intuitive truth "grasped or believed to be grasped for the sake of truth" is in Maritain's view responsible for major evils in present-day education. This has led to a concern with the methods of education instead of its ends, to a psychological worship of the learner and to a neglect of the content of instruction. He agrees with Hutchins that pragmatism is responsible for "the four modern educational cults"—skepticism, presentism, scientism, and anti-intellectualism.

The proposal of Alexander Meiklejohn in *Education Between Two Worlds* may in some respects be classed with the perennialist conceptions.[9] It includes a drastic attack on Deweyan pragmatism and a condemnation of the individualistic tendencies of modern industrial society. On the positive side, it is inspired by the belief in a common human intelligence that leads him to agree that "all human beings should have the same essential education." In his total thought, however, Meiklejohn disagrees with Hutchins and Maritain more than he agrees with them. He makes human brotherhood—not a metaphysical principle—the foundation of a universal education which is to be directed toward the major end of creating a one-world community. He denies that theological religion can serve as the basis of a universal system of values and an international world order. The Darwinian theory of evolution, Meiklejohn holds, precludes the belief that consciousness or purpose is inherent in the cosmos. The task of our era, Meiklejohn concludes, is "to create a non-theological civilization which can carry on the work of intelligence and morality."

Despite agreement with Dewey's humanism, Meiklejohn issues a sharp critique against the latter's pragmatism as ambiguous. He accuses Dewey of vacillating between a defense of the individual and an advocacy of the social and states that despite his passion for democracy he has no clear conception of it. The central weakness of Dewey's position, as Meiklejohn sees it, is its failure to assign a positive function to the state. It limits the state's service to stepping in to solve a problem *after* it has arisen. It lacks the character of a sustained and unified effort to secure equality, justice, and freedom for the whole people. Dewey's conception represents a marriage of convenience between individual interests and group pressures, not a union of sympathy arising from a sense of fellowship and deep-rooted common purpose. In final analysis, Dewey remains "committed to the chaotic individualism of a disintegrated Protestant-Capitalist culture."

Today, Meiklejohn asserts, we need to emphasize the Rousseauan doctrine of the social authority of the absolute and infallible General Will, and not the muddling through to foggy unity of incompatibles as represented by John Locke, to whom he traces Dewey's conception. Dewey's attack on dogma and fixed beliefs served a good purpose in the struggle against the gilded sham values of the Victorian plutocracy. But now that the task is to build a new world, the wholesale condemnation of absolutes stands in the way of constructive thought and action. Meiklejohn's judgment is harsh. "Democracy desperately needs the formation of a positive program of action, both national and international. And pragmatism, in the face of that emergency, does not work. It is irrelevant." To meet the crisis of our age, Meiklejohn exhorts us to teach everyone, young or old, to be citizens of the world and makers of human fellowship. To assure this, the control of education, its planning and supervision should be handed over to the world state!

3

Meiklejohn's conception points in the direction of reconstructionism, the educational position which advocates the participation of the school in the political and economic struggles of our crisis era. However, the several variations of reconstructionism are all friendly to progressive education even when they subject their application to criticisms. A seed of the reconstructionist idea is to be found in *My Pedagogic Creed*, formulated by Dewey in 1897, in which he affirmed the belief: "Education is the fundamental method of social progress and reform." Until the crisis-decade of the nineteen-thirties, this did not imply any direct participation of the school in social change; institutional modifications would result indirectly from the influence of the school on the attitudes of individuals.

A step in the new direction of using education as a means of social change is indicated in the writings of William H. Kilpatrick. In *Education and the Social Crisis* he advocated encouraging the youth, in this era of changing civilization, to envisage a defensible social program and urged the teaching profession to become conscious of the role it might play in achieving a better society.[10] The shift of emphasis is manifested in a notable chapter formulated by Dewey in collaboration with John L. Childs, which appeared during the depression years. They set forth the thesis: "Education must itself assume an increasing responsibility for participation in projecting ideas of social change and taking part in their execution in order to be educative."[11] The experimentalists continued to oppose all forms of indoctrination, depending on critical intelligence and deliberate cooperation to achieve advance. Arguing that "planning" was the only alternative to present-day insecurity and disorder, they made a sharp distinction between a "planning society" and a "planned society."

A more direct expression of the new tendency is exemplified by George S. Counts. In the *American Road to Culture* he subjected American education to criticism for its "philosophic uncertainty." Under the cover of neutrality, he argued, the conventional aims of individual success, social conformity, and mechanical efficiency remain in fact the controlling ideas of American education.[12] Progressive education, he asserted, had no direction, no defined purpose, no theory of social welfare. He defended the thesis that all education involved indoctrination; that the continuous development of society, indeed its very existence, depended on the transmission of a system of values and ideals. In *Conclusions and Recommendations* of the Commission on the Social Studies (in the formulation of which Counts played a leading role), education is described as a high form of statesmanship.[13] The obligation of educational philosophy, in this era of crisis, is to make clear that the individualistic laissez-faire economic order is no longer workable and, through providing the necessary intellectual orientation, to cooperate in bringing about the new interdependent society in the making. Although in accord with the pragmatist outlook, Professor Counts' exposition emphasizes the enduring values of American culture rather than the methodological aspects of experimentalism. He explicitly recognizes the rootage of American culture in the religious and classic heritage of Western civilization.[14]

In *Culture and Education in America* and other works, Harold Rugg has made a plea for "social reconstruction through educational reconstruction."[15] He contrasts the magnificent achievement of American technology with our lagging cultural and artistic activity. He sees in a planned education based on a study of American civilization—its inner striving as well as its external manifestation—a means of bringing together the two creative forces, the materialist drive and the ethical aspiration. There emerges the idea of a school-centered community, under the leadership of the teachers, which will keep the frontier spirit alive and insure the realization of economic abundance and artistic freedom inherent in the democratic promise and the modern technological society. Professor Rugg's emphasis on planning and design carries with it a criticism of progressivism and experimentalism, though he associates himself with both movements. He takes issue with the proponents of the child-centered school which makes "living now" the sole basis of the curriculum, without regard to desirable, predictable goals. In its exclusive reliance on experimental problem-solving, Dewey's instrumentalism neglects the contribution of imagination and intuition. The idea of continuous inquiry leaves us in the lurch in times of crisis when, in the words of Randolph Bourne, "the idealistic focusing of ends is imperative." Experimentalism, although valuable as method, does not provide "objects of allegiance." It lacks purposive force: it is an instrument without power.*

The late Boyd H. Bode, democrat and pragmatist, contributed to the advance of a moderate reconstructionist position in his challenge "growth whither?" addressed to those, not excluding Dewey and Kilpatrick, who expounded the doctrine "growth for more growth." His main attack was directed against the ambiguities of progressive education.[16] Despite their avowed concern with the social aspects of the educational process, the progressives, Bode held, were still rooted in individualistic naturalism, still looking for educational purposes in the impulses and in the desires of the pupil. To try to derive educational aims from the needs and interests of the child apart from their bearing on community life was as fruitless as attempting to find them in the realm of metaphysics. An educational policy could be

* He refers (*Culture and Education in America*, pp. 133-4) to the rift between John Dewey and Randolph Bourne at the time when the United States entered the First World War. A fuller account of this defection from the pragmatist camp is given in Morton G. White, *Social Thought in America* (Viking Press, 1952), Chap. XI, under the title "Destructive Intelligence."

developed only on the basis of a pattern of values embodied in a social order. The confusion in educational theory was a reflection of a conflict in American culture; it could be resolved only through a reshaping of beliefs. This involved, as the great prerequisite, a broadening of the meaning of democracy from a political conception to a comprehensive way of life related to contemporary social interests and needs. If progressive education was to continue to exercise leadership, it would need to direct endeavor toward working out the implications of a democratic social philosophy.

In the decade of the nineteen-forties, a group at Teachers College, Columbia University, under the leadership of R. Bruce Raup, developed a conception of the "uncoerced community of persuasion." This represented an attempt at a synthesis of the idea of planning for social welfare and the non-indoctrination thesis.[17] In accordance with this view, social planning must be guided by ideals and by definite goals; abstract, rigidly held ideologies are to be avoided. Each individual is to share in the shaping of the guiding conceptions of policy and is to assume responsibility for them. New elements in the objectives must be related to the traditions of the people. Plans must be subjected continually to the process of mutual persuasion with the purpose of achieving a consensus on immediate goals—within the framework of long-range objectives. In A Conception of Authority, Kenneth D. Benne, one of the group, expounded the conception further. He assigns to the teacher the function of developing the ideas, the habits of thought, the methods of discussion that would lead in controversial issues to a progressive widening of the area of agreement in the community.[18] More recently another member of the group, William O. Stanley, has emphasized the importance of cooperation between educators and organized interests of the community in winning consent for the social program. Agreeing that education should have a measure of autonomy in the promotion of political objectives, he maintains that such autonomy must be within the framework of purposes approved by the public.[19]

Professor Theodore Brameld has adopted the concept "reconstructionism" for his own position.[20] He has attempted to integrate organismic psychology with the dynamic goal of a new social order. Elements of perennialism, essentialism, and progressivism enter into his synthesis. The idea of "commitment to future-centered goals" is the central theme. Professor Brameld does not hesitate to use the term "blue-print"; nor does he recoil from the concept of a "planned society." His thesis is that, if public education is to fulfill the needs of a developing democracy in this unstable era of vast and violent social change, it must become united with political forces in controlling the giant enterprises that have been created by the new technology. Though he repudiates indoctrination, he accepts "defensible partiality"—that is, taking a stand on controversial issues when commitment to policy arises from a discussion of alternatives and the conclusions are exposed to the test of consequences. He makes group consensus a means of determining such tenable conclusions.

Despite the many-sided criticisms from within and without, the philosophy of neutralism remains central in progressive education. Carleton Washburne, who has had a distinguished career as a leader of the movement, reiterates the non-indoctrination thesis in his popular presentation *What is Progressive Education*.[21] He states its purpose as twofold: the fullest growth of each individual child as a person, and his development as a responsible member of democratic society. Within this broad framework, progressive education can allow for a great variety of aims and methods. "Progressive education," he maintains, "has no fixed creed, it has no unchanging body of knowledge to impart, and it has no one method that is always applied. It is alive and growing." It is guided by the progress of modern science in psychology and pedagogy and "the progress of humanity" in government and economics. It is compatible with various metaphysical systems and is not necessarily dependent on pragmatism and experimentalism. It has no commonly held position in economic or political matters. Dr. Washburne thinks the present reaction against progressive education is due to a lack of understanding on the part of the public of its true purposes, and that the advocacy of definite programs of social reform on the part of progressive educators has added to the confusion.

4

This educational controversy is obviously related to the contemporary crisis in civilization. The discussions are filled with references to economic and political problems as well as to pedagogical issues. Pervading the educational debate is the apprehensive awareness of the destiny-laden struggle to maintain the Western way of life against the new challenging totalitarian philosophies—at the present time, especially against the growing power of communism as a world fact and a world force.

The situation warrants re-evaluation of the experimentalist outlook. The Dewey philosophy, developed in the quarter of a century before the First World War, was the product of a transitional liberalism, moving away from laissez-faire and rugged individualism towards a social conception of education. It retained the impress of modernism in the struggle against clerical authoritarianism, political absolutism, and intellectual dogmatism. Its purpose was to take advantage of the new developments—the march of industrialism, the advance of science and its method, the formulation of the doctrine of evolution, the establishment of the republican form of government —to implement more fully the democratic ideal which had struck roots in the free and abundant American land. The effort of the Dewey philosophy, like the effort of liberalism generally, was to remove obstructions in the intellectual and institutional life so as to release human potentialities and facilitate unhampered progress. The classic and religious foundations of our civilization were not at that time subjected to challenge; criticism was designed to free the rational and spiritual meaning from the rigidities of traditional dogmas. Although a move in the direction of a cooperative socialized form of economy was implied, the purpose was to counteract exploitation and harsh competition; there was no thought of introducing a state-dominated collectivism.

Considered in retrospect even for this earlier period, the Dewey analysis gave a one-sided view of the educational process. It underestimated the part played by institutions in maintaining the existing democratic order and failed to give attention to the significance of formulating ideals in the movement of advance. Seen in the context of the time when it was elaborated, the Dewey philosophy represented a major contribution. But now, new problems confront us. First, there is the need to consolidate the gains of the past and to strengthen the sense of Western society's rootage in its classic and religious foundations. And second—this is the crucial task—it is imperative to formulate the major democratic purposes as a unified social philosophy, to conceive it as a definite system of thought with applications to the social situation. Education for the emerging era must be based on a positive philosophy clear enough to provide guidance on central social issues. The aggressive ideologies of our day cannot be fought with vague statements on the merit of "the democratic process"; they must be met with forceful counter-ideas. Democracy must become a cogent, compelling belief, capable of inspiring commitment and loyalty.

In the critique of the experimentalist philosophy of education to be presented, consideration has been given to the several contemporary schools of thought briefly described above. However, what is proposed has not been conceived either as a synthesis or as a middle-of-the-road solution. Although the conception advanced differs in total configuration from the experimentalist-progressivist outlook, as already indicated in the Preface, it is not a rejection of it but an effort at a constructive revision in which the historical-cultural theme inherent in the Dewey school of thought would become dominant and applied in the light of new situations and contemporary intellectual developments. Emphasis is laid, in this work, on the significance of the traditions in which modern democracy is rooted; the intention, however, is to move not backward but forward from experimentalism.

The first task is to present the major lines of thought in the Dewey-Kilpatrick educational conception which the analysis takes as a point of departure.

NOTES

1. L. Thomas Hopkins, *Interaction: The Democratic Process* (D. C. Heath and Company, 1941), pp. 3ff.

2. Thomas H. Briggs, J. Paul Leonard, Joseph Justman, *Secondary Education* (The Macmillan Company, 1950), pp. 110-111.

3. Herman Harrel Horne, *The Philosophy of Education* (Rev. ed.; The Macmillan Company, 1927), Chap. IX, with special reference to the educational philosophy of John Dewey.

4. Henry C. Morrison, *The Curriculum of the Common School.* (The University of Chicago Press, 1940). John Dale Russell and Charles H. Judd, *The American Educational System* (Houghton Mifflin and Company, 1940).

5. For a detailed study see: Theodore Brameld, *Philosophies of Education in Cultural Perspective* (The Dryden Press, 1955).

6. For a summary of Bagley's views, see my *Education Faces the Future* (Harper & Brothers, 1943), pp. 186-192.

7. Robert M. Hutchins, *The Higher Learning in America* (Yale University Press, 1936), Mortimer J. Adler, *In Defense of a Philosophy of Education*, Forty-first Yearbook (National Society for the Study of Education, 1942), Part I, pp. 197-249.

8. Jacques Maritain, *Education at the Crossroads* (Yale University Press, 1943).

9. Alexander Meiklejohn, *Education Between Two Worlds* (Harper & Brothers, 1942).

10. William H. Kilpatrick, *Education and the Social Crisis* (Liveright, 1932).

11. John Dewey with John L. Childs, "The Underlying Philosophy of Education," in *The Educational Frontier*, (W.H. Kilpatrick, editor) (D. Appleton-Century, 1936), pp. 287-319.

12. George S. Counts, *The American Road to Culture* (John Day, 1930).

13. Commission on the Social Studies, American Historical Association, *Conclusions and Recommendations* (Scribner's, 1934).

14. George S. Counts, *Education and American Civilization* (Bureau of Publications, Teachers College, Columbia University, 1952).

15. Harold Rugg, *Culture and Education in America* (Harcourt Brace and Company, 1931).

16. Boyd H. Bode, *Progressive Education at the Crossroads* (Newson and Company, 1938).

17. R. Bruce Raup, George Axtelle, Kenneth Benne, and B. Othanel Smith, *The Discipline of Practical Judgment in a Democratic Society*, 28th Yearbook of the National Society of College Teachers of Education, 1943. Republished as *The Improvement of Practical Intelligence* (Harper & Brothers, 1950).

18. Kenneth D. Benne, *A Conception of Authority* (Bureau of Publications, Teachers College, Columbia University, 1943).

19. William O. Stanley, *Education and Social Interpretation* (Bureau of Publications, Teachers College, Columbia University, 1953).

20. Theodore Brameld, *Ends and Means in Education: A Midcentury Appraisal* (Harper & Brothers, 1950); *Toward a Reconstructed Philosophy of Education* (The Dryden Press, 1956).

21. Carleton Washburne, *What is Progressive Education* (John Day Company, 1952).

PART ONE

THE REVISION OF EDUCATIONAL EXPERIMENTALISM

What is the matter with the philosophy? One has a sense of having come to a sudden, short stop at the end of an intellectual era. In the crisis, this philosophy of intelligent control just does not measure up to our needs. What is the root of this inadequacy that is felt so keenly by our restless minds? Van Wyck Brooks has pointed out searchingly the lack of poetic vision in our pragmatist "awakeners." Is there something in these realistic attitudes that works actually against poetic vision, against concern for the quality of life as above machinery of life?

—RANDOLPH BOURNE
The Twilight of Ideals

1

THE DEWEY-KILPATRICK
EDUCATIONAL CONCEPTION

The educational philosophy developed by John Dewey is richer and, taken in its totality, better balanced than the conception usually connected with the term "progressive education." In *Experience and Education*, Dewey subjected some progressive school practices and ideas to sharp criticism on grounds similar to those put forward by opponents; namely: that progressive education tended to foster excessive individualism, indulged in day-by-day improvisation, and often confused giving reign to spontaneous impulses with the encouragement of freedom. Some reviewers, not too well acquainted with his other writings on education, rushed to the conclusion that Dewey, after wandering for forty years in the desert of heresy, had finally returned to the traditional views on education. But, of course, Dewey was not expressing opposition to the fundamental concepts of progressive education—its emphasis on first-hand experiences, on purposeful learning, or individual freedom. He was pointing to misunderstandings—to progressive education's failure to work out a positive conception, to the mistaken assumption that the negation of the old type of education would itself lead to a better education.*

1

In its core idea the Dewey conception of the educative process stands in harmony with the central conception of progressive education: namely, that "growth" constitutes a sufficient all-embracing definition of the educational purpose. In *Democracy and Education*, Dewey's most complete statement on education in the light of his

* For an elaboration of Dewey's criticism, see Chap. 13.

philosophical position, the thesis of growth as constituting both the end and the process of education is affirmed in the following explicit and unqualified propositions:

> We have laid it down that the educative process is a continuous process of growth, having as its aim at every stage an added capacity of growth. . . . Since growth is the characteristic of life, education is all one with growing; it has no end beyond itself. . . . Since in reality there is nothing to which growth is relative save more growth, there is nothing to which education is subordinate save more education.[1]

However, the term "growth" taken from the biological field is not self-explanatory. It requires exegesis. To understand what Dewey means necessitates relating it to three other terms in the Dewey analysis: "experience," "intelligence," and "the reconstruction of experience."

A major thesis in the Dewey exposition, one that has had the greatest influence on progressive education, is that learning which leads to growth must be based on the experience of the learner. Here again is a difficulty, since the term "experience," as Dewey well recognizes, is a "weasel word," a slippery concept in philosophical discourse.[2] Essential to experience in the Dewey view is an element prominent in the common usage when one speaks of "having an experience." It signifies an event which has a beginning and a consummation and which makes an impression upon us. An experience is "an active-passive affair"; it occurs when there is a responsive interaction between an individual and his environment. It entails doing something which affects other persons and things and in turn having somethnig done to oneself. It means undergoing the consequences of one's actions either in enjoyment or in suffering. Experience involves consciousness but is not merely or primarily cognitive; it affects the whole person and is accompanied in varying degrees by physical manifestations and emotional involvements. Genuine experience is never a purely internal stream of consciousness; nor does it consist of an external happening which leaves no trace of change on the mind. An event becomes a "real experience" only when we become aware of the fact that something of import has happened to us.

Education, then, in order to be genuine, must be based on experience. But—here is a critical point often neglected—not all experience is educative. Some experiences are trivial and meaningless and others may be miseducative. For an experience to lead to educational growth two further elements must be present: an *increment of understanding* —that is, an increased perception of the interrelationships among the various activities in which we are engaged and, simultaneously, an *increment of added power* in the control of our future actions. The raw experience itself does not have positive educational value: the educational value resides, we may say, in "experience-reflected-upon-in-relation-to-future-experience." In Dewey's own words, growth signifies "a constant reorganizing or reconstructing of experience."[3] The concept "continuity" is stressed; the experience of today must lead to an ever-expanding experience which yields ever-increasing opportunities for growth in new directions.

The educational process develops, and is developed through, the factor of "intelligence," the second term which, along with "experience," is requisite for grasping the Dewey concept of growth. Reflection or thinking, as noted, takes place within a matrix of experience. It consists of tracing the meaningful connections among our activities, in realizing the consequences of what we have done, in noting the bearing of present and past occurrences on possible future experience. Action on the basis of experience so reflected upon would be intelligent action. It is the presence of the factor of intelligence that distinguishes the genuinely educative experience from other forms of learning, such as mechanical habit formation, catering to capricious natural impulses, or so-called experimental procedures of trial and error. However different from each other these methods may appear, they are alike, Dewey points out, in neglecting the crucial element of intelligence—that is, of conscious intention and deliberate control. Whatever their value, the other types of activity fail of being educative in the essential meaning of the word since they do not emphasize thought for the purpose of controlling future action or critical evaluation of the effectiveness of the means for the accomplishment of the desired end-in-view.

The concept of growth, as Dewey uses the term, thus involves three interrelated concepts: experience as the source; reconstruction of experience as the continuing aim; intelligence as the method of this continuous reconstruction. Dewey's technical definition of education is: "that reconstruction or reorganization of experience which adds to the meaning of experience, and which increases ability to direct the course of subsequent experience."[4] In a detailed analysis he contrasts this definition with other formulations of the educative process —preparation for adult life, recapitulation of the past, intellectual discipline—and especially with the contrasting Herbartian and Froebelian conceptions—the formation of the personality from without versus development from within. Each of these views, Dewey agrees, has made a significant contribution to modern educational thought; nevertheless there is an error common to all of them which vitiates their value. This defect lies in the assumption that the purposes of education may be predetermined on some basis other than the genuine needs and interests of the growing child. And to leave no doubt as to where the essential difference lies between his view of education as reconstruction of experience and "all other one-sided conceptions" he states explicitly that his own view identifies the result and the process—that education, being a form of growth, has no end beyond itself.

Dewey recognizes that his identification of the end of education with the process might be challenged as self-contradictory. His explanation of this point is not free from obscurity. But his meaning becomes clear in the light of two other principles: the importance of taking the needs and the interests of the learner into consideration, and the continuing, unending nature of the educational process. When the aim of education remains unrelated to present capacities and concerns of the learners, there is a waste of motive power; there results a tendency to resort to the reward and punishment system or to sugar-coating the educational pill—forms of external sanction of doubtful potency as incentives to learning, which may have the effect of obstructing the wholesome development of the personality. We learn by rote memorization, by mechanical drill, and by various types of persuasive and coercive methods. But such learning is ineffective in comparison with learning when there is "a real motive behind and a real outcome ahead."[5] Only when the interests and purposes of the learner are fully taken advantage of can genuine persistent effort be aroused. Furthermore, the conception that education has an immediate, developing end recognizes that experience is "an ongoing affair," with no sharp line or division between the earlier part of the experience as the source of learning and the later part as outcome. There is no terminus to education; as each end-in-view is reached, it becomes the beginning of another course of experience. The best preparation for the future is the creative use of present capacities; the future emerges insensibly out of the present, and it will, so to speak, take care of itself if the present is fruitfully cultivated.

2

The insistence on the idea of continuous growth coupled with the emphasis on the significance of the present interests of the learners may give the impression that Dewey denies the need of adult direction. He has, by opponents, been charged with advancing individualistic and hedonistic principles. This is a misinterpretation of Dewey's intention. At the turn of the century, when Dewey began to outline his educational conceptions, the child-centered view which laid emphasis on individual self-expression already had strong advocates. Dewey's endeavor was devoted to counteracting the romantic naturalism of the current one-sided concern with the child by elaborating on the social nature of the individual and on the significance of the cultural factor in educational growth. As he later pointed out, "the social phase of education is put first" in his writing.[6] In *Child and Curriculum* he noted: "It will do harm if child-study leaves in the popular mind the impression that a child of a given age has a positive equipment of purposes and interests to be cultivated just as they stand."[7] Native tendencies and present interests were to be utilized in line with social needs and cultural achievements—reconstruction of experience meant *redirection* of experience. The individual as a unique person, it is true, remains the center of concern in the Dewey educational philosophy, but his development is achieved through sharing the knowledge, the purposes, the aspirations of the community to which he belongs, by cooperation in common social tasks.

Not a line in all of Dewey's writing suggests catering to the momentary desires of any individual child. He is as much opposed to the stimulation of casual inclinations, to "making things interesting" when there is no genuine interest to begin with, as he is to inducing attention by the teacher's command or threat of punishment. True interest is developed when considered use is made of native tendencies. In *School and Society* he reviews four groups of tendencies of significance for education: *the social instinct of communication* with oral and written language as the primary means of personal and social intercourse; *the instinct of making* which first expresses itself in play and develops gradually into constructive work in which materials are shaped in accordance with some idea or purpose; *the instinct of finding things out* which is exhibited in children's constant questions and in their manipulative activities to ascertain what makes the thing tick, or in their doing things to see what happens, and which may be taken advantage of for developing habits of scientific inquiry; and finally *the artistic interest* which involves the constructive and communicative propensities as well as the impulse to self-expression and aesthetic appreciation.

The spontaneous activities of children which give vent to the natural tendencies represent potentialities for the development of knowledge, discipline, and social cooperation. The tendencies may creatively be utilized by introducing "occupations" into the school— that is, by reproducing on the child's level the typical activities of the larger, maturer community into which he is to go forth. At the Laboratory School of the University of Chicago, for instance, cooking, sewing, and carpentry were made centers of learning for both girls and boys, not for the purpose primarily of training in these skills but as means of developing social cooperation, scientific knowledge, and a broad, realistic, cultural outlook. In *Democracy and Education*, under the term "conjoint activities," Dewey makes the creative utilization of native tendencies through occupations the fundamental element in the consideration of education as social direction.

Social direction is then essential, but direction is not mainly personal or coercive. Direction would include, on the one hand, "guidance," which implies helping the individual toward an intelligent realization of his capacities and interests, and on the other hand, "control," which connotes the sense of force brought to bear to restrain impulse and propensity. Both guidance and control are usually required in education, but in the favorable situation the element of guidance would be predominant and the factor of control would be transferred into self-control. Through the use of "conjoint activities," educational direction becomes mainly impersonal; it is accomplished by the projects in which the learners are engaged, by the relation of teachers to the pupils, by the influence of the school environment as a whole. In *School and Society* Dewey pictured the ideal school as a "miniature community," a purified reflection of the typical activities of adult society, pervaded with the atmosphere of history, of science, of art, and above all permeated with the spirit of social cooperation.

The conception of education as reconstruction of experience, Dewey points out, has application also to the problem of the relation of the school to social change. Underlying Dewey's analysis is the premise that civilization is undergoing a vast transformation as a result of the advance of science, the revolution in industry, the formulation of the doctrine of evolution, and the spread of the democratic idea. These thoroughgoing changes make urgent a reconsideration of basic ideas in philosophy and in education. Societies in the past have utilized education as a means of reproducing the existing social heritage unchanged in the interest of preserving the established order. Maintenance of the existing mores of the community will always remain a valid element in the educational process. But the progressive society, Dewey holds, will use education to eliminate existing evils and to improve life for the next generation. Education thus has a double social function: on the one hand, it directs the development of children and youth leading them toward participation in the beliefs, knowledge, and aspirations of the community, and, on the other hand, it serves as a constructive agency for improving society.

Recognizing that "the better society" remains a vague and largely meaningless phrase until the nature of the good society is defined, Dewey affirms the democratic conception as basic. However, he defines democracy only in broad terms. Its essence, he agrees, is individual freedom—but not such freedom as connotes primarily an absence of social restraints. The heart of democratic freedom is the ability and the disposition to use the "method of intelligence" as a means of self-direction and as an instrument of social advance. Freedom, in this sense, is promoted by two other features of the democratic society: the extent to which the interests of the group are shared by all its members, and the richness of contacts among the various groups that compose the society.

As an example of undemocratic forces in our civilization, he singles out class divisions. Separation of the people into privileged and underprivileged groups prevents the free interplay of interests and the exchange of experience, thus discouraging diversity, the great stimulant of progressive thought and creative life. The culture of the upper as well as the lower class suffers from the social cleavage: manners become fastidious rather than humane, art becomes artificial, given to display, and culture generally becomes over-refined and sterile. Class lines, moreover, operate to maintain a static society and to obstruct continuous readjustment to changing conditions necessary for social progress. "A society which makes provision for participation in the good of all its members on equal terms and which secures flexible readjustments of its institutions through interaction of different forms of associative life is in so far democratic."[8] Such a society, he concludes, must promote a type of education which would induce in each individual a personal interest in social problems and would develop a mental disposition to secure social changes without introducing social disorder.

3

The educational theory elaborated by Dewey is interrelated with his general philosophic position. That education and philosophy should be intimately connected is a view which Dewey shares with representatives of other schools of thought, but his conception of the relationship differs from the usual position. Those who urge making philosophy basic to education generally imply that we must first accept a conception of the nature of reality—that is, postulate a metaphysics—and then deductively derive a system of educational principles consistent with it. Dewey conceives of the relationship as one of reciprocal interaction between the two fields—educational theory influencing philosophy as much as philosophy affects educational theory. Indeed, he regards educational theory as prior and primary.

European philosophy—as distinct from the earlier metaphysical speculations of the Greeks—Dewey suggests, had its origin in Athens under the pressure of educational problems in an era of intellectual and social change. The Sophists, the first body of professional educators in Europe, were led in their concern with the problem of training the youth to consider fundamental philosophic questions, e.g., the relation of the individual to the state, of traditional opinion to true knowledge, of man and his laws to the character of nature. In the course of generations, however, the discussion of the philosophic questions was divorced from the original connection with the problem of what a good education should be and came to constitute the abstract subject matter of an independent branch of thought. Dewey believes that philosophy would be revitalized if its ancient connection were re-established. "Philosophy of education," Dewey asserts, "is only an explicit formulation of the problems of the formation of right mental and moral habitudes in respect to the difficulties of contemporary social life. The most penetrating definition of philosophy which can be given is, then, that it is the theory of education in its most general phases."[9]

The functional emphasis in this definition immediately suggests "pragmatism," the term by which the Deweyan philosophy is generally designated. Dewey himself, however, has preferred not to use this misunderstood word which has been distorted to mean "that which works is true." The special name by which Dewey's version of the pragmatist philosophy is known, namely, "instrumentalism," suggests that ideas are not photographs of a reality existing apart from man but constitute tools of thought by which we can better understand, and more satisfactorily change, the universe in which we live.

The term "experimentalism," which has in recent years been generally accepted as conveying the essential signification of Dewey's philosophic position, implies that any formulation of truth or value must meet the test of experience before it may be considered valid. Truth is not given to us once for all in perfect form by intuition or authority, and the values we cherish are not to be regarded as "absolutes," as eternal and unchanging. Knowledge and truth, values and ideals, have been worked out gradually through human experience in the course of continuous inquiry in many fields of endeavor and are subject to change by further experience and inquiry. Moreover, our heritage of intellectual and ethical culture was not developed by mental inquiry alone; it grew in the process of all aspects of living, in the ordinary affairs of men.

The term experience which is central in Dewey's philosophy as well as in his educational theory covers a wide range. At one end is the primary raw experience of everyday life pervaded by emotional accompaniments; on the other end are the sciences and philosophies, refined intellectual products. Dewey does not exalt the common sense experience as superior nor does he diminish the importance of the work of science and philosophy. But he thinks that, in the past, philosophers have concerned themselves too much with the abstract concepts of science and with the subtle distinctions of logical analysis, and thus the term experience has in philosophical literature come to have a predominantly psychological and mental connotation. At times the process of refining experience has gone so far in the attempt to make knowledge precise and pure that all the vital kernels of experience have been extracted, leaving only the husks of the verbal formulations. Applying his concept of "interaction," Dewey urges that a continuous interplay be kept alive between the two types of experience, the crude experience of ordinary uncultivated life and the purified experience of the scientist's laboratory and the philosopher's ivory tower, the one type of experience being checked by the other.

As Hans Reichenbach has noted, by emphasizing the import of ordinary experience Dewey has shifted the center of attention to the ethical as against the intellectual aspects of philosophy: "What he intends, . . . is establishing the sphere of values, of human desires and aims, on the same basis and in analogous form as the system of knowledge."[10] To Dewey, the search for truth as pure knowledge is essentially the function of science; philosophy is concerned with the inclusive field of values. Whenever it is relevant truth is all-important, but it represents only one element in value judgments. Truth enters into the judgment of values but it cannot itself create values. Moreover, in the sphere of truth philosophy "is a recipient and not a donor"; it has no private storehouse of knowledge nor a special, mysterious method of attaining it. Philosophy accepts its data from many sources—from tradition, from literature and art, from personal experience as well as from scientific inquiry. Utilizing the best available knowledge of its time, philosophy exercises the function of criticism of established institutions in the light of humane ideals, and its aim is the guidance of action. Philosophy reflects the culture of an era and, in its concern with meaning and value, resembles literature and the arts rather than science.

At the heart of the experimentalist doctrine is an opposition to the dualism between knowing and doing which has characterized both the common sense and philosophic distinction between matter and mind. Influenced by biological and evolutionary conceptions, Dewey sees the mind as an instrument of human survival and adjustment. As differentiated from the mode of adaptation of the lower animals, human adjustment, characterized as it is by mental activity, always involves changes in the environment as well as changes in the human being. Mind is thus an agency of reciprocal adaptation—of organism to environment and of environment to organism. The latter idea, the readaptation of environment to the needs of the organism, is the crux of Dewey's distinctive idea. Its effect is to displace the notion that the mind is a mere spectator in the universe. It makes the mind an active participant in the destiny of the world whose fortunes and vicissitudes it shares. "As the living, and experiencing being is an intimate participant in the activities of the world to which it belongs, then knowledge is a mode of participation, valuable in the degree that it is effective. It cannot be the idle view of an unconcerned spectator."[11]

The term "mind" thus becomes equivalent to "intelligence," which is a process, a mode of responding to problematic situations in which knowing, thinking, and acting are intertwined. The "method of intelligence" approximates the experimental method of the scientist. It is Dewey's thesis that "the method of intelligence," the mode of attack on problems which has brought marvelous scientific achievements, ought to become the method of inquiry in philosophy as well. Philosophy should not begin with the certainties of knowledge, with absolute truths, or with universal values. If we were already in possession of a completely harmonized set of truths and values, adequately embodied in the institutional life, the whole philosophic enterprise would be superfluous. Philosophy begins with the unsolved, with the problematical; it arises when traditional beliefs are challenged and when old institutions no longer meet the needs of life. As in scientific thinking, suggestions for solutions—"hypotheses"—will come to mind which at first are tried out imaginatively. This back and forth movement in the mind as solutions are tried out in imagination constitutes "reflection" in a genuine sense; it is prospective with reference to action to be taken. Genuine reflection is not the remembrance of things past but taking thought for the morrow. The test of the proposed solution can be made only in action. Judgment of the validity of the proposal—here one observes the pragmatic test —can be determined only through its applications; then we can see whether the consequences accord with the anticipation.

Experimentalism as the method of intelligence is not to be confused with the "trial and error" method of chance reaction and fumbling till a solution is found. The "trial" process in reflective thinking is a trial of hypotheses, of conjecture based on accumulated knowledge. Although Dewey deprecates following ideas as ready-made models, he places a premium on having ideas as suggestions of possible solutions. Another misunderstanding arises in assuming that experimentalism raises action to the supreme position, making it the end of all thought. In Dewey's view, activity is as much a means to the advance of thought as thinking is instrumental to better action. The absence of balance between action and thought will leave experience superficial or distorted. In *Art and Experience* Dewey remarks, "Zeal for doing, lust for action, leaves many a person, especially in the hurried and impatient environment in which we live, with experience of an almost incredible paucity, all on the surface."[12] In many places, he protests against regarding pragmatism as a reflex of American practicalism and its worship of success in life and emphasizes its continuity with the stream of European philosophic and scientific thought.

Critical intelligence must be constantly operative, inquiry must be continuous, and reconstruction of experience never-ending. The knowledge we have and the ideas we entertain are products of past experience and of early inquiries; as solutions of former problems, an element of dubiety adheres to them. There is never a guarantee that a settled conclusion will remain settled. The history of thought shows that knowledge, truth, and values are ever-changing, growing in a continuous chain of interaction between experience and thought. Moreover, knowledge, truth, and values have meaning in relation to particular occasions in life—are "relative" in the sense that they are related to definite situations, to time, to place, to special concerns. There are no absolute truths—that is, there are no propositions which are valid for all times, places, and persons or which, once determined, are no longer subject to revision. The term truth, weighted as it is with a notion of correspondence to an unchanging reality, gives a wrong connotation.

In *Logic: A Theory of Inquiry,* Dewey uses "warranted assertibility" in place of the term truth to characterize valid knowledge or belief—

to emphasize that what has been ascertained is still subject to future inquiry. The experimentalist philosophy, as Dewey conceives it, is imbued with a notion that truth must change not only because we increasingly correct for errors and constantly enrich our knowledge but because the universe in which man lives—the only universe he can know—is itself constantly undergoing change by the action of creative human intelligence. The experimentalist view is future-centered: "for we live not in a settled and finished world, but in one which is going on, and where our main task is prospective, and where retrospect . . . is of value in the solidity, security, and fertility it afforded our dealings with the future."[13]

The method of intelligence and the future-centered orientation apply to the problems of society as well as of the individual. What experimentalism aims to do is to create "a faith in intelligence as the one indispensable belief necessary to moral and social life." The world that Dewey speaks of is always a social world; the universe man lives in is a creation of culture. Philosophy itself is a cultural product and can never be isolated from the affairs of social life. Western philosophy, as he points out, had its roots in Greece in a period of great economic and social change when moral values and intellectual concepts were subjected to questioning, and it has always been most creative when the cherished traditional heritage was being challenged by new ideas.

If traced far enough, Dewey asserts, academic philosophies, which on their surface involve abstractions unrelated to everyday life, will be found to have had their origins in cultural conflicts; the subtle disputations about the nature of Being are in final analysis related to acute social controversies. The function of living philosophy is to resolve the sociocultural conflict in the light of a conception of values. At times philosophy will assume a conservationist role; it will endeavor to provide a rationalization of the old social order. But when it is true to its essential critical function it will attempt to reconstruct tradition and to rebuild society in harmony with the growing cultural ideal. Philosophy cannot avoid being concerned with politics and economics if it is not to be evasive. Philosophy cannot undertake to draw a blueprint for the remaking of society, but it can, by consideration of conditions and trends as they interplay with values, suggest the direction of reconstruction.

The major problems of European philosophy have always revolved, Dewey believes, around the continuing struggle between the advancing scientific knowledge and technical power on the one hand and the lagging institutional habits and beliefs on the other. The problem of restoring harmony between our scientific beliefs about the nature of the world in which we live and our beliefs about values and purposes is particularly critical today. The failure to achieve a unity of method for scientific and ethical knowing is responsible for the small progress in the moral sphere as compared with the immense development in the material conditions of life which have resulted from the use of the experimentalist procedures in the field of the natural sciences. The great "imbalance" in our social life, the crisis in our civilization, Dewey maintains, is ultimately due to this failure, the failure being at the core a failure in method. Hence follows the idea of "the supremacy of method"—the affirmation that "intelligent action is the sole ultimate recourse of mankind in every field whatsoever."[14]

4

The educational philosophy of Kilpatrick is not merely a simplified exposition of the views of Dewey, whose influence he acknowledges. It carries the mark of individuality and conviction and in total configuration represents a variant of the experimentalist conception. In fundamentals, nevertheless, Kilpatrick follows closely the Dewey line of thought, developing his own educational theory around the pivotal concept of "growth" with its associated concepts of "experience," "intelligence," and the "reorganization of experience"—or, always preferring the simpler Anglo-Saxon term, the "remaking" of experience. Growth signifies increase in the content and control of experience: it implies the ability to make finer intellectual and moral distinctions, to achieve higher skills and better ways of behavior, to engage in more purposeful activities, to shoulder ever greater responsibilities. "Learn" and "grow" are essentially two ways of saying the same thing, and the aim of education is "continuous growing." The process of continuously remaking experience is the means of the "remaking of life"; learning is not a preparation for life, it is life itself. "The goal for education is to continue to enrich this life-process by better thought and act, and this in turn is education again.

Education thus is in life and for life. Its goal is internal and in the process. Such a goal is the only one that fits a growing world. Continued growing is its essence and end."[15]

In this view learning is to be understood always in behavioral terms. Education must seek primarily an all-round active character needed to live the good life—or, as he prefers to say, "the life good to live." This means nurturing initiative and creativity, self-control and self-direction, through taking thought—and equally and simultaneously fostering a spirit of cooperation and a regard for others as strong as one's regard for one's self. In a democracy every person is an end-in-himself and the self-realization of each individual to the maximum of his potentialities is its goal, but self-realization of the personality requires the full development of the social self, since the human being is social by his very nature. Characteristic of the human being also is purposefulness, which implies consciousness of ends sought, and twin to purposefulness is intelligence, the consideration of probable consequences of a chosen line of action. The democratic society requires "a self-determining person, one not tied to the dictates or direction of others, one who can himself make worthwhile and rewarding choices for his own living and for the common good." Education thus considered has as its central purpose the task of helping youth to "think critically." Since change is an ineluctible factor in the life of the individual and in society, intelligence must confront continuous novelty and the need of readjustment to ever-changing situations. In our present era of unprecedented rapidity and extensiveness of development, consideration of the factor of change in ideas and institutions becomes crucial to an educational policy.

The ideas and procedures of the "old education" are diametrically opposed, Professor Kilpatrick thinks, to the needs of our developing democratic life. It conceives of learning mainly in terms of the acquisition of subject-matter-set-out-in-advance and of training in skills which will be useful in adult life. The old education neglects the primary experience of the pupil and expects him to learn from abstract statements unrelated to his own life. In its dependence on memorization, repetition, and drill, it leaves little if any room for critical analysis, for discussion, or for the expression of differences of opinion. It discourages freedom of thought as it suppresses freedom of movement. The desired behavior in the old-fashioned classroom of single seats fastened down in straight rows was attentive listening to the master up in front. The regime of set-task-sit-alone-at-your-desk makes communication between pupils a meretricious act and discourages anything in the way of cooperative behavior. A premium is set on competition for grades and gaining the favor of the teacher in the fulfillment of the assigned task. Throughout, the attitude of obedience and of uniformity is fostered; it is a system of imposition from above and of indoctrination of fixed principles.

The democratic philosophy and modern psychological science, Kilpatrick holds, unite in requiring a new regime of educational method. The school must become a place of living as well as of learning, of living for the sake of learning. Education should be based on pupil interests, purposeful activity, and sharing of experiences. His idea of the educative process has been embodied in his conception of "the project method," which is recognized as a major contribution to modern curriculum construction. As Kilpatrick has formulated it, the "project" is not primarily a technique for teaching prescribed subject matter. It constitutes a philosophy of education made concrete in a general method involving a radical change in the organization of school work. Instead of basing lessons on assigned portions of specified subject matter, he proposes that the important knowledge, ideas, and skills be organized around units involving purposeful activities, around projects each of which embodies a "whole-hearted purposeful activity proceeding in a social environment."[16]

Projects would be diverse, and might be utilized in various areas—in science, social studies, the arts, and in practical community service. To counter the usual tendency to identify the term "project" with manual or motor activity, Kilpatrick describes four major types: the creative or constructive project; the appreciation or enjoyment project; the problem or intellectual project; the drill or specific learning project. In each case there would be doing and learning elements, the doing for the sake of learning and the learning for the sake of better doing; every project would be a group affair involving the learners' working together for the fulfillment of common ends; every project would involve knowledge and values of interest to the individual learner and of concern to the community.

The project method utilizes the interest of the learner, guides action to clear goals, supplies motive power to keep the learning process going on until its purpose is achieved. It provides a many-sided learning situation: "primary learnings"—the objectives of the immediate learning situation; "associate learnings"—auxiliary learnings of scientific, social, or aesthetic import; "concomitant learnings" —methods of study, attitudes, and standards of broad significance for all learning situations. Through the use of projects, the relatedness of various aspects of knowledge and their connections with real life are made clear. Most important, in Kilpatrick's opinion, are the ethical values inherent in the concomitant learnings of the project method—its encouragement of the use of knowledge for social ends, of the spirit of cooperative inquiry, of the working together in the fulfillment of common tasks.

During the decade of the nineteen-thirties, Kilpatrick developed his ideas further along both social and psychological lines. For a time he joined those who believed that the technical changes under industrialism demanded a reconstruction of our economic system and that the teaching profession should become conscious of the part it might play in promoting desirable social changes. But he opposed the indoctrination of a definite conception of a new social order such as some of his colleagues at Teachers College were advocating. In the psychological sphere, he drew away from the specific bond psychology of E. L. Thorndike and adopted the organismic conception with its emphasis on goal-seeking, on the complete interrelation of person and environment, and on the importance of "inner acceptance." Both trends, the social and the psychological, enforced his teaching that a well-integrated personality, in this period of vast change and crisis, could be achieved only through a reconstruction of education which would give due consideration to the principles of critical intelligence, purposeful activity, and shared experience. The interrelationship between learning and living remained the keystone of his conception. In recent addresses and writings he has epitomized his view thus: "We learn what we live, we learn each item we live as we accept it, and we learn it in the degree that we accept it."[17]

5

Differences between Dewey and Kilpatrick in their delineation of the educative process are partly due to the different audiences they addressed. Professor Kilpatrick's work was with teachers and other school personnel whose concern with education was practical and whose interest in philosophy was limited. His mode of influence was oral, through lecture and discussion. His penchant for the use of homely Anglo-Saxon English and his gift for epitomizing philosophical ideas in arresting phrases made for effectiveness and clarity, but it also led to oversimplification and one-sidedness. While Dewey's early educational writings—based on addresses to teachers, parents, and educators and related to the experimental work which he guided in Chicago—are easily readable, his later writings published when he was concerned mainly with philosophical problems are difficult. To students with inadequate training they appear obscure and hard to follow as he works his way through the thicket of philosophical concepts. Kilpatrick, moreover, is the preacher of a new gospel, casting out the devil of the old education. Dewey surrounds his statements with qualifications which often militate against lucidity but preserve a better balance of ideas.

The variations are not in the direction of opposition to the Dewey concepts but of more extreme assertion of them. In the question of the relation of thought to action, Dewey himself goes far in stressing the functional character of ideas, and he allows himself to say, "action is at the heart of ideas." But this and similar statements are counterbalanced by others which stress the intermediary role of action in developing meanings and values. For Dewey, understanding of the world is as deep a human need as improving it. Kilpatrick also recognizes the importance of the interaction of thinking and doing but the final impression conveyed is that thinking has as its end doing, and that thinking which is not connected with action is culpable, even immoral. A favorite phrase, "activity leading to further activity," has become identified with his conception of growth. His biographer gives the following interpretation of his position: "Thought and thinking had for him significance only as they affect deeds and outcomes; only as they were concomitants of socially useful problem solving."[18]

Similarly, in the discussion of "change" as a central concept in educational and social thought there is a difference. While Dewey constantly admonishes against taking the past as rival to the present or as model for the future, he considers the study of the past as of great significance when its vital connection with the present is realized. He praises the study of history as a rich source for the imagination, as adding a new dimension to life. The study of history if properly conducted could yield an understanding of the part that mind has played in the advancing of civilization and provide insight into the connection of morality with social processes. Kilpatrick, no doubt, would subscribe to these views, but in total effect his teaching tends to associate the past with staticism, authoritarianism, and dogmatism. In Dewey the necessity of change is assumed but his emphasis is as much on the need of continuity in change as on the desirability of change itself. Kilpatrick, however, stressing the theme of the unprecedented changes of our era, urges that the philosophy of education "must somehow base itself on change." The theme is that we need a radical, separative change from the past to an unpredictable future.

A tinge of rebellion against institutionalized authority colors Professor Kilpatrick's writings. In *Education for a Changing Civilization*, particularly, he uses strong expressions: "Education is prostituted," he says, "and becomes a training to a pre-ordained set of habits and attitudes or an indoctrination in a prior system of thought, and the individual is denied his very personality." Imposition of standards he contends is harmful today in the face of the decline of the family, the church, and the local community life. Since external authority is no longer effective, the argument runs, we must help the youth "to find the only real authority that can command respect, the internal authority of how it works when tried." Parents must resist their inclination to fix their children's thinking and must let them work out their problems for themselves. The teacher must refrain from offering solutions; his function is to develop understanding of problems and provide guidance in the use of intelligent methods of attack. Indeed, "that teachers do not know the answers to the problems will help, not hurt, the work."[19] In Dewey we shall also find strong emphasis on individual thinking, as is indicated in the famous aphorism, "The phrase, 'thinking for one's self,' is a pleonasm. Unless one does it for one's self, it isn't thinking." This, too, may be challenged, but read in context it does not imply a diminution of the directive function of community life.

The communal nature of education is a primary assumption in Dewey's analysis. This is well illustrated in the opening chapter of

Democracy and Education, where he discusses the function of education for social survival—for the survival, that is, of definite communities and their characteristically significant cultural contributions and spiritual aspirations. Education secures social and cultural continuity by gradually inducting the young into the life of the community through communication to them of common understandings, similar emotional and intellectual attitudes, and like ways of responding to requirements. He does not underestimate the importance of the individual: "for how can there be a society really worth serving unless it is constituted of individuals of significant personal qualities." And he is conscious of the need of interchange between person and person and of the necessity of mutual interdependence. But the background of a community culture is ever present. Kilpatrick on his part recognizes the importance of cultural heritage in the formation of good character, but the focus is always on the individual personality. The personality he advocates is the socialized self, to be sure, but socialization for him means essentially the interaction of one person with another. That the individual is socialized primarily through participation in the communal and institutional life does not stand clear.

It is important to note the differences between the Dewey and the Kilpatrick versions of the experimentalist philosophy because it is the latter which has most directly influenced the formulation of the current progressivist educational concepts. The impress of Kilpatrick's teaching is visible in emphasis on pupil purposings; on activity for further activity; on the doctrinal opposition to indoctrination; in the tendency to identify authority with authoritarianism; and, not least, in exalting "process" as the all-prevailing principle of life and education. In Kilpatrick's writings these ideas are developed in a context which takes account of countervailing considerations. In the concluding chapter of his *Foundations of Method,* for instance, he warns against hasty and superficial application of the progressive pedagogical doctrines.[20] In the teaching of some followers all restraint is abandoned; organized subject matter as such is represented as authoritarian since it represents the aims of the teacher and not the needs of the pupils; the children should have a major share—not only a share—in making their own curricula. The impression is given that the problems of living or morality, of politics and economics, could be reasonably solved if the youth would be taught to make use of "the coordinated thinking of the cooperative group."

Professor Kilpatrick, of course, cannot be held responsible for the extravagance of thought and expression of his disciples, but resemblance of these pronouncements to the ideas propounded by him is too great to permit a denial of paternity even though he may take no delight in these misshapen offspring. It is, however, by no means the intention to imply that the difficulties in the progressivist position are due to overemphasis of some of its aspects by Kilpatrick or by other representatives of the experimentalist position. The major criticisms to be made in the following chapters apply to the careful formulations by John Dewey as well as to the views of his followers.*

NOTES

1. *Democracy and Education* (The Macmillan Company, 1915), pp. 60-63.
2. *Experience and Nature* (Open Court Publishing Company, 1925), p. 1.
3. *Democracy and Education*, p. 89.
4. *Ibid.*, pp. 89-90.
5. *The School and Society* (University of Chicago Press, 1915), p. 9.
6. Katherine C. Mayhew and Anna C. Edwards, *The Dewey School* (D. Appleton-Century, 1936), p. 467.
7. *The Child and the Curriculum* (University of Chicago Press, 1902), pp. 20-21.
8. *Democracy and Education*, p. 115.
9. *Ibid.*, p. 386.
10. Paul Arthur Schilpp, editor, *The Philosophy of John Dewey* (Northwestern University, 1939), p. 162.
11. *Democracy and Education*, p. 393.
12. *Art as Experience* (Minton, Balch Company, 1934), pp. 44-45.
13. *Democracy and Education*, p. 178.
14. *The Quest for Certainty* (Minton, Balch and Company, 1939), p. 252.
15. William Heard Kilpatrick, *Education for a Changing Civilization* (The Macmillan Company, 1928), p. 134.

* The exposition of the experimentalist educational philosophy presented by John L. Childs is discussed in Chap. 14.

16. *The Project Method* (Teachers College, Columbia University, 1918).

17. *Philosophy of Education* (The Macmillan Company, 1951), p. 244.

18. Samuel Tennenbaum, *William Heard Kilpatrick, Trail Blazer in Education* (Harper & Brothers, 1951), p. 174.

19. *Education for a Changing Civilization*, see pp. 132, 82, 110.

20. *Foundations of Method* (The Macmillan Company, 1925), p. 369.

2

INADEQUACIES OF
EDUCATIONAL EXPERIMENTALISM

CRITICISMS of the experimentalist position might be met in part by giving themes now recessive in the Dewey exposition a more dominant place than is usual in the prevailing interpretations. But this would not be enough. The Dewey educational philosophy even at its best needs more than a revision—it requires a reconstruction, to use one of its favorite terms.

In this reconstruction the concept of "continuous growth" as an all-sufficient definition of the aim of the educative process will be abandoned. The conception that education involves personal development is indispensable, but the validity of the biological approach with its corollary that the "life process" gives us the clue to an educational philosophy is to be denied. Moreover, the modification of the biological viewpoint by integrating it with the social approach still leaves us without an adequate basis. The bio-social concept represents an advance over the individual-centered naturalistic emphasis, but it omits an essential—the clearly conceived ethical aim. The educational philosophy to be outlined takes its departure from the cultural and spiritual achievements of man and not from his biological and natural origin. It asserts that education must be based on clear beliefs and definite commitments. A triune definition of education is necessary, a biological-social-ideal synthesis in which the last term—the formulated ideal—and not the first—the biological need—will provide the directives for educational policy.

1

We may begin by a denial of the experimentalists' assumption that philosophy of education is to be based on "the life process" in the sense of a process of continuing activity, change, and growth. This thesis is set forth by Professor Kilpatrick in the following words: "It is essential, therefore, for philosophy to make the study of the life process central if it is really concerned with the living of people, if it wishes its study of basic assumptions, of values, of worthwhile aims, of means of validating, to flower in more satisfying living."[1] The life process, the central consideration, is interpreted in biological and evolutionary terms: man is described as ever-active, like the lower animals, striving to fulfill wants. Man differs from the lower animals to the extent that he is conscious of his wants and subject to the need of choosing among them. Purposeful activity is an essential characteristic of human life, and this ultimately leads to setting up values and to the construction of philosophy. Nevertheless, desire and activity are characteristic of the human as well as of the lower organisms and, accordingly, "the successful and happy life is active life."

The dubious idea that a philosophy of education can be based on features of existence which man has in common with the lower animals will later receive consideration. First we may question the assumption that life represents a process of continuous change and activity. On ordinary observation it would appear that the life process like all existence can better be understood in terms of a cyclical rhythm—of motion and rest, of activity and recuperation, of growth and maturity. If we carry the analysis into the heart of nature, we must conclude that existence itself consists of intermittent transformations of energy into matter and of matter into energy. Process without form would be veritable chaos; all creatures exhibit vitalities within definite stable structures. Evolution in the levels below man involve changes in anatomy along with changes in behavior and species remain fixed for ages even if we cannot consider them forever unchangeable.

In human life where biological patterns of behavior are modified and supplanted by cultural forms, evolution takes place by stages. History, as Reinhold Niebuhr notes, may be conceived as a process in which inherent vitalities periodically break down established social forms and create new orders of vitalities.[2] Progress does not take place as uniformly accelerated motion; there are periods of change and eras of the consolidation of change. Advance in civilization does not take place in a single line of upward inclination; we lift ourselves from step to step, and progress, we may say, is not primarily in the movement but rather in the new position attained on the rational and spiritual plane. Shall we not value contemplation, the reflection on our activities, as much as the activities themselves and shall we not esteem the joys of the Sabbath as well as the satisfactions of the workday week? And should we not supplement the nineteenth-century poet whose lines Dewey quotes in *Experience and Education:*

> . . . all experience is an arch where thro'
> Gleams that untravelled world, whose margin fades
> For ever and for ever when I move.

by the lines of another poet of our own age who says:

> We must be still and still moving
> Into another intensity
> For a further union, a deeper communion.

The exaltation of change to the position of a first and highest principle is another metaphysical absolute as dogmatic as the opposite idea of a universe of unchanging reality. Its adoption involves a self-contradiction, for the concept of change has no meaning except in the background of stability. The value of any particular change is subject to judgment: some changes are desirable, others undesirable. Even growth is not always desirable, as in the case of cancer, monopolies, and our megalopolitan cities. An empirical view would study the actual changes taking place in the life of the individual and society in the light of some conception of the good and attempt to indicate which are to be promoted and which retarded.

In accordance with the biological life-process conception, values are regarded as arising when the individual experiences a conflict of wants and finds it necessary to choose among them. When the choice is made on the basis of "thinking through" the conflict of wants, and a principle of action decided upon, a value ensues. Values, in this sense, are no more than wants which have been critically examined and found worthy of choice. Out of such process of evaluation continuously employed the individual develops a guiding philosophy of life. Kilpatrick sums up: "We saw that out of behavior came wants; out of conflict of wants came evaluation and resulting values; out of study of these, through an aggregate consistent and defensible at the bar of reason, came what we have called philosophizing. The cumulative result of this philosophizing is one's philosophy of life, built, as we have just seen, upon the life process itself. In this way are essentially related the life process, values, and philosophy."[3]

There is in this presentation no suggestion of the need of a prior standard of judgment by which to evaluate desires. Apparently, each individual makes his judgment independently by comparison of the several separate wants which impel him, making his decisions as to which will give him the greatest degree of satisfying activity. The phrase "defensible at the bar of reason" seems to beg the questions at issue—the possible conflict between the individual's judgment and the social judgment, between judgment of the day and of life-long experience, between the ideal and the pressures of daily life. Since his values lack specific content, the experimentalist is led to confine himself to circular phrases, e.g., "a richer personality," "more promising ideals," "a better society," "a sense of direction in which to move." Their practice being better than their theory, experimentalist educators as individuals do have standards of judgment and at times specify them clearly. When stated the ideals of the experimentalists are revealed as having their source in the cultural heritage, past and present, and not in the biological life process.

In recent years this has been more explicitly voiced in some of the experimentalist writings in which philosophy of education is conceived as being a branch of social philosophy. In this view, the purposes of education are based on social experience, not on individual experience: an educational philosophy would rest on a double inquiry, on a survey and interpretation of existing social conditions and trends; on a formulation of "the deeper and more intangible aspirations, purposes and values, in our own American scene and life."[4]

2

Ambiguity permeates the experimentalist discussion of the relation of the individual to society. To be sure, the social nature of the individual is constantly referred to; a central theme of the experimentalist philosophy is the need of developing a cooperative, community-conscious, socially responsible individual. But there is something in this of the nature of a "joker," since in final analysis, by "social" the experimentalist means "individuals-in-their-relations." Kilpatrick conceives of social-mindedness as developing when one person interacts with another in the "self-other" process.[5] Inadequate consideration is given in the elaboration of the experimentalist conception to the system of institutions and the heritage of mores through which the interpersonal relationships are mediated.

Except in the intimate contacts of private life—perhaps not always then—our relations with others involves the taking on of social roles.[6] We relate ourselves to each other in the sphere of the family as husband or wife, as father or mother, as son or daughter, as brother or sister; in our vocational capacities as physician or patient, as lawyer or client, as teacher or student, as businessman, employee or colleague; in the less definitely structured societal relationships, as members of the lower, middle, or upper class; as belonging to the Protestant, Nordic, white, so-called "majority" group; as one of the many minor communities with their denominations, varied ethnic descent, and diverse national extractions. Each of these roles involves inhibitions of behavior, limitations of as well as opportunities for intercourse and communication.

In theory, the experimentalists recognize that each individual lives within a definite social *milieu*. But somehow in the end this gets lost and the discussion proceeds on the assumption that the development of the personality results from the process of interaction among individuals who possess characteristics of their own apart from their position in the social structure. In the effort to illustrate the idea that "society" is not an abstract entity but that it consists of people joined together in interlocking associations, Kilpatrick describes the case of Mr. Smith, a traveling salesman for a hardware firm in a small or middle-sized American city.[7] Consistent with his upbringing—his father having been a Methodist minister—Mr. Smith is an active member in the local church and teaches a Sunday School class for businessmen, something which keeps alive old family friendships and at the same time strengthens his position with his firm. Mr. Smith is married, owns his own home, and has three children who attend the public schools. Mrs. Smith, too, is all that she should be; she grew up in the same city and has friends and relations in and about town. Mr. Smith is an active member in the Rotary Club; Mrs. Smith belongs to several women's clubs. He plays golf and she plays bridge, while the children swim in the pool attached to the country club to which the family belongs. Through the women's clubs, Mrs. Smith plays an active part in politics; "Mr. Smith more guardedly so."

Kilpatrick's graphic thumbnail sketch is designed to show how opportunities and satisfactions of life are dependent on many associations, to stress the fact that the welfare of one individual is bound up with the welfare of many. His point is that what society can give the individual depends on the individual's support of law and order in society. "What society can give is dependent on what the aggregate of individual men like Mr. Smith can think and do." Obviously, however, as Kilpatrick's short history indicates, what the average individual may think and do will depend to no small extent on his position in the social class structure. Is "society" an aggregate of Mr. Smiths whose interests and attitudes determine law and order, or is law and order the result of the stability of institutions and the security of the mores? In Kilpatrick's analysis the solution of social problems is seen largely in terms of the elimination of individual selfishness and the development of a positive intent to serve others. Mr. Smith is admonished to think not only of his salary but also of the success and good name of his firm; while the firm is admonished to think not only of its profits but also of serving the customers well, for in the end the good of each in involved in the good of all. The very factors, however, that make for increased association of Mr. Smith with other members of his class and circle set up barriers between him and other citizens. What is his attitude toward members of other faiths? What is his relation to the people who live on the other side of the tracks? What is his position likely to be on labor issues?

The weakness of the individual-centered experimentalist analysis shows up in the discussion of economic problems. In his faith in the reasonableness of individuals, Kilpatrick is led to say that if labor and management could only learn to "confer honestly on a basis of getting at the best possible solutions of their difficulties, we would be spared many, if not most, of our industrial quarrels." But, obviously, the controversial economic issues of our day are terribly complex— not just a matter between an individual employer and his employees, or an individual enterprise and a local union. Labor problems involve intricate complexes of factors of national and international scope not subject to anybody's good will in any decisive measure. Some industries have succeeded better than others in working out peaceful modes of settling labor disputes. Better attitudes have no doubt contributed; but the main advances in employer-worker relations have been gained after much struggle and have been achieved through institutional changes brought about by labor organization and legislative action. While "social change" may redound to the general welfare in the long run, we should not blink the fact that it involves a conflict of interests that cannot often be resolved by appeal to good will and intelligence. In the best compromise some are bound to lose. In instances, changes in wage rates may endanger the survival of an industry or threaten the economic security of a whole community. Inadequate considerations of institutional arrangements has led to wishful thinking despite the appeal to "the method of intelligence."

The fact that the important relations between individuals are within definite social structures, that they are mediated by ideas, that they involve conflict as well as cooperation, is noted by the experimentalists. But the importance of a consideration of the social structure and social conceptions in the development of personality, for its fulfilment as well as for its limitation, is really not taken into account. The experimentalist has endeavored to discount "rugged individualism" by elaborating on the "social theme," but the failure to give due weight to the part played by institutions and by established ideas in the realization of the self has to no small extent neutralized the proposed antidote to individualism.

3

The individualist bias reveals itself also in the emphasis laid on personal experience as the basis of knowledge and thought. Again we find a certain inconsistency: the social nature of human knowledge is expatiated upon; still it is the experience of the individual that commands authority. Despite the assumption that scientific thinking involves cooperative inquiry and public verification, the ultimate reliance on the individual breaks through in Dewey's oft-quoted aphorism: "The phrase 'think for oneself' is a pleonasm. Unless one does it for one's self it isn't thinking." To this, in the text, is added: "Only by a pupil's own observations, reflection, framing and testing of suggestions can what he already knows be amplified and rectified."[8]

But clearly we could not get far in our thinking if we depended largely on our own observations and reflections. Dewey is nearer the truth when he points out that intelligence is not an individual possession, that the level to which the average man can rise depends upon the degree that science, art, and ideas are embodied in the existing social institutions.[9]

In the experimentalist analysis of the thinking process, the part that mastery of the organized knowledge in any field plays in effective thinking is strikingly underestimated. The primary factor in stimulating thought, it may be suggested, is not method, but a plenitude and diversity of knowledge. While scholarly erudition does not of itself necessarily make for originality of thought, the great creative thinkers, in the field of science certainly, were men exceptionally well versed in the fields related to their interest. It is a truism, though often forgotten, that all genuine advances in thought rest on the accumulated social heritage of knowledge and ideas. This is the case in science no less than in other areas. As Newton said, "If I have seen farther, it is by standing on the shoulders of giants." He could never have formulated the law of gravitation if he had not built on the work of Copernicus, Kepler, and Galileo. Einstein's imaginative genius would have failed to produce the relativity theory if there had not been a Newtonian theory to modify—and if Max Planck, Maxwell, and Lorentz had not prepared the ground. It is one thing to say that we owe no rigid allegiance to the cultural heritage either in science, art, or morals; it is quite another to suggest that each individual is able, or called upon, to check on what is accepted in any field as competent knowledge and warranted belief.

Connected with this overemphasis on the importance of personal experience is the rejection of reasoning on the basis of *a priori* assumptions as the negation of scientific method. We may, of course, deny the idea that true statements about the world can be made without reference to any experience whatsoever, and then proceeding on the assumption that the statements are self-evident, go on to build our knowledge on the predetermined conceptions without ever questioning them at all. But such a denial of the sufficiency of deductive reasoning by no means exhausts the issue. All thinking—surely all scientific thinking—as well as all purposive behavior involves assumptions, beliefs, and hypotheses which are prerequisite for carrying on the action or inquiry to its conclusion. They are *a priori* in the sense that they are prior to the enterprise in hand; and whether we designate them principles, assumptions, or hypotheses, they must be considered to be true for the period of the enterprise at least. It may be necessary, at times, to change our hypothesis in the midst of the stream of thought or action, but in such a case we would need to formulate another hypothesis to enable us to ride to a successful conclusion.

Experimentalism has gone a step ahead of empiricism which relies wholly on induction by introducing the idea of "hypothesis," that is, of a possible explanation which directs the organization of the experiment or of the observations to be noted. But this advance is negated when the hypothesis is regarded as something that can easily be disregarded, like a railroad time-table, "subject to change without notice." In any genuine scientific procedure the hypothesis is a careful—even though imaginative—construction based on the best knowledge available and on painstaking logical analysis—and it will be held to by the investigator even though apparently incompatible with the facts or some of the facts. It will be yielded only when it is no longer at all tenable, or when a different hypothesis solves the difficulties successfully. Every hypothesis relates to a definite area of investigation, and is framed within some broader system of conceptions assumed to be true. These broader systems are more enduring than any particular hypothesis. Underlying the Darwinian idea of natural selection is the general evolutionary hypothesis, and behind the latter is the theory of naturalism itself. Deductive reasoning, then, is not a method to be discarded: it enters into all contemporary statements on the nature of scientific method as an indispensable element.

The conception of experimentalism prevalent in educational circles suffers from the misunderstanding that scientific method consists of a trial and error procedure which involves some form of manipulation. Galileo, cited as a pioneer of experimental induction, is represented as having arrived at his law of falling bodies through "experimenting with actual balls." However, the story of the dropping of the two balls from the Leaning Tower of Pisa first narrated by a romantic disciple is now generally regarded by historians as without factual basis.* It finds no confirmation in the writings of Galileo himself. That two bodies of similar material but different weights would, if dropped from a height, fall to the ground at the same time had already been suggested by predecessors on the basis of reasoning which Galileo seems to have accepted. In fact, experiments of dropping bodies from elevations made by Galileo and others gave opposite conclusions—as they actually would on account of the factor of air resistance. But Galileo continued to hold the non-Aristotelian belief *despite* the fact that the experimental evidence did not confirm the new view but tended to support the traditional common sense belief that heavier bodies fell faster than lighter ones.[10] This was not because he did not value experimental evidence, but because he thought that the particular experiments made were not decisive as against the rational arguments that supported the new view.

Surprise is sometimes expressed that "the false theory" of Aristotle should have been taken for granted for two thousand years without being questioned, still less put to the test of trial. As Herbert Butterfield makes clear in the discussion of the broader question of the nature of motion: ". . . the Aristotelian teaching, precisely because it carried such an intricate dovetailing of observations and explanations—that is to say, precisely because it was part of a system which was such a colossal feat in itself—was hard for the human mind to escape from, and gained a strong hold on medieval scholastic thought."[11] The Aristotelian view could not have been refuted by "the test of actual trial" within the framework of the prevailing system of ideas. The weakness of the Aristotelian view lay in its dependence on the belief that all movement—except falling bodies— had to be initiated and sustained by an impulse from without. Galileo's great achievement in approximating the law of inertia resulted in part from his aptitude in thinking through imaginary situations which Aristotle, dominated by common sense, regarded as unthinkable—as, for instance, when Galileo considered what would happen if an object sailing away toward infinity continued rectilinear motion into empty space.

* Charles S. Peirce, the founder of pragmatism, noted many years ago: "A modern physicist on examining Galileo's works is surprised to find how little experiment had to do with the establishment of the foundation of mechanics." See *Chance, Love, and Logic,* edited by Morris R. Cohen (Harcourt, Brace and Company, 1923), p. 159.

Observation, the use of instruments, and experiment—modes of scientific inquiry not as unusual in his day as popular accounts would have us believe—unquestionably played a decisive part in Galileo's discoveries. But an essential point is lost if one fails to note the conceptual background, the thought-frame in which he placed his observations and experiments. There is agreement among students of Galileo's works that he was greatly influenced by the Platonic view of nature as representing a geometrically ordered, rational universe. His tendency and his ability "to geometrize" a problem—along with his proclivity toward envisaging ideal situations—was a factor that led to his major contributions. Students of the history of science agree with the conclusion of Morris R. Cohen "that it was the Pythagorean conception of the book of nature as written in simple mathematical terms that led Galileo to look for and ultimately to see the simple law connecting the increased velocity of a falling body with the time of the fall."[12] He was imbued with the outlook that nature represented a system which was "inexorable and immutable," governed by exact laws which could be understood only through the language of mathematics through "triangles, circles and other geometric figures." Galileo's opposition to relying on common sense observation alone was as strong as his lack of faith in pure logic. He had an unbounded admiration for those who, like the ancient Aristarchus and the modern Copernicus, dared to defy common sense and to trust to reason instead.

The achievements of Galileo, and of modern science in general, must be seen in the framework of the new intellectual climate that began to affect men's outlook in the period of the Renaissance. Basic to the changed Weltanschauung was a great interest in nature; with this was associated the belief that there was a single lawful order that applied to both earth and the heavens. This denial of the Middle Age division between the supernatural and the natural made it possible to resurrect old conceptions that had been suppressed by scholastic authority. In his evaluation of the factors that brought about the modern scientific revolution Butterfield places the highest estimate on the factor of the transformation in the prevailing intellectual outlook: "We shall find that in both celestial and terrestrial physics—which hold the strategic place in the whole movement—change is brought about not by new observations or additional evidence in the first instance, but by transpositions that were taking place in the minds of the scientists themselves."[13]

Scientific method in any period rests on a complex system of beliefs partly recognized, partly subconscious which supplies the framework of inquiry and of valid reasoning. It is in reference to such bodies of belief that intellectual problems occur, are defined, and resolved. This view should be congenial to the distinctive Dewey conception which asserts that thought takes place in a cultural context. But as in other aspects, the experimentalist emphasis on individual experience counteracts a constructive insight. The current interpretations of experimentalism in educational circles imply that the method of intelligence modeled on scientific method is opposed to any use of deductive reasoning—that effective thinking can be carried on without making presuppositions. It lays the emphasis on the concept of "hypothesis" in the sense of tentative holding of a suggestion. It encourages the suspension of judgment, expatiates on the provisional character of truth, leaves the impression that the individual "thinking for himself" plays the main part in creating valid knowledge.

Science rests on assumptions and theories; it is only in intermittent periods that foundational concepts in any field are modified or changed—even then historical continuity is discernible. The scientific attitude implies a readiness to give up old assumptions and conclusions when those are no longer tenable in the light of new factual evidence, or when a new theory offers a more comprehensive system of explanation. But scientific method does not require eternal universal doubt any more than it needs to posit eternal and universal truth. When there is doubt, the purpose of inquiry is to arrive at better conclusions than hitherto held, not to pursue inquiry for the sake of further inquiry. Moreover, the contribution that any individual can make is small in comparison to the accumulated heritage of knowledge and research.

4

The idea that experimental method is identical with scientific method must be greatly qualified even when we deal with the natural sciences. It becomes wholly inapplicable in the field of ethics and social philosophy. If the experimentalist concept of controlled inquiry were carried out with any degree of consistency, it would require revolutionary changes in economics, politics, and the general social structure several times in a generation. The experimentalist, of course, does not intend to apply the laboratory idea to life in any mechanical fashion, recognizing the need of special "social instrumentalities" for the solution of social problems. But the experimentalists have not indicated what their techniques of social study should or could be. For the most part nothing more is offered than a reiteration of the notion that experimentalism requires, in Dewey's italics, a *"willingness to reexamine and if necessary to revise current convictions, even if that course entails the effort to change by concerted effort existing institutions, and to direct existing tendencies to new ends."* This reasonable common-sense attitude hardly requires the defense, or is worth the designation, of scientific method. Moreover, Dewey prefaces this mild formulation of what is meant by "experimentalism in moral theory" by a statement that many a conservative would endorse: "In moral matters there is a presumption in favor of principles that have had a long career in the past and that have been endorsed by men of insight. . . . Such principles are no more to be disregarded than are scientific principles worked out in the past."[14]

Despite the qualifications he introduces, Dewey insists to the end on the principle of "a common logical pattern in scientific and moral knowing."[15] In a rejoinder to critics, he endeavors to meet the objections to this view in a technical and abstruse argument. He asserts that his critics misunderstand his position because they assume the traditional theory according to which knowing involves an accommodation of the self to conditions already fixed, while his own view is based on the idea that scientific knowing, as indicated in the use of experiment, involves a "qualitative transformation of antecedent conditions," a deliberate modification through operational ideas of what previously existed. This view that all knowing involves operations of transformation, reconstruction, control, and union of theory and practice manifested in experimental activities, Dewey attempts to show, is derived from a transfer of traits usually implied in moral judgments to modes of attaining valid conclusions in the natural sciences. His point is that since the experimental method is drawn from moral judgments in life situations it is, in the first instance, applicable to the sphere of ethics. To put the matter on the level of ordinary discourse, Dewey believes that scientific and moral inquiries have a common root in the need of meeting the problems that men face in life's affairs and hence are subject to a common method of attack.

This subtle analysis, assuming that it is correct, hardly helps us in the practical problems that we must confront in social life and in education. We may grant that, as seen by the physicist, all the colors of the spectrum are refractions of the common element of white light and that from the physicist's view of the matter this may have important consequences. Still, in a large part of the world's work we must deal with color in its multitudinous appearances. Even if we grant that at certain levels of generalization, Dewey's conception of thought as a qualitative reconstruction of antecedent experience has meaning for all areas of inquiry, nevertheless for the field of education, which is a practical art, the usual distinction between judgments in the field of science and in the field of morals cannot be left out of consideration. If we should go so far as to concede that there is only a difference of emphasis—to which Dewey agrees—in the practical application, this might be decisive. Moreover, to say that the fields of science and ethics are distinct, requiring in practice different modes of judgment, does not necessarily imply a "splendid isolation" of moral values, or a "rigid dualism" between scientific and moral knowing. Scientific knowledge may influence morals and morals may influence our use of science or limit our experimental procedures. On the contrary, only as we differentiate between the two fields can we recognize the possibilities and the limitations of the mutual interaction.

At the risk of belaboring the obvious we may assert that science is concerned with what is, not with what ought to be. It is properly defined as the persistent search for precise and systematic knowledge, for objective general truths about the world we live in. Science studies the facts and relations among the facts, arranges them in accordance with a scheme of order, propounds theories to explain observed phenomena and aims to predict what will happen in given conditions. It is concerned with existence, its limitations and its possibilities. The scientist must state what he finds whether the findings are pleasant or unpleasant, beneficial or harmful, immediately useful or seemingly irrelevant. Science is best pursued in a spirit of detachment. The true scientist is the one who can say with Santayana: "The truth is cruel, but it can be loved, and it makes free those who love it."

In the field of ethics, on the other hand, we are concerned with action, with principles for the direction of conduct, with what ought to be done in a given situation. In the field of science, suspension of judgment until all or sufficient facts are in is a virtue; different hypotheses may be held simultaneously and experimented with in different research projects. In the field of action, delay may sometimes be wise, sometimes fatal; in any case, to act soon becomes necessary. Every day brings a problem requiring a moral decision on the part of each one of us. In the field of science we can arrange an experimental situation, in the field of morals whatever choice we have is narrowly limited by the existing social organization. In the former the test lies in the future, in the observed consequences of the experiment; the essence of the moral difficulty lies in the fact that we cannot know the consequences, however carefully we calculate. In all moral decisions the emotional core of personality is engaged: needs, wants, aspirations struggle with each other; the issues cannot be judged wholly from the outside.

These many differences between the nature of science and the demands of ethics would be sufficient to disqualify the experimentalist method as a means of establishing the principles of conduct. But there is even a deeper difficulty. In the field of science objective evidence is possible. Theories of nature are subject to the judgment of nature. In Bacon's phrase: we "put Nature to the question." We ask nature about herself; if we know how to formulate the question we can get the truth out of her, at least an approximate truth. At times we may be able to coax her to respond by skillful questioning, at times we may need to use instruments even as Bacon said to commit violence upon her to extract her secrets—as we do in nuclear physics today. In ethics we can only refer to the opinions of other men. In science, we can have the impersonal evidence of an experimental *test*. In morals, we can have only *testimony*, the testimony of men of vision, of the poets, the saints and the philosophers, of men whose lives and whose words evoke a response in us.

It is far-fetched to ascribe the crisis in contemporary life as Dewey does to divergent methods of inquiry in the field of morals and the field of science. On the face of it the "imbalance" in our civilization is to be found in the gap between the humane ideals of Western civilization and its actual social, political, economic organization. The causes of the disparity are multiple and many-sided and can be understood only in the light of historical and sociological analysis. The age-long struggle in the world of ideas is part of it; but underlying is a bitter conflict of material interests—between family groups, classes, nations, regions, and races—a struggle for bread and for power. The study of history reveals a conflict between man's vision and the actual circumstances of his nature in a world that is given, between his divine image of himself as a rational, just, and merciful being and his existential character as a biological creature with the need of survival and mastery—even at the expense of his mate, his friend, and his neighbor if necessary. And for most men apart from the discipline of a religious or philosophic culture it has always seemed necessary.

To summarize: Experimentalism fails to provide a basis for educational theory. It is one-sided in its view of life as a process of continuous change; it is in error in making the biological process central since education is always the expression of a definite culture; its interpretation of scientific method is questionable and misapplied to social affairs. Its emphasis on the social aspects of personality is weakened by its reluctance to establish clear social aims and definite criteria of value. It thus opens itself to the charge that, in effect, it promotes egoistic individualism which as one of its major purposes, it aims to combat. As an antithesis to policies based on the bare metaphysical idea of an unchanging reality, it has value in counteracting tendencies to social staticism. But in so far as it denies the necessity of definite assumptions, clear principles of action, and well defined aims, as it tends to do in current formulations, it falls short of fulfilling the essentials of a philosophy of education.

As used in the field of educational philosophy, experimentalism turns out to be a vague term, connoting hardly more than an antagonism to dogma and uncritical traditional positions. It does not distinguish itself with sufficient clarity from positivist empiricism or from the broader concept of experience. Empiricism which draws its conclusions from observation of existing situations is a more reasonable approach than experimentalism to social investigation in so far as science can aid in suggesting specific reforms. The term experience is a broader and a richer concept: it suggests the wisdom of ideas as well as knowledge of facts. But before the concept of experience can be accepted as a basis for education, two provisos must be introduced: that the experience referred to is the experience of a community and not alone of an individual; and that the experience is evaluated with reference to its merit in promoting defined ends. The experience of a community is significant for education because it has left a deposit of valid beliefs and cherished ideals.

The experimentalist, echoing the dictum, "not philosophy but philosophizing," defines philosophy primarily as a method of continuous inquiry. But if philosophy is to be of aid in the formulation of educational policy, it must not only raise questions, it must give answers. The philosophic enterprise begins with criticism. But the task of philosophy is not done until it reinstates beliefs—either a rationalized return to old beliefs, a modification of them, or a proposal of new beliefs.

NOTES

1. William H. Kilpatrick, *Philosophy of Education* (The Macmillan Company, 1951), p. 13.

2. Reinhold Niebuhr, *The Nature and Destiny of Man*, I, *Human Nature* (Charles Scribner's Sons, 1941), Chap. II.

3. *Philosophy of Education*, p. 15.

4. John Dewey and John L. Childs, "The Underlying Philosophy of Education," in *The Educational Frontier*, edited by William H. Kilpatrick, (D. Appleton-Century, 1933), p. 294.

5. See particularly *Selfhood and Civilization* (Teachers College, Columbia University, 1941).

6. Karl Mannheim, *Freedom, Power, and Democratic Planning* (Oxford University Press, 1956), Chap. 9, and especially his discussion of George H. Mead's conception of role-taking as developed in *Mind, Self and Society*.

7. *Philosophy of Education*, pp. 82ff.

8. *Democracy and Education*, p. 353.

9. *Liberalism and Social Action* (G. P. Putnam's Sons, 1935), pp. 67-70.

10. Herbert Butterfield, *The Origins of Modern Science* (G. Bell and Sons, London, 1949), pp. 68-71.

11. *Ibid.*, p. 3.

12. Morris R. Cohen, *Reason and Nature* (Harcourt, Brace and Company, 1925), p. 77.

13. Butterfield, *op. cit.*, p. 1.

14. John Dewey and James H. Tufts, *Ethics*, (rev. ed., Henry Holt, 1932), p. 366.

15. Paul Arthur Schilpp, *The Philosophy of John Dewey* (Northwestern University, 1939), pp. 578ff.

3

BELIEF, AND THE PRAGMATISMS
OF PEIRCE AND JAMES

Emphasis on the significance of clear beliefs for the formulation of educational policy indicates a deviation from the prevalent experimentalist line. But it is not inconsistent with pragmatism as exemplified by Charles S. Peirce who originated it and by William James who popularized it. In both instances, the term "belief" plays a central part, although each is concerned with a different aspect of the concept.

1

The first published essay in which Peirce presented his conception was entitled "The Fixation of Belief." As the title suggests, he is concerned with achieving secure beliefs, not with challenging existing beliefs when these still stand firm. He attacks the Cartesian position which directs us to begin the philosophic inquiry by questioning everything. Where no doubt troubles, Peirce is content not to raise any. It is only when accepted belief is found inadequate or inconsistent with facts observed—that is, when a belief is really doubted at heart—not merely questioned for the sake of starting a philosophic argument—that inquiry is demanded and becomes urgent. The purpose of inquiry, moreover, is not further inquiry but the finding of a solution that would terminate the doubt and reestablish belief. Peirce lays down the fundamental proposition: "the settlement of opinion is the sole end of inquiry."[1]

Before presenting his own conception of how secure beliefs are to be arrived at, Peirce reviews three methods which are usually employed in the settlement of opinion. The first of these is the method of tenacity, the simple procedure of sticking to one's own opinion and refusing to give consideration to contrary views. Unless one isolates oneself completely, this method is self-defeating, since each dogmatist must clash with every other dogmatist of diverse opinion, and his confidence in his own belief will ultimately be shaken. So, it becomes necessary to fix belief in the community as a whole, and this brings us to the method of authority. This involves the creation of an institution with power to define the correct doctrines, keep them before the people, teach them to the young, and prevent contrary doctrines from being advocated or expressed. But this, too, is bound to fail, since no institution can hope to regulate opinion on every subject, and no state can completely shut out the ideas emanating from other countries.

The third method is that of the philosopher who accepts as true and "agreeable to natural reason" the consensus of views arrived at as a result of discussion. This method stands on a higher plane than the other two—the methods of tenacity and authority—and often leads to the adoption of scientifically determined conclusions. But in final analysis, it amounts to no more than affirmation of beliefs congenial to a period.

Peirce concedes that these methods have their advantages and indeed are necessary for the maintenance of social stability. But if a man has chosen the truth as his loved and reverenced bride, to follow Peirce's style of expression, then these methods will appear inadequate. "To satisfy our doubts, therefore, it is necessary that a method should be found by which our beliefs may be determined by nothing human, but by some external permanency—by something upon which our thinking has no effect."[2] He hastens to add that such security of belief cannot be obtained by private inspiration from on high as mystics imagine. It can only be achieved by a form of inquiry which leads to common agreement, by a method of investigation open to public scrutiny, which will end in conclusions concurred in by all the investigators. When a belief becomes untenable, the method of science demands proposing another belief, which is to be held as an hypothesis to be tested by an arranged experiment devised specifically for the purpose. If the consequences anticipated from applying the hypothesis and the consequences found to occur as a result of the experiment are the same, then we may call the hypothesis valid: it becomes a belief. By this method perseveringly applied we would arrive at ever more dependable beliefs, which though always in some degree fallible, would steadily approximate more closely an ideal truth existent in the universe.

In Peirce's conception, the testing of any hypothesis had to be open to observers; conclusions were to be subjected to public criticism; agreements were to be established by the consent of the community of scientists. "The opinion which is fated to be ultimately agreed upon by all who investigate is what we mean by the truth, and the object represented in this opinion is the real." This emphasis upon the public and cooperative nature of inquiry has misled some writers into thinking that Peirce believes that truth is a convention, the result of a consensus arrived at in group discussion. Indeed, he employs expressions which taken out of context support such a view, as when he speaks of his "social theory of reality" in accordance with which "reality involves the notion of community." Nevertheless, this interpretation is an error: in Peirce's view the inquiry carried on by the experimentalist method *had* to lead to a general agreement. Scientific inquiry *compelled* agreement, not as a result of the exchange of opinion, but because of the verification of the hypothesis by objective evidence.[3]

Peirce's pragmatism cannot be understood unless it is realized that he was a philosophic realist, his whole conception of scientific method being predicated upon the possibility of achieving universal truth. As the basis of his method of inquiry he asserts: "Such is the method of science. Its fundamental hypothesis, restated in more familiar language is this: There are Real things, whose characters are entirely independent of our opinions about them; those Reals affect our senses according to regular laws, and though our sensations are as different as are our relations to the objects, we can ascertain by reasoning how things really and truly are; and any man, if he have sufficient experience and he reason enough about it, will be led to the one True conclusion. The new conception here involved is that of Reality."[4]

At times, Peirce uses the term "truth" to signify this objective Reality, whereas at other times he means by it the beliefs about reality arrived at by scientific investigation. There is no genuine inconsistency between the two conceptions of truth. The scientific truth at any particular stage is not a perfect truth; on the other hand it is not a mere shadow of the truth, an appearance in the sense of an illusion. The scientific truth is an approximation of the real truth; but an approximation of the truth can only have meaning in relation to a conceived existent truth which it approximates. What we know of truth is an infinitesimal part of the whole realm of truth; and for what we know of it we cannot claim exactitude, certitude, or universality. At the same time, the knowledge we have, in so far as it has been the result of experience and experimental investigation must, at any stage, be regarded as reliable as far as it goes. The implication of his conception is twofold: on the one hand it instills a faith in historically developed beliefs as embodying validity; on the other hand, it insists on the necessity of renewed inquiry when old beliefs are challenged.

When doubt arises, then the method of resolving doubt is the method of experimental inquiry. In the field of knowledge, the rule to be inscribed on every wall of the city of philosophy is: "Do not block the way of inquiry." But the purpose of inquiry is the settlement of opinion and the attainment of belief, which Peirce defines as "the demi-cadence which closes a musical phrase in the symphony of our intellectual life."[5] As belief terminates doubt, thought relaxes and comes to rest for a time, and belief becomes a rule for action. As the belief is applied to action, it may again raise doubts; and thus belief is a starting place for thought as well as a stopping place. Thought and action while interplaying with each other are distinct and intermittent not continuous and identical. An important contrast should be noted: in the stage of inquiry the element of doubt must prevail; in the stage of action conviction is essential. "If a proposition is to be applied to action, it has to be embraced, or believed without reservation. There is no room for doubt, which can only paralyze action."[6]

2

In a second article, "How to Make Our Ideas Clear" Peirce proposes using the experimental method—which involves doing something to prove the validity of an idea—as a device not for the establishment of beliefs, but for the primary task of ascertaining the meaning of propositions. He takes his point of departure from Descartes' view that the clarity of an idea is an indication of its validity. Peirce approves of the underlying assumption that logic requires, as a first step, the clarification of ideas, but he points out that the Descartes method of establishing what ideas were clear was vague and largely subjective. Peirce then develops the essence of the pragmatic concept: that the meaning of an idea cannot be adequately determined by verbal definition alone; that in the end, the meaning of an idea can only be established through the application of the idea to action. In the last analysis, if two ideas embody different meanings, the differences must come to light in applying them to relevant situations; if, though worded differently, they have no differential effect, then the two ideas mean the same thing, or mean nothing. ". . . there is no distinction of meaning so fine as to consist of anything but a possible difference of practice." Thus "for the attainment of clearness of apprehension" he arrives at the so-called pragmatic maxim: "Consider what effects, that might conceivably have practical bearings, we conceive the object of our conception to have. Then, our conception of these effects is the whole of our conception of the object."[7]

In the course of discussion, Peirce makes statements which give the impression that thinking is primarily instrumental to action, the idea which under the influence of William James came to be widely accepted as the essence of pragmatism. In this essay, he says without qualification, ". . . the whole function of thought is to produce habits of action." In his last formulation, under the title "Pragmatism in Retrospect" he recalls the fact that his early reflections on the subject were stimulated by Bain's definition of belief, as "that upon which a man is prepared to act," a notion, Peirce remarks, of which "pragmatism is scarce more than a corollary." However, even in these instances, it is clear that Peirce was concerned not with the immediate application of thinking to particular acts, but with the influence of rational processes on general principles of action which would serve as guides in the conduct of life. His interest was in the relation of the logical to the ethical, not in the relation of thought to practical results in the popular sense.

In later years, when James' interpretation of pragmatism led to the misconception that it subordinated thought to action, Peirce asserted sharply that if pragmatism "really made Doing to be the Be-all and the End-all of life, that would be its death. For to say that we live for the mere sake of action, as action, regardless of the thought it carries out, would be to say that there is no such thing as rational purport."[8] Writing to James the day he received a copy of *The Varieties of Religious Experience,* he expresses his accord with the viewpoint of the book in that it stressed the power of ideas, and remarks: "Pragmatism is correct doctrine only in so far as it is recognized that material action is the mere husk of ideas. . . . the end of thought is action only in so far as the end of action is another thought."[9] Although it is true that Peirce believed that intellectual concepts had genuine significance for life, for him personally as scientist and logician, the import of pragmatism lay in its contribution to the clarification of the meaning of abstract terms. In saying that the experimental method was but an application of Jesus' principle, "By their fruits ye shall know them," he emphasized the word *know.*

Peirce's main interest as a philosopher lay in the natural sciences, in logic, and in mathematics. To what extent he meant to employ his pragmatic conception with its experimentalist implications to the field of ethics and religion is a difficult question to answer. Undoubtedly, he regarded inquiry in these fields as legitimate and desirable. In one of his later essays, he refers to the problem of extending and modifying our beliefs in the face of the great changes wrought by modern science. "It is above all," he writes, "the normative sciences, esthetics, ethics, and logic, that men are in dire need of having severely criticized, in their relation to the new world created by science."[10] But he adds: "The needed new criticism must know whereon it stands; namely on the beliefs which remain indubitable." He had a high regard for the primary beliefs embedded in the common experience of mankind, with reference to the existence of cosmic order, of the reality of God, and the significance of love. He seems to have thought that such concepts had a basis in human instinct, and that intuitive beliefs though general and vague, were more trustworthy in the deeper issues of life than the results of scientific research which, attempting too great accuracy and too precise definition in dealing with the broad concepts of common sense were likely to fall into error.

In discussing the religious question he says: "So, then, the question being whether I believe in the reality of God, I answer, 'Yes.' . . . where would such an idea, say as that of God, come from, if not from direct experience? As to God, open your eyes—and your heart, which is also a perceptive organ—and you see him. . . . Now the only guide to the answer to this question lies in the power of the passion of love which more or less overmasters every agnostic scientist and everybody who seriously and deeply considers the universe."[11] In his conception of the nature of evolution, he made agapism, the law of love, the central controlling force, as it interplayed with chance (tychism) and with the principle of continuity (synechism) in developing the universe to ever higher stages. Justus Buchler in his introduction to *The Philosophy of Peirce* touches a key problem in the thought of Peirce and of pragmatism generally when he raises the question "whether the experimentalism and the agapastic idealism of Peirce are congruous."[12]

In final analysis, the pragmatism of Peirce emphasizes continuity in development rather than the factor of change, the communal agreement as against the individual judgment, the importance of habit along with the recognition of spontaneity, the value of clear logical thought rather than creative intelligence.* He conceives of beliefs as dubitable and subject to criticism. This provides for progressive development, but the new is to be seen in terms of a substratum of the historically developed body of truth. Perhaps we need not go as far as Ralph Barton Perry who says "In short, for Peirce a conception had meaning only in so far as it expresses and promotes the idea of a well-ordered life." But the balance of his view leans distinctly toward appreciation of the general and the universal, which make for uniformity and stability. As Professor Perry says, "For Peirce the good lies in coherence, order, coalescence, unity; for James in the individuality, variety, and satisfaction of concrete interests."[13]

3

There are common elements in the pragmatisms of James and Peirce. Both wished to liberate thought from vague and meaningless verbalisms and to make abstract ideas effective. But taken as a whole

---

* James Feibleman points out that Peirce's concept of chance mingled as it is with the factor of love carries the seeds of its own supplanting by order, and that his theory of probability logically leads to a denial of the validity of individual judgments and to positing an unlimited community of mankind as ultimate criterion of right and truth. See *The Revival of Realism* (Chapel Hill, North Carolina: University of North Carolina Press, 1946), pp. 40-43.

the two conceptions differ greatly. It was James who gave to pragmatism the connotations with which it is now usually associated in the popular mind: that truth means successfully working belief, that it is significant only when it leads to action, that it is made by man, having no independent existence outside the human mind. As so baldly stated, these popular notions would not have been endorsed by James. Throughout his writings there are qualifying comments: any single favored belief must be in harmony with other beliefs one holds, a new truth to be satisfactory must be related to the fund of truths already achieved by mankind, the pressure of fact and the force of logic will limit our freedom in "truth-making." And not least when James speaks of truth as the better belief, he says he means, "Better either intellectually or practically." He regards pragmatism as a mediating philosophy which attempts to satisfy the "tender-minded" rationalist who goes by principles as well as the "tough-minded" empiricist who goes by facts. In a broad sense, both James and Peirce were concerned with satisfying the claims of both reason and experience.

Undeniably, however, in their total impact the two pragmatisms create divergent impressions. Part of this is due to differences of temperament, vocation, and mode of expression. Peirce, the solitary student and scientist, was mainly devoted to working out ideas. "My book," he wrote in an autobiographical note, "will have no instruction to impart to anybody. Like a mathematical treatise, it will suggest certain ideas and certain reasons for holding them true; but then if you accept them, it must be because you like my reasons, and the responsibility lies with you. Man is essentially a social animal: but to be social is one thing, to be gregarious is another: I decline to serve as a bellwether." James was the teacher *par excellence*, easily at home in the lecture hall and on the public platform. He was concerned to show that philosophy had a real meaning for conduct, to persuade that it could help man to build a good life.

Interested as he was in the direction of conduct, James made central the activist implications of Peirce's conception. This is indicated in the title of his address, "Philosophical Conceptions and Practical Results" delivered in 1898 when he introduced the term "pragmatism" to the public and inaugurated the new philosophic conception as a movement in American thought. Making full acknowledgment for the use of the term to Peirce—who had explored the conception and employed the word in discussions but refrained from using it in print—he gave it the active emphasis: "The ultimate test for us of what a truth means is the conduct it dictates or inspires." In *Pragmatism*, which carries the subtitle "Popular Lectures on Philosophy," he makes many statements which give support to the popular misconception of pragmatism: ". . . an idea is 'true' so long as to believe it is profitable to our lives. . . . What, in short, is the truth's cash-value in experiential terms? . . . Truth is *made*, just as health, wealth, and strength are made, in the course of experience. . . . *'The true,' to put it very briefly, is only the expedient in the way of our thinking, just as 'the right' is only the expedient in our way of behaving.*"[14] As noted above, there are qualifying statements, but these are so to speak "recessive"—the dominant theme is that "truths" are good beliefs which are satisfying and useful.

The difference between Peirce and James did not result mainly from the latter's use of vivid language in the effort to put the message of pragmatism across. There are genuine disparities in philosophic outlook. Peirce's view is grounded in objective realism while James' outlook is nominalistic, strongly tinctured by subjectivism and individualism. Peirce seeks general principles of explanation and the development of stable habits of action, whereas James characterizes pragmatism as looking away from first principles toward the facts and as encouraging the new and diverse.

In the former view, truth is independent of what any one thinks it is, and the chief merit of the pragmatist method is that it progressively eliminates the element of judgment; in the latter, all truth has a human ingredient, and a reality independent of human thinking is regarded as very hard to find.

In James' forceful words: "We receive, in short, the block of marble, but we carve the statue ourselves."[15] And further: "In our cognitive as well as in our active life we are creative. We *add*, both to the subject and to the predicate part of reality. The world stands really malleable, waiting to receive its final touches at our hands. Like the kingdom of heaven, it suffers human violence willingly. Man *engenders* truths upon it."[16] Peirce recognized the gulf between his own view and that propounded by James, and suggested renaming his brain child "pragmaticism," a designation he thought "ugly enough to be safe from kidnappers." It was, however, James' conception which prevailed, as Ralph Barton Perry epitomizes the situation: "Perhaps it would be correct, and just to all parties, to say that the modern movement known as pragmatism is largely the result of James' misunderstanding of Peirce."[17]

Professor Perry's epigram should not be taken too narrowly—it was not entirely "misunderstanding" on James' part. In the first place, it is undeniable that the implications of Peirce's conception are in the direction of James' insistence that to influence conduct is an essential function of ideas, although Peirce, more immediately concerned with problems in logic and science, did not choose to develop this aspect of his pragmatic proposal. James did not so much misunderstand Peirce as draw out the implications of the view with reference to the ethical and religious questions with which he was mainly concerned.

In the second place, James was by no means merely a follower of Peirce. He, James, was in his own right a creative thinker, subject to the trends of thought similar to those which had led Peirce to formulate the pragmatic conception. In any case, as both Peirce and James assert, pragmatism is a new name for some old ways of thinking. James' use of the term "truth" when he means a warranted belief, and the term "useful" when he means significant as well as practical, has caused much misunderstanding. But his insistence that philosophic conceptions ought to have meaning for life, not merely for science and logic, constitutes a wholesome redirection of the philosophic enterprise, and brings back philosophy to its basic meaning as a love of wisdom.

James' interpretation of pragmatism is looser than that made by Peirce and subject to just criticism on logical grounds, but in some aspects it represents an advance in thought not a regression. Peirce had suggested that "the rational purport of an idea lies in the future." James took this line out of Peirce's writings and wrote his own chapter. Following the trail that the founder of pragmatism had blazed, he developed the idea that truth depends not on precedents of the past, but on possibilities of action in the future. Pragmatism's central doctrine, the import of the consequences of a belief looks toward the future, the future of a world of many possibilities still in the process of becoming, a world which men can still influence by taking thought.[18]

In the *Will to Believe* James makes his major contribution. This title is unfortunate, as James later realized—"And the critics neglecting the essay, pounced on the title." That the will can create truth in the face of contradictory facts, that, by mere willing, the false can be turned into the true, or that strong wishing is sufficient to accomplish a desired goal, James along with his severest critics would certainly deny. He should, as he noted, have called his essay, "The Right to Believe." James' point was that in the great issues of life, not susceptible to decisive evidence, men have a right to hold fast to their ideals. We are, in any case, forced to believe or not to believe, and our belief is itself a factor in determining the future course of events. To discover whether our belief is a true one, it is necessary to act on the basis of our belief, and our acts are turning places in the road of life. Will harnessed to vision can change the world in which we live. We are not mechanistically controlled by the past.

In the transition from Peirce, the logician and the scientist, to James the psychologist and moralist, the experimentalist concept underwent a radical change. In the former, experimental method is a procedure designed to transform a hypothesis into a conclusion, in the latter, "experiment" implies taking a chance, trying out something new. Accordingly, the word "belief" carries in each case a different connotation: in Peirce, a belief is a habit of thought, an assertion of a principle warranted by experience, whereas in James a belief is a hope allowable in the context of accumulated knowledge and logical inference—a hope which requires human effort to make it come about. Both conceptions of belief—that warranted by inquiry and that which is warranted by faith—are valid, but it is necessary to keep the two meanings of belief clearly distinguished in our minds. Only the first is based on experience, the second being grounded in vision; and the essence of the matter is that it may be held despite ordinary experience. Between faith and experience—however closely they may be related—a gap exists; this is always an element of tension between the actual situation and the conceived ideal.

In its tendency to assimilate all knowing to scientific knowing and all thinking to experimental inquiry, the Deweyan view falls between the two stools of the Peircean and Jamesian pragmatisms. The merging of the concepts of truth and belief in Dewey's neutral term "warranted assertibility" obscures the indispensable distinction between that which is warranted in fact and that which may be asserted in faith. Experimentalism is thus itself guilty of the major fallacy it ascribes to the European philosophic tradition—its overoptimistic view of the harmony of reason and nature. Through a logical *tour de force*, experimentalism makes what amounts to no more than a verbal reconciliation of the ineluctible struggle in human existence—the conflict between man's vision and the world that is given. It glosses over the recalcitrance of nature to human will and, as a consequence, fails to emphasize the necessity of commitment to the moral and rational ideal, if it is in any measure to prevail.

Following the pragmatisms of Peirce and James, we may say that educational policy must be based on beliefs—in two complementary senses. There are beliefs we must accept as truths, and there are beliefs going beyond truth but not inconsistent with it which we may entertain as foundations of faith. Within the cosmological framework described by the sciences, more than one way of life is possible for man. A degree of choice is granted. Once the choice is made, however, there are corollary actions that become necessary, so that the "may" of belief, once accepted as a commitment, becomes a "must," carrying with it subsidiary obligations. Just as the Catholic has definite articles of faith under the heading, "What Every Christian Must Believe," so the communicant of every other faith, including the democratic faith, must also have certain credos to affirm. The credos of the non-dogmatic faiths may be broader and more flexible, lending themselves more easily to change and to individual variation in application. But a framework of beliefs is essential for education: of what we must believe in the way of knowledge, and what we must believe if we wish the rational and moral vision to come true.

NOTES

1. Justus Buchler, ed., *The Philosophy of Peirce: Selected Writings* (Harcourt, Brace and Company, 1940), p. 11.

2. *Ibid.*, p. 18.

3. For a discussion of this point see: Justus Buchler, *Charles Peirce's Empiricism* (Harcourt, Brace and Company, 1939), pp. 144-149.

4. Justus Buchler, *The Philosophy of Peirce: Selected Writings*, p. 18.

5. *Ibid.*, p. 28.

6. *Ibid.*, p. 46.

7. *Ibid.*, p. 31.

8. James Feibleman, *An Introduction to Peirce's Philosophy* (Harper & Brothers, 1946), pp. 298-299.

9. Ralph Barton Perry, *The Thought and Character of William James* (Little Brown and Company, 1936), Vol. II, pp. 424-425.

10. Justus Buchler, *The Philosophy of Peirce: Selected Writings*, p. 297.

11. *Ibid.*, pp. 375-378.

12. *Ibid.*, "Preface," p. xv.

13. Perry, *op. cit.*, pp. 410-411.

14. William James, *Pragmatism, A New Name for Some Old Ways of Thinking* (Longmans, Green and Company, 1908), pp. 197-235.

15. *Ibid.*, p. 247.

16. *Ibid.*, pp. 256-257.

17. Perry, *op. cit.*, p. 409.

18. For the prospective outlook of James' pragmatism see Dewey's essay, "The Development of American Pragmatism" in *Philosophy and Civilization* (G. P. Putnam's Sons, 1931), especially pp. 24ff.

4

THE UNIVERSE OF NATURE
AND THE IDEALS OF MAN

THE divergences from the experimentalist view expressed in the preceding chapters are rooted in a difference of judgment as to the relation of man's ideals to natural existence. The experimentalist is always at pains to stress the continuity of human nature with all nature, denying that "the social and natural are oppositional conceptions."[1] He sees the physical, the vital, and the mental in terms of an ever-widening evolutionary spiral with "the social" as the highest and most comprehensive category involving all the others. A balanced view, however, would give consideration to the aspect of discontinuity as well as continuity in natural evolution and in social development. Strife as well as harmony is an ineluctable feature within nature and of man's relation to nature. Evolution is not automatic: the higher forms of life, unless fixed by a supporting environment, are ever in danger of reversion to lower forms. The physical, vital, mental, and social categories represent contrasting orders which stand in relation of potential conflict as well as of cooperative association. Indeed, the view proposed here sees significance in the traditional dualistic distinctions of matter and spirit, of body and mind, and of animal and human nature, and underlying all, the dichotomy between man and nature.

1

The word "Nature" is properly used to signify "the familiar setting of human history" if we mean by it that part of man's environment which was not created by man himself.[2] Nature comprises "the vast and varied universe," that long existed before mankind appeared on the terrestial scene and which provides the stage for the human drama.

76

Man has grown within the womb of Nature and continues to live in her and through her. Man is dependent on Nature for his continued existence, for his sustenance and his pleasures. But he is also subject to her inexorable demands, to her irregularities as well as to her laws. Although man is dependent on Nature, she seems oblivious of his existence, often careless of his welfare.

Regarded from man's point of view some of nature's forces are good, serving his survival, ministering to his wants, helping him to fulfill his dreams. Other forces are, from mankind's point of view, evil, limiting his achievements, frustrating his desires, leading to his destruction. In balance, nature is roughly favorable to man's survival and permissive of his development, otherwise we would not be here. The earth provides a livable home; and nature has yielded to man's efforts to make the world he lives in more responsive to his needs, more conducive to his pursuit of happiness, and more expressive of his aspiration for order and beauty. But man's process of raising himself from the state of nature to civilization has been attended by toil and struggle; the basic needs of the masses of men have never been adequately met, and achievement has always fallen short of the vision. Man has exhibited extraordinary ingenuity in transforming nature's potentialities to his own uses, but he has also learned that he must conform to nature's limitations and excesses. Often he has found it the better part of wisdom to accept what was given and to seek consolation through inner peace. There are both orders and contingencies in nature, but neither the orders nor the contingencies are harmoniously adjusted to man's character.

Man's struggle is not only with original nature; it is also with the social orders which he has contrived out of nature. Nor is it merely an impersonal struggle of men against things and institutions. The conflict with his fellow men is more pervasive, certainly more bitter. Man's struggle with man, moreover, is not only with his avowed enemies; it goes on between kith and kin, between the truest of lovers, between the well-married husband and wife. Deepest of all is each man's conflict with himself. These many conflicts have to do with the struggle for the satisfaction of wants, no doubt. But underlying them is, also, a struggle of man against his own nature, a struggle not only of need with need, but of need with desire, and of desire with aspiration. Like nature itself in its relation to man, man's nature is dualistic, and it may be added, ambivalent.

The idea that man has a dual nature, part material, part spiritual, part animal, part divine, is deeply embedded in the commonsense tradition of mankind. The religious teaching of the Western world, generally supported by the philosophers, has emphasized the opposition between body and mind, attaching a moral condemnation to the intellectual distinction of the two kinds of substances. The struggle between the good and evil instinct in man is conceived as a struggle between the satisfaction of the material, animal body and the salvation of the spiritual, divine soul. Characteristic of the view is that man is a unique creature who possesses a psyche, a mind-soul, which although situated in an animal body, affected and distorted by contact with its sensuous instincts and inclinations, nevertheless has a separate immortal existence of its own. There have, of course, been other views from earliest times. The disillusioned lay preacher, once King of Jerusalem, bewailing the mortal destiny of all living creatures, cries out in despair, "the superiority of man to beast is naught," and there are occasions which justify the pessimistic view. The philosophers of the golden mean have taken a more amiable position, and sought to find a balance between bodily desires and spiritual aspirations, not generally denying, however, the opposition between the two aspects of man's nature. The idea of man as a dual nature, that he is ever vacillating between the two poles, the divine and the creaturely, has been the prevailing belief, maintained not only by the priesthood and the people, but also by the scholarly elite.

Modern naturalism, in its various forms, has tried to dissolve this dualistic conception into a unitary body-mind view in which the mental and spiritual are regarded as developing out of the material and sensuous. The eighteenth-century version of the materialistic conception, as illustrated in La Mettrie's *L'Homme Machine*, reduced man to a mechanism: human perception and judgment resulted from a more complex organization of the nervous system than that of the lower animals and plants. There was no essential difference between man, the lower animals, the vegetable world and inorganic substance; all alike were guided by the same laws, all alike were the development of an original "matter." So strongly was La Mettrie imbued with his view, that he believed an ape—which he likened to a deaf-mute— might be transformed into a human being by a proper scheme of education. With the development of the Darwinian conception, the earlier cruder conception gave way to the idea of the formation of new species by chance variation and survival of such types as were successful in the struggle for existence. But the tendency to explain human behavior in terms of a more complex development of animal behavior persisted, indeed became for a time, at least, intensified in the field of psychology.

As Dr. Adolph Meyer relates, a superintendent of the Utica State Hospital in 1870 was proud of eliminating "mental and moral" factors from his list of the causes of mental diseases, on the prevalent theory that "mind cannot become diseased, but only the body."[3] Only a generation ago Dr. John B. Watson created a stir with his barren behaviorism which attempted to reduce thought to physiology and to erect a human psychology on the basis of the "conditioned reflex"—although its originator, Ivan Pavlov, had wisely applied the concept only to the life of animals with which he had experimented. Edward L. Thorndike developed a much broader form of behaviorism which took into consideration observable intellectual and emotional behavior as well as external motor responses. But he, too, regarded human behavior as a more complex form of animal behavior, and entertained a low estimate of the impulsive power of ideas.

In the analysis made by Dewey, there is a great step forward due largely to the introduction of the social factor into the biological frame of reference. Dewey recognizes three levels of reaction in nature: a first stage dominated by material-mechanical reactions; a second, characterized by biological-organismic responses; a psycho-physical form of behavior, typical of the higher animals, especially of man, in which association and communication are essential. In the last most developed form, the environment is "spread out"; the eyes as "distance receptors" make it possible to respond to features in the environment with which the animal is not in direct contact; a vague prehension of the state of affairs relevant to success or failure develops as "feeling." He concludes that: " 'mind' is an added property assumed by a feeling creature, when it reaches that organized interaction with other living creatures which is language, communication."[4]

This analysis goes far in ascribing significance to language as "a system of signs," as well as to the social character of the environment, in giving to human life its distinctive quality. Nevertheless, Dewey does not liberate his conception entirely from the "reductionist fallacy" of explaining the higher levels in terms of more complex organization of lower forms. He still builds his system on the organismic pattern of stimulus and response, his analysis of the thinking process is avowedly influenced by the biological survival theme, and he conceives of mind as falling within the psycho-physical level of behavior characteristic in general of animal response. He regards the social and the ideal as outgrowths of the natural, rightly emphasizing the continuity between the physical and the vital, on the one hand, and the mental and the spiritual on the other, but failing to recognize the possible opposition between them. The fact that the various levels of behavior so often do stand in opposition is the real problem in the organization of the ethical life.

Likewise, the contemporary trend in psychology toward a biosocial approach linked with *gestaltist* and organismic conceptions represents an advance over previous individualistic views whether mentalist, mechanistic, or biological. In the field of psychiatry as well as general psychology the biosocial approach is leading to a more realistic consideration of the actual societal forces at work in the formation and maladjustment of personality, as against exclusive concern with instinctual factors, the libido and power drives taken independently. But like the whole of modern naturalism, the bio-social approach still suffers from a failure to give adequate consideration to the sociological structure and to institutional forms. The "social" is defined largely in terms of the relation of one individual to another, in terms of "interpersonal relations." The part that the mores, ethnic affiliations, religious denominations, economic institutions play in forming the personality—as well as in affecting it detrimentally—is, generally speaking, underestimated. More serious, perhaps, is the tendency, due to the dominance of the biological stimulus-response pattern, to neglect the part played by ideas in mediating reactions to situations.

Naturalism has made an invaluable contribution in turning attention to the aspects of continuity between the mind-soul and its material basis, in stressing the fact that the body and mind are ever joined together, that higher forms of life have grown out of lower forms in the evolutionary process. The moral gain is no less than the scientific advance. Naturalism has led to a more favorable disposition toward the wants of the body, a greater attention to its needs, a more generous tolerance of its vagaries, a friendlier attitude toward pleasures in and of themselves. Not least, it has given us understanding of the significance of the satisfaction of bodily needs for the release of mind and spirit. By the same token, naturalism has brought about the realization that the mental and the spiritual do not always serve the truth and the humane ideal. The pure idea may be mistaken and the high-minded ideology may become fanatical—more destructive of the individual and of society than the carnal vices and the earthly vanities against which priests and puritans have ever fulminated.

However, in its reaction against the sharp dualisms of the traditional religious and philosophic positions, naturalism has gone to the opposite extreme of a denial of the subsistent antagonism between the aspects of the personality indicated by the terms "physical" and "natural," on the one hand, and those symbolized by the words "mental" and "spiritual," on the other. We may agree that human nature exhibits continuities with animal nature, that the social has a natural basis. But we must at the same time recognize that there is a constant struggle between matter and spirit, between the humane and the brutish, between the impulses of the individual and the achieved social organizations. Our Western religious and philosophic tradition asserts that man is endowed with a psyche, with a rational-moral-spiritual soul, different in essentials from the physical or natural body. The error in the classic Christian formulation lay in confusing distinct aspects of the personality with two kinds of substance, material and immaterial, and in holding that the soul had a separate immortal existence and could continue to live in a realm of its own, released from bodily cares and disturbances. But its insistence on an essential distinction between material and spiritual, and its insight into the continuous struggle between the two cannot be dispensed with. The ancient Zoroastrian conception of a battle between the Power of Light and the Power of Darkness which has been absorbed into Judeo-Christian tradition remains a necessary idea. Our prosaic age may prefer depersonalized symbols but the traditional view of the unending struggle between God and Satan for the possession of men's souls represents a reality that finds an echo in human experience of all epochs and civilizations.

2

The acceptance of the Darwinian hypothesis does not compel us to explain human purposes in terms of the responses of the lower animals. No matter what the course of evolution has been, the vegetable, the animal, the human, must be studied empirically each on its own merits, each in its own area and in the context of the relations in which it is found in the present stage of development. Obviously all things have common characteristics as things, and all organisms have common characteristics as organisms. But the character of any genus, species, or variety, as well as of any individual, must be defined in what distinguishes it, not only in the qualities it shares with beings of the larger class of which it is a part. Each type of organism has a life-experience which cannot be transferred to that of another type. As Ernst Cassirer has stated it, "The experiences—and therefore the realities of two different organisms are incommensurate with one another." Quoting the biologist, Johannes von Uexküll, he goes on to say, "In the world of a fly we find only 'fly things,' in the world of a sea urchin we find only sea urchin things."[5]

If this applies to lower stages of animal life, should we not assume that it is valid for the higher stages? Writing in the naturalist idiom, George Santayana observes in *Dominations and Powers*, "Mankind is a race of animals living in a material world." He does not make this as a statement of the whole case, but rather as a starting point of analysis. But even so, it is misleading as a presupposition of any inquiry into human affairs. There are all sorts of "animals," ranging from the vegetable-like barnacle that lacks the power of mobility characteristic of animals to the anthropoid apes whose behavior on superficial examination in some respects reveals resemblance to that of man's. But there is, nevertheless, a tremendous gap between the highest type of ape and man and it is the recognition of this difference which must be the starting point. A discussion of human affairs must be related to what is distinctive in the nature of man.

In the usual accounts, man is distinguished from the lower animals by three great differences. First, as Aristotle impressed on Western thought, man is by nature a political animal, or better, "by nature a civic creature." From the time that he is recognizable as man, the human animal has always lived under some form of social—that is, institutional—organization. A second characteristic, strongly emphasized by anthropologists, is man's tool-making proclivity; man lives in a world of artifacts, in a world of arts and crafts. Along with this, as universally recognized, man is distinguished from the dumb animals by his power of speech.

There is a crucial distinction between the cries of animals, as a germinal form of speech, and the highly developed speech of man. The language of animals is emotional and subjective; it can communicate a presence, a feeling, and a desire, but it can never describe objects or state a proposition. Human speech is not only a call, or a cooing; its major expression is in connected thought: "The difference between *propositional* language and *emotional* language is the real landmark between the human and the animal world."[6]

The divergence, as Ernst Cassirer explains, may be described in terms of the difference between the use of "signs" which are part of the physical world and of "symbols" which are part of the human world of meaning. Animals are susceptible to signs; only the human being can make use of symbols. Man can properly be called *animal symbolicum*, for it is his ability to use symbols to stand for things and experiences that distinguishes him. "As compared with the other animals man lives not merely in a broader reality; he lives, so to speak, in a new *dimension* of reality. . . . No longer in a merely physical universe, man lives in a symbolic universe. Language, myth, art, and religion are parts of this universe. They are the varied threads which weave the symbolic net, the tangled web of human experience."[7]

The symbol-using capacity rests in turn on man's ability to conceive images. Man is *par excellence* the image making, idea creating animal. Wolfgang Köhler, whose *Mentality of Apes* constitutes a historic study, concludes that the wide gulf which separates the anthropoids, despite their intelligence and sociability, is due to this narrow range of "image-life." There may have been beginnings of the development of the image-making capacity among the higher apes, as there were in the province of tool-making, association, and communication, but as Cassirer says, ". . . they did not reach the threshold of the human world. They entered, as it were, a blind alley."

What is unique about man is that he has the power of imagination. The human being can disengage himself from the immediate particular situation in time and place and view it from a more distant and wider perspective. He can recall the past and in a sense live in it; he can try to divine the future and plan for it. He can see himself in a different country from the one he actually lives in, and not least in significance from the moral point of view, he can put himself in another person's place. Man's power to construct hypotheses which plays so important a part in scientific thinking depends upon a fruitful imagination disciplined by knowledge. Man dreams, has visions, constructs ideals; he can "create another world to live in," which Santayana remarks in the *Life of Reason* is what we mean by having a religion. Man does not react directly to the actual world of nature; his imagination is interposed between himself and the physical universe. He cannot avoid living in a world of spirits and symbols whether this helps him or hurts him: he lives in a world of imaginary evils as well as in a realm of hoped-for goods, in a world of illusion as well as in a world of conceived rational order.

Imaginative thought divorced from proper relation to natural existence may evanesce in mystic communion, run riot in speculative disorder, even lose itself in deviations of insanity. Nevertheless, all higher intellectual and moral life is dependent upon it: this is the essential meaning underlying the Platonists' appeal to the reality of the Idea which we can grasp by the aid of the sixth sense. The image-creating power makes it possible for us to perceive stable relations within the flux of experience and to construct them in mental patterns or ideas. Man can abstract and generalize, and, on the basis of generalization, classify objects, formulate scientific principles by which he can better understand the world and to a degree, control it. By means of his imagination each man can see his present experience in terms of a framework of cosmic space and time, and as D. H. Lawrence has beautifully said "see the little life in the circle of the greater life."

The intellectual merges into the moral. The highest function of the sixth sense of imagination is, as in the Platonic conception, in the service of the ethical, in the Idea of the Good. Man can form an ideal of conduct by which he can guide the personal life, a standard transcending his own experience by which he can measure his actions; by the same means he can devise an ideal of a better world by which to transform the present world. The achievements that lend distinction to man's life—science, philosophy, art, and religion—are the consequences of man's power to separate himself from the domination of the immediate need and the particular experience and live, and act, and create, in the light of some ideal by which the sensuous stimulation and impulsive drives are mediated and transformed. Imagination, abstraction, universalization, idealization are the essential attributes of man. Instead of the naturalist presupposition "that mankind is a race of animals living in a material world," it would be truer to say, "man—in so far as he is *man*—is a unique creature living in a universe of spirit."

This unique ability to guide action by ideas, however, is a recent mutation in animal development; it has as yet not attained the strength or stability of an instinctive reaction. To speak of man as *homo sapiens* contains more of hope than of actuality. Man endeavors to fix his conceived better ways of managing life in material and mental tools and in social institutions. But the vital energies which express themselves in instinctive impulses remain as disturbing forces which press against the confines of institutionalized forms. In a memorable passage Santayana has described the life of reason as: ". . . the happy marriage of the two elements—impulse and ideation —which if wholly divorced would reduce man to a brute or to a maniac. The rational animal is generated by these two monsters. He is constituted by ideas which have ceased to be visionary and actions that have ceased to be vain." As in common life, however, one may remark, it would require a fortunate conjunction of events and characters to bring about a happy marriage and maintain it securely, and even in the harmonious union, conflict, it would appear, is rarely absent.

It is this basic fact of human existence that our religious tradition reflects in terms of the struggle between the spirit and the flesh—a struggle between man's divine image of himself and what he actually is under the press of impulse or circumstance. Man acts on various levels of behavior. To the many designations that have been made—as *homo sapiens, homo faber, homo ludens*, we may add another, namely *homo ambivalens*. Man wavers between the two poles of his nature, the animal and the divine. Organisms below man have achieved a stable relation with their respective environments, their structure and functions being well adapted to their usual surroundings. But man, a recent emergent in the line of evolution, lacks by nature a fixed character. A lion acts like a lion, a lamb like a lamb; and a human being created in the image of God but a little lower than the angels, may achieve saintliness. But he may also act in a way that justifies calling him a "wolf," a "pig," or a "rat." Man can sink below the beasts into bestiality.

3

Original nature endows man with potentialities but not with definite character. Man acquires his human nature by a twofold process —through participation in the institutional life of society and through living in a universe of conceptions and ideals. The institutions which have developed in the course of cultural evolution give expression to natural impulses, canalizing them at the same time into orderly forms. We sometimes speak as if men possessed rational and moral faculties within themselves; it would be nearer the truth to say that reason and morality have been built into, and subsist in, the institutions of civilization. Insofar as the great majority of men live a decent life above the level of impulse, it is because elements of the good, the true, and the beautiful are embodied in the laws, the mores, the arts, the sciences, the religious practices, of the communities with which they identify themselves. A higher degree of humane living is achieved when men become aware of the ideals that are implicit in social practices and attempt consciously to guide their own actions and to rebuild the institutional life in the light of their ideals. Less frequently, men aspire to direct their lives by a conceptual pattern of values which transcends any particular society as is the case of the saint and the philosopher.

Both ways of life, the social-institutional and the religious-philosophical, involve the organization and control of natural impulses by means of supra-natural standards. There can be no "self-control" apart from relation to a system of institutions or a pattern of ideas. The self-discipline imposed by ancient schools of philosophy, Stoicism and Epicureanism, involved a regimen of life as well as a system of beliefs. And what is true of these philosophies is even more palpably the case with the religions. Life on a moral-rational plane always involves a tension between the line of least resistance—the instinctive or routine way—and the conceived possibly better way. There is ever a gap between the overflowing vitalities and the unlimited vision on the one hand, and the most liberal opportunities offered at any time by social organization. There is a distance between our instinctive desires and the possibilities of fulfillment, between actual practices and approved mores, between locally approved social norms and the ideals of the national community, between the national and denominational ideal, however broad, and the striving toward the perfection of the religious, philosophic, and social utopias.

Human beings have the power of choice—that is their glory; but they also have the necessity of choice and that may often be their undoing. Freedom means a liberation of energies; it also involves a limitation. As on the chess board every choice opens some possibilities and closes others. There is point to the paradoxical definition of freedom as implying conformity; i.e., Spinoza's view of freedom as conformity to cosmic necessity, Bacon's adage that we master nature in the measure that we obey her, Montesquieu's idea that freedom consists of adherence to law. And the testimony of the great saints that the good life can be achieved only through renunciation of the goods of life cannot be disregarded. These opinions may be one-sided, perhaps not applicable to all men, to all times, or to all places. The good life in which a measure of freedom is essential, it may be said, requires an equilibrium of expanding vitalities and ordering restrictions. But the doctrine of the need of limitation is no more subject to error than the contrary view that the good life means emancipation from the restraints of the institutional life.

Education is the process of transforming a creature of nature into a human being. This requires socialization—in the sense of habituation to institutional life—and idealization—in the classic sense of deliberately forming human character in accordance with an ideal. The liberation from the confinements and rigidities of institutional life cannot be achieved by the rejection of law and convention but by their continuous reconstruction through the agency of ideas. When the ideal of the good life is too far removed from the needs of the common, garden variety of mankind as in the ascetic aspirations of the saint, this may lead to withdrawal from the communal life and to a precious concern with the salvation of one's own soul. When the institutional structure does not permit the satisfaction of basic needs or suppresses man's urge to freedom, resort may be had to revolutionary action for the purpose of a radical reformation. There are occasions when both types of rejection of the existing political and social constitution may be regarded as falling within the category of the rational. But where the ideal itself grows out of the needs and

the aspirations of man living in society, a continuous dynamic interaction takes place between the ideals and the institutional life. There
occurs, to borrow a phrase which the late Charles A. Beard liked to
use, "the involution of ideas and interests moving forward in time."[8]

We return in summarizing to the thesis that a philosophy of education must be predicated on a clearly formulated conception of a way
of life in a definite society. Tension is established between the conventional way of life embodied in the existing laws and customs and
the ideal way approved by our reason and conscience. The conception
of an interaction between the ideal and the actual is in harmony with
the experimentalist mode of thought. The point here made in diverg-
ing from the experimentalist emphasis is that in order that there may
be an interaction the ideal must be formulated as a firmly held belief.
Those who assert that nature has no clear destiny for man need all
the more to draw a design for living out of man's vision and
experience.

NOTES

1. John Dewey, *Philosophy and Civilization* (G. P. Putnam's Sons,
1931), p. 81.

2. Frederick J. E. Woodbridge, *An Essay on Nature* (Columbia
University Press, 1940), p. 3.

3. Alfred Lief, editor, *The Common Sense Psychiatry of Dr. Adolf
Meyer* (McGraw-Hill, 1948), p. 5.

4. John Dewey, *Experience and Nature* (Open Court Publishing Company, 1925), p. 258.

5. Ernst Cassirer, *An Essay on Man* (Yale University Press, 1944),
p. 23.

6. *Ibid.*, p. 30.

7. *Ibid.*, pp. 24, 25.

8. Charles A. Beard, *The Open Door at Home* (The Macmillan Company, 1938), p. 157.

5

ETHICS AND POLITICS AS BASIS
FOR A PHILOSOPHY OF EDUCATION

A DEFINITION of philosophy in terms only of process and inquiry is inadequate for educational policy. While the idea of a continuous quest must ever remain an element of living philosophies, the search insofar as it is to lead to action in any given society must eventuate in a clearly formulated communally accepted pattern of beliefs. A philosophy need not lay down the law in specific cases, but it must be definite enough to suggest a policy, it must support conviction on major issues of principle, and, in some instances, involve a commitment to "absolutes."

1

Schools of thought which avow absolutes as a basis of education usually derive them from a conception of ultimate reality, the search for which they identify with metaphysics.[1] "Metaphysics," as a characteristic statement has it, "is the real support of ethics, or the theory of the good life and right conduct. It is clear that one's conduct in important life situations depends on one's scale of values, itself depending on one's idea of ultimate reality."[2] Underlying this conception of the nature of philosophy is an ancient view that there are two worlds—on the one hand, the world of human experience which is a world of appearances, and a world of reality, a good and a true world that lies behind it which we may come to know, or at least to glimpse, by some power—revelation, intuition, or pure reason—which transcends ordinary experience. The belief that we can attain secure knowledge by a method which by-passes human experience is, of course, out of harmony with the outlook that underlies the position taken in these pages. Santayana's opening sentence in *The Life of*

Reason is to be accepted as the beginning of wisdom: "Whatever forces may govern human life, if they are to be recognized by man, must betray themselves in human experience." This, however, is the beginning of wisdom, not the end of it. The rejection of a transcendental metaphysics and the acceptance of experience as a basis, it must be admitted, does not get us far.

A conception of metaphysics of some significance for educational philosophy is presented by the late R. G. Collingwood. His view is that there are two different conceptions of the nature of metaphysics discernible in Aristotle's writings: one, that metaphysics is ontology or the "science of pure being"; the other that, "Metaphysics is the science that deals with the absolute presuppositions underlying ordinary science."[3] The definition of metaphysics as the science of pure being he regards as self-contradictory and nonsensical, long a source of confusion in European thought. "Ontology will be my name," he says, "for a mistake people have made, Aristotle first and foremost, about metaphysics." His point is that science, as generally agreed, is systematic thinking about problems arising out of special subject matters involving special methods of inquiry, and accordingly a "science of pure being" is a contradiction in terms right at the start.

But the second meaning of metaphysics as the deliberate study of the absolute presuppositions made in any sphere of thought or activity Collingwood regards as of primary importance. In the last analysis, all thinking involves assumptions, some made consciously, others so deeply imbedded in consciousness and so fully accepted at a given period that we may not be aware of the presuppositions that we entertain. These assumptions as requisite for the conduct of an inquiry or activity Collingwood designates "absolute presuppositions." There are absolute presuppositions in any system of culture at any period in all the major fields of thought—in science, religion, politics, and in education.

Metaphysics, Collingwood insists, is a historical descriptive study. It has only one function, namely, "to find out what absolute presuppositions have been made by this or that person or group of persons, on this or that occasion or group of occasions, in the course of this or that piece of thinking."[4] The absolutes revealed by the study of metaphysics are not verifiable or deniable, not because their truth is established for all time, but because the question of truth is not involved. It is enough that they are fully accepted and do not stand in contradiction to other presuppositions held. Nor are the absolutes to be conceived as eternal truths. On the contrary, metaphysical truths must change when absolute presuppositions suitable for previous periods are no longer acceptable in the new frame of thought. There is never a complete unity among the presuppositions in various areas of culture in any period. It is the tension among the presuppositions that leads to historical development. "When there is no strain there is no history."

The presuppositions which underlie various aspects of any culture —political, religious, scientific—manage after a time to achieve a workable unity, but the idea that they ever can achieve a complete harmony, Collingwood believes, represents a pernicious error in philosophic thought. "A reformed metaphysics will conceive of any constellation of absolute propositions as having in its structure not the simplicity and calm that characterizes the subject matter of mathematics but the intricacy and restlessness that characterize the subject matter, say, of legal and constitutional history."[5] One stage of culture changes into another when the strains are so great that the precarious coexistence of presuppositions becomes unstable and gives way to a new set which are "consupponable" to use Collingwood's own term.

We need not subscribe to Collingwood's limitations on the nature of metaphysics, or to his analysis of how strains in systems of culture come about. But the assumption that all ideas including metaphysical absolutes cannot be divorced from their historical-cultural setting is indispensable for the formulation of educational policy. Nevertheless, Collingwood's analysis is not fully adequate: it denies to philosophy the function of criticism and unification, of evaluation and selection from among the several sets of presuppositions that are made at any particular time and place. Thus it divests philosophy of the function of lessening the strains that are brought about by different types and rates of change in civilization. It takes from philosophy its purpose of deliberate direction of social life.

A view that comes closest to representing a valid conception of the philosophy of education is referred to with approval by Dewey although he makes only partial use of it. He points out: "Whenever philosophy has been taken seriously, it has always been assumed that it signified achieving a wisdom which would influence the conduct of life. Witness the fact that almost all ancient schools of philosophy were also organized ways of living, those who accepted their tenets being committed to certain distinctive modes of conduct; witness the intimate connection of philosophy with the theology of the Roman church in the middle ages, its frequent association with religious interests, and, at national crises, its association with political struggles."[6] Dewey makes this statement to illustrate the idea that philosophy aims not only to achieve a unified intellectual outlook but that it implies also a reference to conduct within a definite society. But there is more in the quotation than Dewey makes explicit. For in both instances, in the schools of ancient philosophy which were fraternities as well as in the Catholic Church, the organized way of living was based on an acceptance of a definite system of beliefs.

To sum up: educational policy cannot be based on a metaphysical position in the usual sense, e.g., naturalism, idealism, realism or pragmatism taken in abstraction out of a social context. A philosophy of education must be related to the more inclusive and yet more definite range of considerations implied in the term "philosophy of life"—as illustrated by Stoicism, Catholicism, Communism, or Democracy. A philosophy of life, hence an educational philosophy, will have two indispensable planes of reference—a definite community and a correlated pattern of beliefs.

On the one hand, a philosophy of life implies membership in a community with responsibilities toward it. It involves a conception of the relation of the individual to the political and economic organization and this is the case even when it deprecates or denies the value of life in the world. On the other hand, a philosophy of life, whether religious, political, or merely conventional, is associated with ideas and value-judgments, with convictions that transcend the confines of any particular society.

A fully unified conception of educational philosophy would require an elucidation of a view with reference to man's relation to the cosmos, a view of nature and of the character of man. But the heart of any philosophy of life is the pattern of personal and social behavior which it prescribes or inspires. The ethical—as connoting the ideal type of behavior in relation to others, to the community as a whole, and not least, to one's own self—is the keystone of any philosophy of life. The term political as here used refers to the social-institutional structure; as in the original Greek sense, it bears the signification of membership in a community, and as in Plato and Aristotle, it implies the economic basis as well as the procedural forms of government. A philosophy of life aims at the integration of the political as representing an actual socioeconomic community organization, and the ethical as representing an ideal type of human relationship—both framed within a conception of the nature of being. The word "aims" is used with deliberation, for it is of the essence of human life that a perfect synthesis is not at the highest levels attainable in the contingent world of existence. There is ever strain and struggle between the ethical and the political; the arena of this struggle is the realm of history.

2

This proposed conception of educational philosophy is indebted to Greek classic thought as later modified by attitudes prevalent in the Hellenistic world. In Socrates we find clearly exemplified the interplay of ethical and political—and the conflict between them—within an assumed metaphysical frame of reference. Socrates aimed to replace the customary morality by an ethics based on knowledge and reason. He believed that a true conception of the good life could be achieved by subjecting one individual opinion to the criticism of another. The examination was conducted in public and the aim was to arrive at a consistent position against which no further argument could be brought. "The purpose of the Socratic dialogue is, by discussion with other men on a subject of incomparable interest to all concerned—namely, the highest values in human life—to reach an agreement which must be recognized as valid by everyone."[7] Here we must guard ourselves against the anachronism of thinking that Socrates believed we could arrive at the truth by a consensus of common opinion. The process of Socratic questioning serves to bring out contradictions, the elimination of which leads to the eduction from the consciousness of the divine truth innate in the human mind. The quest begins with the thought "that the unexamined life is not worth living for man," and this is joined to the idea "that we must follow the argument wherever it leads." But the assumption is that it will lead to the remembrance of the true good as it has been implanted in the human soul by God.

The ideal that Socrates set before men was self-discipline, not in the sense of an ascetic suppression of desire but in the characteristic Hellenic meaning of self-control through knowledge—knowledge which was at the same time reason (*logos*) and life's wisdom (*sophrosyné*). Socrates' conception of the good life was a universal one, appropriate for man as man at any time and in any country. But he was not a cosmopolitan in the sense that his service was dedicated to humanity in the abstract; he was "heart and soul bound to Athens." Although his conception of the good life, as he himself saw it, was based on the distillation of an ideal truth inherent in the individual soul, yet, as a matter of fact, as Jaeger has discerned, he "argued his way to an agreement with his fellow citizens about a common idea, presupposed in every such conversation, and rooted in the common origin and common home, common history and tradition, common laws and constitution. This sharing in a common knowledge or belief gave concrete content to the universals he was always seeking."[8] Out of the common experience he drew an ideal conception of the good life which transcended the common experience. Custom and law were not to be repudiated or supplanted by an abstract universal idea; they were to be elevated by better custom and by an ideal law.

Classic Greek thought assumes that individual virtue and civic virtue, the good person and the good state, are in essence harmonious. That a high ideal of personal ethics is not easily combined with loyalty to an existing state is evidenced by the trial and martyrdom of Socrates. In the end he had to decide whether to obey God or man, and he chose to obey God. To some even in that day, as represented by Aristippus in the *Memorabilia* of Xenophon, the conflict between the ethical person and the political community seemed to be inevitable. The only solution for men of reason who did not wish to undergo martyrdom was to withdraw from civic activity and devote themselves to the enjoyment of a life of intellectual pursuits. Plato, in the *Republic*, however, continued to believe in the possibility of a union of rational ethics and political order, but he realized that a complete reorganization of the state, in economic foundations, in political structure, and in educational regimen would be necessary.

Plato carried to an extreme the process of generalization and idealization which Socrates had begun and made ideas, envisioned in pure thought, the models for the life of the individual and the community.

To the "Idea of the Good" so conceived he attributed a super-mundane existence, possessed of eternal value, a truth which reflected the unchanging aspects of the "really real." But his affirmation of an absolute good was not in the interest of supporting existing society; on the contrary, the plan of the *Republic* was radically utopian. The ideal could be attained only when the state would be ruled by philosophers or when philosophers became kings. He attempted, so it seems, to have his idea tried out in Syracuse, where apparently he completely failed. In the *Laws*, he projected a second-best state, in which stable order and the welfare of the whole would be achieved through subordination to an ordained law, not through the cultivation of reason. Insofar as he continued to believe in philosophy, he conceived it as "a method of dying," of emancipation from the needs of the body so that one might the better pursue the aspirations of the soul.

Aristotle, like the younger Plato, sees no absolute antithesis between the rational and moral good of the individual and the good of the state. The state exists for the perfection of the individual and the perfection of the individual is conducive to the welfare of the state. Lacking the imaginative power of Plato, he sensed even less the genuine difficulty of a reconciliation of a rational conception of the good and life in the state. In balance of emphasis, both Plato and Aristotle make the welfare of society as a whole, the ethics of the community predominant over the welfare of the individuals who compose the state. Aristotle anticipates the principle that "as is the state so is the school." Education is a means of preserving the character of the state—in an oligarchy it should be oligarchal, in a democracy, democratic. The good state would promote the arts of peace and leisure as well as the arts of war and business which were, after all, only means for the former. But he recognizes that the highest good, the contemplation of the universe, is an individual pursuit, not a civic activity.

Ernest Barker suggests the inescapable tension between the ethical and political elements in Greek classic thought. "Plato is at one with Aristotle, and both are true to Greek tradition, in upholding the primacy of the educational function of the State. Education exists for the sake of the initiation of the citizen into the spiritual life of his state; and conversely the government of the state exists for the sake of education. . . . Yet there is another aspect of Plato's theory of education. Education is indeed a social process, and, as such, it is intended to adjust the individual to his society; but it is also the way to the vision of absolute truth, and that vision is a vision of the individual soul. Apart from society and from social values, education is good in itself and for its own sake; its ultimate good is rather the contemplation of the reality which lies behind time and existence than a life of action among earth's vain shadows—though we must always, Plato bids us, play our part like men among the shadows, and refuse to forget our duty to our fellows in the ecstacy of the contemplation."[9]

3

With the downfall of the city state and the rise of empire, philosophy tended to turn more and more to a concern for the welfare of the soul, for *eudaimonia*, happiness for the individual. The idea of *cosmopolites*, of citizenship in a conceptual world-order was substituted for membership in an actual city-state. This brought with it, at least in the abstract, a broadening of the sense of human kinship, so that in the Stoic view barbarians, slaves, and women come to be counted within the fraternities of men. With the denial of the opportunity of effective participation in political activity, men endeavored to give order to their lives through "ways of life" organized around a conception of values related to a view of the nature of the cosmos. The bond of union through membership in the city-community was replaced by a sense of fellowship based on a community of ideas. Along with the decline of interest in political affairs went a lack of faith in the possibility of achieving happiness through secular satisfactions. Despite the variety of views and styles of life which they expressed, all the great philosophic movements of the Hellenistic age are marked by a rejection of worldly values. Stoicism teaches dispassion (*apatheia*), indifference to whatever befalls us whether of joy or sorrow, in the resolute pursuit of reason and duty. Epicureanism counsels freedom from distraction (*ataraksia*), and the seeking of the sweetness of life through tilling the soil and through affectionate friendships. Neo-Platonism calls for, as its first condition, the purging of the soul (*katharsis*) from all contamination with the sensuous body. There is one faith they all exhibit in common, as Gilbert Murray sums up: "Faith in the absolute supremacy of the inner life over things external."[10]

With Christianity the movement toward the separation of the individual's happiness from the welfare of the civil community becomes crystallized and later embodied in an institutional form. Concentrated on the problem of salvation for the individual soul, the Christian was prepared to sacrifice membership in the state for the sake of the beatitude to be achieved in living under the sovereign will of God. For loyalty to the city there is substituted allegiance to the church in which all who accept salvation through Christian faith are regarded as equal, and from which in the words of Paul "neither Jew nor Greek, bond or free, Barbarian or Scythian, male or female" are to be excluded. When Rome adopted Christianity as a state religion, Jesus' instruction, "Render unto Caesar the things which are Caesar's," became an established principle. But this acquiescence in the demands of the state only served to strengthen the fundamental principle that the spiritual and ethical life could not be lived within the political community; it could be attained in the monastery, in the inner life of the soul, and in the world to come. St. Augustine—who, as Ernest Barker notes, wrote "the first great treatise on the theory of human community since Plato's *Republic* and Aristotle's *Politics*"— brought the conception to a climax in his *Civitas Dei* and laid the foundation of the dualistic conception of the Middle Ages, of history as the conflict of the two cities.[11] In Santayana's celebrated formulation this was an all pervasive conflict between "two moralities, one natural, the other supernatural; two philosophies, one rational, the other revealed; two beauties, one corporeal, the other spiritual; two glories, one temporal, the other eternal; two institutions, one the world, the other the church."

Underlying the several antitheses is a dichotomy between the ethical and the political aspects of life. In no matter does the dualism of medieval Christian thought express itself so patently as in the conception of equality within the community of Christians, and the acceptance of a sociological structure of inequality in the life of the world. The idea that men are equal before God is strictly limited to the religious sphere. "It is an equality," as Ernst Troelsch has emphasized, "which exists purely in the Presence of God, and in Him, based solely on the religious relation to God as the centre of the whole."[12] The slave as well as the free, the woman as well as the man, the poor as well as the rich, can participate in the Supper of the Lord as the festival of brotherhood, can lead in the public worship and is eligible for the gift of salvation. Even here, in the religious phase, the equality before God does not signify a claim on God, but rather a negative equality in common human dependence in the presence of the infinite power and holiness of God. It is by no means certain that all men have an equal right to redemption on the basis of merit alone; predestination of one and rejection of another lies within the unlimited decision of God's omnipotent and sovereign Will. Be that as it may, when it comes to the question of applying the doctrine of equality to secular relationships and institutions, it is abandoned completely.

The characteristic medieval Christian ethic required that men should love each other, that the rich give charity to the poor, that the poor should be grateful and not envy the rich, that those in authority should as stewards of God care for those of low estate, and that those in the subordinate positions should respectfully obey, and that all should act in humility. But before modern times, there is no idea of removing the inequalities among men, or of improving social conditions as a foundation for the moral and spiritual life: "nowhere is there any talk of improving living conditions, but only of enduring them and making them inwardly fruitful." The germ idea of equality remains undeveloped: throughout the Middle Ages the church supported a hierarchical social structure based on gradations of authority and subordination. The obligation of every man was to remain in his class, whether high or law, and to discharge his responsibilities to members of the other class. "The Christian virtues are not progress and change, but the preservation of healthy organizations and contentment with one's present position in relation to the whole."[13]

4

The modern age which began with the Renaissance represented in its major presuppositions a direct antithesis to the medieval system. As against the idea of a "fixed order of God," as it has been called, the thesis of progressive change becomes central. A sense of breaking of bounds, of revolt against tradition, of adventure into new realms, pervades the Western world. Freedom becomes more precious than salvation, and success in worldly life more to be desired than saintliness. The principle of hierarchy of ranks and classes is supplanted by the conception of a fluid society in which each man attains a position consistent with his native abilities. The individual takes the center of the stage, the self-made man of business vies with the well-born aristocrat, the man of science challenges the authority of the clerical elite. Science replaces revelation as the source of secure truth, and society is conceived, not as patterned after a divine plan, but as the work of men to be fashioned by human intelligence.

The movement is in the direction of naturalism, secularism, and humanism. It is impelled by the idea of breaking down the medieval dualism of this-worldly and other-worldly orders. The dichotomy of spirituals and temporals is denied and a uniform world grounded in nature's laws is set up in its stead. Along with this general dissolution of the medieval dualisms, there is a return to the classic Hellenic ideal of citizenship—now conceived in terms of allegiance to the national community. The conviction gains ground that the good of the individual and the welfare of society are bound together. The cosmopolitan ideal of the union of peoples under the direction of a universal church gives way to the conception of a secular international organization, a "Concert of European Nations" in which the sovereignty of the nation-state is preserved and the diversity of national cultures encouraged.

The movement toward breaking down the division between the natural-secular order and the supernatural-moral realm reaches a climax in the eighteenth-century doctrines of enlightenment and republicanism. In the new scheme of thought, man is conceived essentially good—as are all things that come from the hands of the Author of nature. Society is infinitely perfectible; archaic institutions are due to ignorance and to superstition. Reason, tolerance of differences, free discussion of ideas, inquiry into the laws of nature, experiment with new social forms—these are the agencies of continuous human progress. Education—the general diffusion of knowledge and the promotion of a scientific attitude of mind—comes to be regarded as the chief means for achieving individual freedom and advancing the good society.

To these rationalist beliefs of the intellectual elites of the enlightenment, the political declarations of the revolutionary period add a radical democratic creed: that government must be based on the natural rights of man, and on the principle that all men are created free and equal. This represents a radical attempt to make man, formerly conceived as equal before God, truly equal in the society of men. In part, it is a return to classic thought in that it reflects an endeavor to unite an ethical aim with a political constitution. But it is unprecedented: for the first time in human history government is to be founded on universal principles, of human right and of natural law that make no distinction of race, of class, or of church affiliation.

The new philosophy of life may be termed "liberalism" if the word is used in a broad sense. Like all conceptions, it was compromised in the course of applying it. In its restricted meaning as formulated under the leadership of English thinkers during the nineteenth century, liberalism was tailored to fit the interests of the rising industrial middle class. The Benthamites, who formulated the utilitarian position, rejected the conception of natural rights as a basis for government in favor of what they considered the more practical doctrine of utility and they made the security of property pre-eminent above the principle of equality. Nevertheless, liberalism, in its narrower as well as in its broader sense, retained the belief in a progressive realization of freedom and welfare. Its expounders hoped, indeed were confident, that under its direction a gradual but steady improvement in the life of individual and society would be achieved.

In the countries which accepted it, new levels of achievement in industry and in science were attained. Society moved in the direction of a humane order of existence. There developed a greater regard for human personality. The standard of living was raised for an ever-widening group of people; education became widespread, almost universal; freedom of speech, of the press, of association, and religious toleration were established as principles. Dogmatism tended to decrease, a broader, less parochial attitude of mind accompanied growth of the liberal temper. But, as we realize now, its success was limited and partial. Liberalism won out in only a relatively small part of the world, and even in countries of the Western world and in the United States, where it took root, its achievements were partial and its ideals much qualified in practice. Today, the failures of liberalism tend to obscure its achievements.

Toward the end of the nineteenth century, the economic doctrines and individualistic impulsions of liberalism began to be subjected to sharp criticism. Its capitalistic structure and its rugged competitiveness were attacked from many sides. Christian moralists and secular humanists united in condemning the worship of financial success and the vulgarization of culture in a civilization dominated by the money-making drive. Socialists, utopian and Marxist, accused liberalism of joining with capitalism in betraying the revolutionary principles of equality and fraternity and of distorting the idea of liberty to mean freedom for the owners of property to exploit the working classes. Although liberalism held its own as the directing principle of social thought well into the twentieth century, the criticisms increased and gained in force after the First World War.

In the last generation, new ideologies have risen which challenge the basic principles of liberalism. Communism rejects not only its capitalist foundation; it distrusts the spirit of free inquiry, denies the validity of the parliamentary system of government, and substitutes the method of revolution for gradual reform. Fascism repudiates liberalism in its entirety, its moral attitudes as well as its political doctrines; it denounces the basic principle of the Western ethic, the essential equality of all men, in its secular as well as in its religious forms. Existentialism, a new way of redemption for the disillusioned intellectual, turns its back on the modern effort to embody ethical ideals in the institutional life. The liberals of today are divided among themselves; they reveal a loss of nerve as bemused they face a world that has disappointed their hopes and seemingly rejected their faith.

5

The opening of the second half of the twentieth century found an anxiety-ridden world. Although the cities which were ruined in the Second World War were slowly being rebuilt and the pinch of austerity relieved, it was evident that Europe had lost the leadership in civilization advance which she had enjoyed for five hundred years. Instead of the hoped-for one world, a two world system of West and East was becoming entrenched, the former led by the United States upholding the liberal tradition in the name of democracy, the other, directed by Soviet Russia aggressively advancing the ideology of communism. The steadily increasing destructive power of nuclear weapons deepened the widespread feeling of insecurity and apprehension. In the atmosphere of perplexity and dread, there was a growing curtailment of liberty of thought and of academic freedom—at times defensible, at times reprehensible. The temper of war and the fear of treachery do not permit niceties in any case, and there have always been political jackals ready to prey on fear and hatred for their own purposes. But justified or not, the jailing of Communist leaders and the harassment of fellow travellers mark the passing of the old liberalism.

To what degree has the decline of liberalism as a "life structure for the modern world," to use John Haynes Holmes' expression, been due to historical factors, to the unreadiness of the larger portion of the world—ruled by autocracies and steeped in ignorance and superstition, held back by poverty—to accept its enlightened and forward-looking doctrines? Or is the weakening of its influence, in recent decades, the result of error in its presuppositions, of failure to modify its doctrines in the light of intellectual and social change?

The changes in thought and in life in the last half century by far exceed the changes that occurred in the previous half millenium since the Renaissance. Most evident are the material developments that have transformed industry and greatly affected our whole way of life. Of even more critical significance is the social ferment which interplays with the technological forces. There is rebellion against class domination and revolt of suppressed nationalities against imperialistic control. There is an "upsurge of the masses" which, in the backward countries in the world, expresses itself in the cry for a decent subsistence and which, in the more advanced nations of the West, in a drive for a fairer share of the good things that modern technology can produce.

The present attempt to sketch the outlines of an educational philosophy is directed by the belief that we are entering a new stage in world civilization—a stage continuous with the previous liberalist era but which differs from it in a number of essentials. There is no final knowing of what man will do with his many inventions—but there is hope as well as the possibility of doom in them. What we are facing in the world is a new effort under the aegis of democracy to unite an ethical conception with a political structure—to apply more genuinely and on a world-wide scale the eighteenth-century doctrines of liberty, equality, and fraternity. To this all-pervading social struggle of our age, educational policy must be related. The failure to do so makes the greater part of what is written in the field of educational philosophy of marginal significance when it is not wholly irrelevant.

In this, there is a return to the classic Greek conception—as exemplied in *The Republic*—of relating education to ethics and politics. The content of an educational philosophy for our own age will of course differ, because of our divergent conceptions of cosmic and human nature, of the relation of reason to experience, most of all because of our deliberate democratic purpose. A crucial point of difference resides in the fact that Plato believed that education was a means of maintaining the good society after it had been once established while the democratic philosophy gives education an indispensable part to play in bringing about the good society. At the same time, the gradualist implications of the democratic process deter from projecting utopian blueprints. Utopias have their uses in opposing passive acquiescence in the present state of affairs, in suggesting the ultimately possible and pointing to its direction. But as a basis for policy, the utopian ideal may be destructive. In the formulation of a social policy as framework for educational endeavor we must face the future—not the distant future but the emerging era.

In the endeavor to base educational policy on some conception of the nature of the emerging social order, the present analysis parts company both with essentialist and with progressivist whose views were discussed in the opening chapter. The former would have us confine education to the transmission of the heritage of the past and to adjustment to present-day institutions of society. The progressivist would shun any definite formulation of policy as tending to fixity of position, particularly in view of the fact that we live in an era of "rapid change and an unknown future." But, it is submitted, we know the immediate future better than we know the past for it is to an extent only the present seen in dynamic terms. We are already living in the emerging future. If we take into account the observable trends we can minimize the element of error, an element always present in this world of contingency. If we hold to our principles without dogmatism, we can readjust our plans to the needs of practice and to the test of events.

The future of society is not a mechanical development forever predetermined: to an extent our beliefs, clearly and firmly held, enter into the formation of the future.

NOTES

1. John S. Brubacher, *Modern Philosophies of Education* (McGraw-Hill Book Co., 1950), pp. 22ff.

2. Michael Demiashkevich, *An Introduction to the Philosophy of Education* (American Book Company, 1935), p. 42.

3. R. G. Collingwood, *An Essay on Metaphysics* (Oxford, The Clarendon Press, 1940), p. 11.

4. *Ibid.*, p. 47.

5. *Ibid.*, p. 77.

6. John Dewey, *Democracy and Education* (The Macmillan Company, 1916), pp. 378, 379.

7. Werner Jaeger, *The Ideals of Greek Culture* (Oxford University Press, 1943), Vol. II, p. 63.

8. *Ibid.*, p. 75.

9. Ernest Barker, *Greek Political Theory: Plato and his Predecessors* (Methuen & Company, 1947), p. 182.

10. Gilbert Murray, *Five Stages of Greek Religion* (Oxford, The Clarendon Press, 1925), p. 147.

11. Ernest Barker, *The Politics of Aristotle* (Oxford, The Clarendon Press), Introduction, p. xx.

12. Ernst Troeltsch, *The Social Teaching of the Christian Churches* (The Macmillan Company), 1931, p. 72.

13. *Ibid.*, p. 291.

PART TWO

THE EMERGING DEMOCRATIC ORDER

> We cannot recover the past, but we can, within the limits set by nature and history and our own intelligence and resolution, make the future. We do make the future in any case. Even if, apathetic and resigned, we are content to let things ride; even if, afflicted with the impervious conservative mind, we strive in vain to return to the good old days—even so, we help to make the future. But in that case we make it by default; and since we help to make the future in any case, it is better to help make it, not by letting things ride, but by having some idea of where things ought to go and doing whatever is possible to make them go in that direction.
>
> —CARL BECKER
> *How New Will the Better World Be?*

6

ENDURING IDEALS
AND TEMPORAL DEVELOPMENTS

THE following chapters are devoted to outlining the ethical-
political position requisite for a reformulated educational policy. Contemporary trends in science and religion will be considered. But the
central issues lie in the area of social thought. The main problems in
educational philosophy are connected with the struggle of democracy
with the totalitarian ideologies, with the effort to preserve its values
and embody them more fully in the light of new conditions and possibilities. The movement in contemporary social thought might be
characterized by Stephen Spender's phrase, "Forward from Liberalism."[1] The characteristic features of nineteenth-century liberalism will
be reviewed and the fundamentals that have been challenged by communism and fascism discussed. From this analysis we may proceed to
formulate the main lines of a reconstructed conception of democracy.

The term "democracy" is eminently fitting as a designation of the
pattern of ideas requisite to guide the educational purpose: it has both
ethical and political implications. It has outgrown its earlier limited
connotation as a method of government and assumed the character of
an all-embracing philosophy of culture. Implicit in American life at
the outset, it came to maturity in our own century in the first struggle
with German autocracy, achieving global dimension in Woodrow
Wilson's proclamation: "The world must be made safe for democracy." The struggle with fascism and communism in our own day has
made the word "democracy" a symbol of the Western tradition and
way of life.

As a consciously held social philosophy, democracy may be said to
be a creation of American life. But the ideals that we call "democratic"
transcend any particular national experience. They are derived from
a heritage of religious, philosophic, and political conceptions that

reaches back to classic times. If there is warrant for the faith in the ultimate victory of democracy as a basis for a one-world order, this is because it embodies universal ethical aspirations and political principles which have found expression ever more fully—although always imperfectly—throughout the course of civilization.

"Definitions," as a recent statement has it, "acquire their full meanings in the course of the historical process. They cannot be used intelligently unless we concede that their penumbrae are not easily penetrated by linguistic short cuts."[2] It is important to emphasize the historical perspective as a corrective to current educational discussions of democracy. As noted in previous chapters, one fault of progressivist educational theory is the failure to give adequate consideration to the structural aspects of society. The other is the tendency to neglect the historical background of ideas. As a result, the discussion of democracy in pedagogical literature tends to circle around the generalities of self-government, cooperation, intelligence, group participation, and the like. Important as such conceptions may be, without relating them to social realities and to perennial ideals, the discussion tends to lack content and to evade the difficult problems that must be faced in the attempt to implement democratic ideals.

A review of the pivotal concepts that have gone into the making of modern democracy will exemplify the continuity in Western thought. It will illustrate the power of ideas in human history. It will, also, make apparent, as Lord Acton says, "that pure reason is as powerless as custom to solve the problem of free government; that it can only be the fruit of a long, manifold, and painful experience." The difficulties are not due to human failings alone; they are due as much to man's striving for perfection; not only to the obstruction that matter places in the way of vision but also to the struggle of one ideal with another. Every great principle has its antinomy: the will to freedom versus the need of law; the urge for equality versus the need of security which property brings; the impulse for self-realization versus the obligation to the state; the necessity of civil law for each state versus the ideal of a universal law for the whole of mankind.

1

The germinal concepts of democracy as the aspiration for an ideal social order lie deep in the soil of the Judeo-Christian and the Classic-

Stoic traditions. First of all is the primary Hebrew concept of the infinite worth of the person as made in the image of God with which is inseparably joined the idea of the unity of the human race as descended from the single ancestor, Adam. A corollary of this twin conception is the principle of the equality of all men, the dynamic force in the evolution of the democratic conception. A second principle which enters into the heritage of Western civilization is the conception of a rule of universal law as against the legislation of the state, of a transcendent law which aims at a justice alike for all men as a matter of right. In the Judeo-Christian view, the universal law is the commandment of God; in the Stoic philosophy it is the counterpart of a rationally ordered Nature. In both is expressed the same aspiration—to govern life by a principle that transcends the self-interest, the error, and the arbitrariness that mar merely human legislation.

There is a third momentous idea—the crucial idea of freedom which aims to liberate men from governmental tyranny and spiritual restriction, from the rigidities of priest-like legalism as well as from slavery to the caprice of princes; and on the positive side to allow men to live a life in accordance with what is believed to be God's will or in harmony with a reasoned conception of the Good. And to this triune idea, of personality, of universal law, and of freedom, may be added a fourth—the longing for civil peace, for cessation from war when men shall beat their swords into ploughshares, and for peace of mind which is given to us when the Lord lifts up the light of his countenance toward us.

The ideas of the prophets and teachers of ancient Israel are expressed in a religious and poetic universe of discourse. The Jews never created a state in harmony with their spiritual vision. Insofar the ideal of fraternity and equality found expression in communal form it was through the congregational fellowship of the synagogue. The rationally minded Hellenes, whose center of life was in the city-community, contributed, along with their philosophic conceptions of the nature of the state, the major political principles of democracy. Chief among these is constitutionalism, the principle that the rulers whoever they may be, princes or people, are subject to a fundamental law which sets limits to what the legislators can decree. In the Greek view, the essence of tyranny, or as we would say, of dictatorship, was not op-

pressive one-man rule; tyranny would be exercised by a whole band
of men elected by the populace when they flouted the underlying constitution of the state. Between the laws passed from time to time by
the assembly and the fundamental law of the city, a basic distinction
existed. The latter, as *nomos*, as a way of life, had a deeper rootage
in the traditions of the community; to it was attributed the sanction
of divine origin. In this unwritten law of *nomos*, the ethical ideal of
justice is linked with the ideal of equality in a threefold sense—
equality before the law (*isonomia*), equality of personal dignity
(*isotimia*), and equality in the right to speak before the assembly
(*isogoria*).[3]

Basic to Greek politics was the principle of citizenship, the idea that
the governed participate in the control of government. This represents
an epoch-making advance over theocracy and monarchy, the political
modes of the ancient East, despite the fact that citizenship in the
Greek states was limited to the free-born descendents of the founders
of each city-state, and excluded besides slaves, all "aliens"—Hellenes
as well as Barbarians. An associated idea was the supremacy of the
popular assembly, subject only to constitutional limitations which
conferred on the whole body of citizens, in their several classes, the
power to legislate and made the magistrates and other officers of government responsible to the will of the people. In practice, one class or
another—the large landowners, the merchants and manufacturers, the
farmers, artisans and sailors—usually exercised political control. In all
forms of government, however, there were provisions for checking
the influence of one class by that of another, so that all Greek governments were based on the principle of a "mixed constitution." Discussion played a major part in the procedures of the assembly and the
law courts, and thus the democratic principle of persuasion was substituted for coercion as the major element in social control.

To these principles, Rome added the emancipation of citizenship
from the connection with descent. Citizenship became a social honor
and economic privilege which could be conferred on any person without regard to race or nationality. This gain was, however, counterbalanced by diminution of the element of political participation.
Already in the first century before the Christian era, the popular
assembly had lost all real influence on legislation; under the Empire,
the ruler exercised absolute control. A vestige of the democratic idea

remained in the legal fiction that the power of Caesar had been dele-
gated to him by the people. The Roman lawyers continued to insist
that the state existed for the welfare of its citizens and that no government was legitimate which did not derive its authority from the
will of the people, and this theoretical legal position, a heritage be-
queathed to the Middle Ages, became an important factor in the
struggle for democracy in later times.

With the extension of the Roman Empire, the Stoic idea of a *jus
naturale* reflecting a rational order in nature became merged with the
jus gentium, the body of law applied to cases in which citizens of
foreign states were involved and which followed principles common
to different communities. In practice as well as in theory, law freed
itself from reliance on separate national traditions and from the control of particular states and came to be conceived as based on rational
principles rather than on precedents alone. Law was no longer merely
lex, the custom of the ancestors, it aimed to be *jus*, a conception of
justice to which civil government must conform. As A. D. Lindsay
points out, the Roman law "helped to create the conception of a community greater than the state, to which men belonged—a common
civilization within which men were governed by common principles
in their relation to one another."[4] Roman law played a major part in
making Europe one single civilization and one community, despite
its separation into many states.

2

The era of a thousand years between the sixth and the sixteenth
centuries has generally been regarded as representing, in its emphasis
on authority and obedience and in its support of a hierarchical social
structure, the very antithesis of democratic principles. There is no
period in history in which the professed ideal and the actuality stood
so starkly in contrast. The masses of the people, held in serfdom, were
badly exploited, vice and ignorance among all classes were widespread,
physical torture was accepted as a usual means of social control.
Despite its high aspirations of charity and loving-kindness, the church
itself was only too often guilty of the common evils of the times.
Nevertheless, looked at from the perspective of its own development,
the Middle Ages, taken as a whole, must be regarded as a period of
progress and not of retrogression. The synthesis of classic thought,

Christian religion, and indigenous ideas and institutions which was brought to fruition in the twelfth and thirteenth centuries was immeasurably in advance of the primitive native, Gallic, Teutonic, and Celtic cultures which it replaced, and in its totality spiritually richer than the antique civilizations of Greece and Rome.

The recognition of the two jurisdictions, of the prince over secular affairs and of the church over spiritual concerns, served as a check on absolutism. The royal power as avowedly Christian acknowledged the spiritual supremacy of the church. Although the theory was as often honored in the breach as in the performance, this acknowledgment constituted an admission that political organization was subject to moral law. To the conflict between the church and royal power modern democracy owes a debt for the subsequent victory of the right of religious freedom and the closely connected civil liberties. The separation of authorities stood in the way of the rise of Oriental despotisms on the lines of the Byzantine empire, and has left with us a heritage of deeply rooted abhorrence of the totalitarian state.

A related contribution was the affirmation of a conception of an ideal morality sanctioned by an authority that stood above the positive law. There is a continuity of thought between the Stoics and the teaching of the Christian divines in the assertion of the principle of a higher law—as the source of human right, of freedom, and of equality. The ideal, it was assumed, could only be lived in the world of the church, and in practice even there the ideal was often corrupted. But the very assumption of a morality of perfection, even though only poorly embodied, was an ever-present reminder of the inadequacy of existing institutions. Modern humanitarian social theory, even when it repudiates clerical authority, stems from the commingling of the sanction of the *jus divinum* with the *jus naturale*. The medieval system of thought created a tension between the socially accepted moral code and the ideal of a higher standard. A primary conception of medieval thought was that "obedience was due less to men than to principle."

A centrally important application of this idea was the subordination of the sovereign to the law of the land. United with the notion that the voice of the people echoed the voice of God, the theory of the subordination of the king carried in it the germs of modern constitutional government. Marsilius of Padua, the able leader of the Ghibel-

lines who defended the authority of the head of the Holy Roman
Empire against papal imperialism, made a formulation which anticipates the liberal theory of John Locke. "Laws," he said, "derive their
authority from the nation, and are invalid without its assent . . . ;
and as all men are equal, it is wrong that men should be bound by
laws made by another." The monarch was responsible to the nation
and its law, and the people had the right to dismiss him if he disobeys
the constitution. "The rights of citizens are independent of the faith
they profess; and no man may be punished for his religion." His great
opponent, Thomas Aquinas, of the party of the Guelphs who sought
to subordinate Christian government to Papal authority, and who was
far less liberal in matters of freedom of belief, nevertheless goes quite
as far as Marsilius does in limiting the princely power by constitutional law. "A king who is unfaithful to his duty forfeits his claim
to obedience. It is not rebellion to oppose him, for he is himself a
rebel whom the nation has a right to put down."[5]

There were also institutional curbs, in medieval times, on the domination by a single centralized governmental authority. Representative
government was, in some form or other, fairly widespread, elected
national assemblies being frequently called together for consultation
by the king. The recognition of autonomous corporations and guilds
for industry and commerce, and, as illustrated in the universities, for
the pursuit of knowledge and truth, laid the basis for the modern
pluralistic state with its wide range of voluntary associations. Feudalism—generally regarded as the very antithesis of democracy—was paradoxically, in certain respects, the most powerful of all restraints on
monarchical absolutism. The relation between lord and vassal involved
a code of rights and duties, and the failure of the lord to carry out his
obligations was held to justify the withdrawal of allegiance. The
Magna Charta, popularly regarded as the root of English and American conception of liberty of all subjects from arbitrary action on the
part of the government, was in the first instance obtained from the
king for the benefit of feudal claims and privileges.

3

The dominance of absolutism which we often associate with the
Middle Ages was characteristic rather of the periods of transition
before the rise of liberalism in the seventeenth and eighteenth cen-

turies. Ultimately, the new forces at work led to an increase of liberty
and equality. But at first the breakdown of the medieval system of a
balance between the power of the church and that of the state—both
under a sovereign law—gave way to an ascendency of absolutism, in
both the realms of the church and the state. For the impersonal authority of law was substituted the personal authority of the king; the
doctrine of the sovereignty of divine rule was supplanted by the idea
of the unfettered competence of the nation-state. "All the religious
authority which had been behind the law and the church was transferred to the king."[6] The new system of monarchical supremacy was
generally supported by the people and by the intellectual elite. It
worked in with the rising spirit of nationalism; it led to strong government felt to be needed at the time; it curtailed exploitation by local
barons and diminished the burdens imposed by the church. Jesuit
and Calvinist theologians supported and rationalized the substitution
of the authority of the sovereign for the authority of law. And the
philosophers each in his own way fell in line with the new trend.*

Nationalism, which at first supported the royal power—as against
the local lords—later allied itself with the middle class and provided
the mass support needed to overthrow monarchical absolutism. The
Reformation, in part a reflection of national and middle-class movements, underwent a similar change. There was much in Calvin and
Luther that supported absolutism in government as well as dogmatism
in religion. But the doctrines of the direct relation of every person to
God and the emphasis on access to the Scriptures were factors in the
development of individual freedom. The multiplication of sects,
moreover, made imperative the toleration of dissenting opinion. The
"Puritans of the Left"—particularly the Congregationalists, Independents, and Quakers—made positive contributions to the development
of democratic conceptions and attitudes. Their congregations constituted self-governing bodies in which each member was equal. Each
congregation was a fellowship united by common belief; discussion

* As Lord Acton, with more than a trace of irony, details for us: "Bacon fixed
his hope of all human progress on the strong hand of kings. Descartes advised them
to crush all those who might be able to resist their power. Hobbes taught that
authority is always right. Pascal considered it absurd to reform laws, or to set
up an ideal justice against actual force. Even Spinoza, who was a Republican and
a Jew, assigned to the state the absolute control of religion." (Gertrude Himmelfarb, ed., *Essays on Freedom and Power*, p. 75). Bertrand Russell in his
History of Western Philosophy explains Spinoza's position: "In Holland, the
state was more tolerant than the church."

and consensus without the use of compulsion represented the approved method of achieving decisions.

The developments in nationalism and religion illustrate the principle that the significance of social forces cannot be evaluated apart from their relation to the political and economic factors at any given period. The same may be said of science and its purported method of unprejudiced empirical inquiry. Here, too, the effects were in diverse directions. On the one hand, the realm of science represented a commonwealth, a new international fellowship indifferent to class or to religious affiliation, composed of men dedicated to the advance of objective truth. At the same time, the Newtonian conception of a world made up of separate hard and solid particles was calculated to lend support, in this period of expanding competitive industrial order, to the conception that society was a collection of isolated rugged individuals. Newton's suspicion of the method of deduction from *a priori* assumptions and his diffidence toward the use of speculative hypotheses—which with him were cautionary measures in scientific inquiry—could be employed to constrain social vision and to defend a narrow utilitarianism.

A counterbalancing element is the concept of "utopia." The sixteenth century gave birth to two distinct types. The former, humanitarian in outlook, is best represented by Sir Thomas More, who describes the ideal society as a commonwealth where all engage in useful labor and all share the product of agriculture and industry in accordance with need. More's utopia was not an escapist reverie; it was the work of an able business man and financier and though imaginative in design was meant to be a guide to social reform. The scientific utopian idea, best represented in Sir Francis Bacon's *New Atlantis*, was, in a sense, a counterproposal to More's *Utopia*. Bacon does not touch on the question of the evil effects of private property; his interest lies in the increased productivity to be brought about by the progress of science and its application to human life. Modern thought, it may perhaps be said, seeks a synthesis of both factors, the social democratic concept of More with the practical, scientific, technological approach of Francis Bacon.

4

With the political revolutions of the seventeenth and eighteenth centuries, the ideas which were fermenting in the preceding periods were distilled and formulated as clear beliefs. In the conceptions of John Locke, who wrote, after the fact, the apologia for the English revolution of 1688, and in the ideas of Rousseau who helped to bring about the French Revolution, we find crystallized the major political concepts of the modern era. Both accepted the social compact principle but their varying interpretations of it reveal the ineluctable conflict in democratic theory between the natural rights of the individual and the general will of the community, between the claims of property and the demands of equality.

Locke's political conceptions must be seen in the context of his great plea for the toleration of religious dissent. Whatever is permitted to the members of one religious community should be permitted to all Christians. "Nay," as he says in one of his letters on toleration, "if we may openly speak the truth, and as becomes one man to another, neither pagan, nor Mohametan nor Jew, ought to be excluded from the civil rights of the commonwealth, because of his religion." This implies the foundation principle of modern democratic government: a clear distinction between the functions of state and church and strict separation of their competences. The state authorities are charged with the protection of civil interests, such as life and health, liberty and property, but salvation is beyond their powers and should therefore be beyond their meddling. Nor should the church, which is a free and voluntary association, interfere with the functions of the state or assume its coercive powers in order to force men to accept one faith rather than another.

His attack on clerical power is joined with opposition to political absolutisms. In the time-honored popular formulation: All men have natural rights of life, liberty, and estate; for the protection of these rights men establish governments; if any government fails to fulfil the purposes for which it was created, the people have the right to change it; and if the government resists, the people have the right to resort to revolutionary means. In the historian's more exact exposition: Government is based on a contract and holds power only as long as it fulfils the trust imposed in it. The government, as the executive chosen by society may forfeit its position if it violates the terms of its trust but society itself remains and is entitled to choose another executive to protect the natural rights of the people.[7] The second version makes clear that Locke's political theory asserts more than the responsibility of government to the people; it limits both government and people by historically developed law as a means of preventing infringement of man's natural rights. Sabine formulates Locke's position as follows: "Legislative power can never be arbitrary, for even the people who set it up have no such power; it cannot rule by extemporary decrees, since men unite to have known law and judges."[8] As George N. Clark, our historian, states it: "Revolution, on this theory, is the ultimate safeguard of law." Law—not the arbitrary will of the people—is the basis of freedom.

The active political citizen, the voter, that Locke had in mind, was an owner of property. Locke's defense of the rights of property represented a broadening of the political base since he demanded rights for those who had acquired property by their own efforts in commerce and industry, as well as for those who inherited it. Charles Beard has summarized Locke's doctrine as "the right of citizens to overthrow governments that took their money or their property without their consent."[9] This is hardly fair, for prerequisite to Locke's conception is a belief in the inalienable rights of all men for protection of life and freedom of conscience—no small matters in the light of present-day developments. But Beard's overstatement reveals important points— that the gains made for democracy in modern times were associated with economic struggle, that the advances made in political organization redounded mainly to the benefit of the middle, the manufacturing, and commercial classes, and that Locke had little concern with the common man or the poverty-stricken laborer of his day.

There was a sharp contrariety, if not a contradiction, in the fundamental assumptions implicit in Locke's conception. On the one hand, echoing medieval political theory transmitted through Richard Hooker, he regarded government as responsible to the community as a whole and as concerned with the common good of the nation. On the other hand, persuaded by the logic and psychology of Thomas Hobbes, he looked upon government as an agency for protecting the private interests of individuals conceived as the components of society. Like the liberals of the later period, he did not face up to the fact that the preservation of the common good and the protection of private rights might come into sharp conflict. Locke's compromise might be defended as the best practical reconciliation of interests possible in his day; however this may be, the fact is that the idea of the common good became recessive in his political theory, and the idea of protection of the liberty and property of private persons from interference by the community became the dominant principle. "The curious result in his social philosophy," Sabine remarks, "was a theory markedly tolerant and critical in defending religious freedom and capable of being highly dogmatic in defending rights of property."

The political thought of Rousseau whose doctrine began with the same double-barrelled assumption as did Locke's, namely, that government existed to preserve the natural rights of the individual and to promote the well-being of the community, led in the end to an emphasis quite opposite to that of the English philosopher. Rousseau's doctrines placed the emphasis on the need of subordination of the individual to the general welfare, on the exaltation of the will of the people as against the preservation of personal freedom. Fundamental to Rousseau's outlook is an insistence on political and social equality. He rejected the view that property qualifications or differences of wealth could justly have any influence on political organization: every man should have one vote and a vote of the same value. For equality, Rousseau sacrificed individuality. Each individual, in the Rousseauan version of the social contract, was to contribute all of his person and all of his power to the government when he voted for it, accepting henceforth its supreme direction as representing the general will of the collective community. By thus losing himself in the corporate body, a voluntary union of free men, the citizen regained himself enhanced as an individual part of the whole.

The "general will" to which he had thus surrendered, Rousseau maintained—echoing the medieval idea that the voice of the people is the voice of God—was always in the right. If the individual had cast a vote or expressed a view which turned out to be opposed to the general opinion he must have been in error. Anyone who refused to obey the general will should be compelled to do so, and such compulsion of the individual by the corporate body of the community, far from being coercion, Rousseau avers "means nothing less that that he will be forced to be free." Consistent with this conception, Rousseau leaves no room for the active cooperation of the dissenting minority in the government organization; he deprecates discussion among the citizens as tending to obscure the general will which developed fully only when each citizen in the first instance thinks only his own thoughts; he favors the plebiscite as against the parliament; he deprecates party organization and free association within the state as possible rivals to the absolute and indivisible sovereignty of the general will of the community as a whole.

Beginning with an exaltation of the natural right of the individual to freedom, Rousseau ends with a glorification of the collective will. He transfers both ecclesiastical infallability and monarchical absolutism to the mystical entity of "the people." In its extreme form the idea of the general will could be used, as it has been in our own day, to give support to the fascist domination of a minority which claimed to reflect "the community of blood and soil." In Rousseau's day, the concept of the "general will" gave support to the revolutionary denial of the privileged position of the clergy and the nobility. The bourgeoisie, who came into power, limited the suffrage by property qualifications. Nevertheless, the grandiose phrases of Rousseau, who spoke with fervor of man as created free and equal, were not without effect in advancing the cause of universal suffrage and in converting the idea of democracy from a method of government to the broad social principle.

The culmination of the long historical evolution in European civilization of the ideas of freedom, equality, and human right comes in the great declarations of the eighteenth-century revolutions. The singular significance of the American and French proclamations resides in their deliberate intention to base government on enduring principles, in the conviction that no free government can be preserved but, as the Virginia Declaration sets forth: "by a frequent recurrence to fundamental principles." These principles are rational and moral in essence, they have a sanction which transcends the judgment of any one age or nation.

The usual analysis attributes the American Declaration mainly to the influence of Locke, but it would seem that the Rousseauan interpretation of the social contract greatly affected Jefferson's formulation.* His substitution of the phrase "life, liberty, and the pursuit of happiness" for Locke's "life, liberty, and estate" is expressive of a different spirit than that which animated the property-minded Eng-

* This does not necessarily imply that Jefferson read much of Rousseau, since the thought of the period was pervaded by the French sentiment and its appeal to the conscience of mankind. See Carl Becker, *The Declaration of Independence*, pp. 27-28.

lishman. The Constitution, the instrument of government, follows
the practical British tradition; the Declaration of Independence, in its
memorable opening paragraphs, reveals the broader French humane
vision. The English talked in terms of the "free-born Englishman."
The French publicists spoke of citizens primarily as men; they
grounded their views on universal reason; and they believed that universal reason was a manifestation of the mind of the Creator who
endowed all men with rights that no human power could justly take
from them.

This universal outlook served to connect the modern development
with Judeo-Christian and the Classic-Stoic heritage and was destined,
after the period of the liberalist compromise of the nineteenth century, to supply the dynamic toward international organization and
world unity which our own epoch is struggling to achieve.

NOTES

1. Stephen Spender, *Forward from Liberalism* (Random House, 1937).

2. Max Horkheimer, *Eclipse of Reason* (Oxford University Press,
1947), p. 165.

3. H. Lauterpacht, *An International Bill of the Rights of Man*
(Columbia University Press), 1945, p. 18.

4. A. D. Lindsay, *The Modern Democratic State* (Oxford University
Press, 1947), p. 57.

5. Lord Acton, *Essays on Freedom and Power*, Gertrude Himmelfarb,
ed., (The Free Press, 1948), p. 65.

6. Lindsay, *op. cit.*, p. 73.

7. George N. Clark, *The Later Stuarts, 1660-1714* (Oxford University
Press, 1940), p. 142.

8. George H. Sabine, *A History of Political Thought* (Henry Holt &
Co., 1938), p. 534.

9. Charles A. Beard and Mary R. Beard, *The Rise of American
Civilization*, 1927, p. 187.

7

THE NINETEENTH-CENTURY LIBERALIST COMPROMISE

The eighteenth-century declarations of the rights of man continued to act as a social ferment throughout the subsequent era and exerted a profound effect on the character of the modern state. But these idealistic proclamations did not as a matter of fact become the basis of actual policy. The principles which guided social organization and constitutional development during the nineteenth century resulted from the interaction of the revolutionary ideals with historical forces and with class interests—particularly with the struggle for position and power of the newly risen class of industrialists.

To the body of social thought which evolved, the term "liberalism" still applies. In its broadest sense liberalism signifies the principles that have been held up as ideals in recent centuries: belief in popular government, exaltation of the liberty of the individual, tolerance of diverse opinion, faith in reason, in free discussion, and in education as a means to social reform and continuous progress. In this general meaning, liberalism had its conservative as well as its radical exemplifications, its Christian as well as its secularist interpretations.

In a more specific sense to be discussed in this chapter, liberalism refers to the pattern of ideas formulated by the "Philosophical Radicals" in England under the leadership of Jeremy Bentham. Adam Smith, Ricardo, and Malthus laid the economic foundations; James Mill expounded the doctrine and won many followers for it. His son, John Stuart, and colleagues of the Utilitarian Society organized in 1823, made it the regnant position of progressive intellectuals in the second and third quarters of the nineteenth century.

Though far from consistent, the compound of ideas associated with laissez-faire and utilitarianism held together as an effective working

philosophy and exerted a decisive influence on the course of Western
civilization in the last one hundred years. It is this heritage of liberalist
principles which until recently was widely accepted in Europe and
America as the core of progressivism. In some of its aspects it still
remains the basic philosophy of Western life. But as is now generally
recognized, the vast changes that have taken place since its formulation, joined with long-standing criticisms of its moral and intellectual compromises, demand a revision and reconstruction.

1

The component of liberalism which remains its lasting contribution
to the democratic conception of society is the substitution of popular
representative parliamentary government for the system of absolute
monarchical rule which immediately preceded. The liberal state of
the nineteenth century was strongly influenced in its actual working
by the laissez-faire principle which attempted to minimize political
control over economic enterprise. But its political conceptions and
practices retained, to a greater extent than Benthamism, a connection
with the notions of natural law and natural rights. Political liberalism
goes back to Locke, and through him to the deep and varied source
of ideas in European history. In some aspects, as in the division of
powers and in the pluralistic conception of social organization, it
reveals medieval influence. In others, as in the participation of the
body of citizens in government and in the concept of a mixed constitution within a framework of law, it harks back to classic times.

It is in its assumption of the primacy of law and the inalienability
of civil rights that liberalism in its total configuration must be evaluated. The separation of powers between the judiciary, on the one hand,
and the legislative and the executive on the other was designed as a
curb on the concentration of rule in any one branch of government.
But it had another, it might be said, a transcendental significance.
The independence of the judiciary places the whole scheme of
democratic government under a framework of law that has developed
in the course of time and stands above the present and the particular
in an enduring continuity and universality. In the American system,
this is explicit in the recognition of the Constitution as the framework
of legislation. In the British tradition which adheres to the principle
of parliamentary supremacy, the high regard for precedents and for

the morality of lawful procedure achieves essentially the same purpose. In both we find the concept of the Bill of Rights which legislation and the courts may interpret and modify for the purpose of ever better realization but which no human power can take away or transgress.

It was the tacit assumption of the sovereignty of historically developed law that made workable the counterbalancing principles of majority rule and minority rights which characterized liberalism. Underlying, moreover, was a strong feeling of national cohesion, a sense of membership in a community with a common destiny. The principle of nationality was still in the nineteenth century joined to the impulse to liberty and popular rule. It worked to offset doctrinal differences and to moderate class divisions to some degree. Common language, common history, and a common heritage of values, as well as of common law, provided firm bonds of social unity.

Although the liberalist conception is generally interpreted as having made the individual the unit of social organization, the right of association which it included as an essential of civil liberty necessitated giving large place to group life and to autonomous institutions. Liberalism allowed a wide range of independence to the family, the church, and the school. While liberalism opposed the establishment of a single religion as authoritive, and although it tended in its typical forms toward secularism, the principle of the freedom of worship encouraged the organization of churches. The family with its right to bequeath property and its prior responsibility for the education of the child, was implicitly regarded as the very foundation of the national life. Toward organization in the economic field, liberalism's position was compromised. Despite its opposition in theory to any combinations either as among employers or workers, it early acquiesced in the corporate organization of business. It was antagonistic to trade-unionism, but the principle of free association won out in the end also in the field of labor.

The individualistic impulsions which Benthamism stimulated were nourished by its alliance with laissez-faire capitalism; they were not derived from its political conceptions. In its opposition to the mercantilist system which required strict regulation of trade and manufacturing on the part of government, economic liberalism formulated the doctrine of free enterprise which aimed to emancipate economics from political control and allow it to develop in accord with its "natural laws." Through free contract between employer and workers, through the automatic regulation of the market by supply and demand, through freedom of trade among the nations, production would continuously expand and bring about an increase in the national wealth. Freedom of enterprise would result in a true justice: wages to labor, profits to the capitalist, rent to the landowner, would all fall into a balanced equilibrium. As David Ricardo who formulated the basic principles of the classical capitalist economy averred, in the free competition of all with all, "the interests of the individual and that of the community are never at variance."

On the supposition that society was the sum of the individuals who composed it, the doctrine of the fusion of interests was perhaps not implausible. Nevertheless, it was recognized that there were difficulties in the simple arithmetical conclusion. To bolster the optimistic view of the beneficent working of natural law in economics, the French thinkers of the eighteenth century postulated "a pre-established harmony" in the universe and Adam Smith invoked an "invisible hand" which directed each individual, without his knowing it, to labor in the interest of the general welfare. However, the evidence provided by the classical economists, as Élie Halévy has shown, reveals a sharp "natural divergence of interests" not a natural identity of interests among the several classes, landed aristocracy, capitalists, and labor.[1]

Ricardo, the founder of classical economy, asserted: "There is no other way of keeping profits up but by keeping wages down." In keeping wages down, he believed, he had the help of nature, as Malthus, his friend, had convinced him. The natural propensity to reproduce led to a steadily increasing population against a relatively limited food supply with the result that the hungry worker competing with other hungry workers could never receive more in real wages than the amount he needed for subsistence for himself and his family. The real problem was with the landlord. Since the supply of land was limited, the owner of it, in periods of increasing population and advancing industry, was in a seller's market, to use our own expression, and could place a burden of larger ground-rents on the capitalist. Protected by the corn laws, he could charge a high price for the foodstuffs produced on his land, thus indirectly forcing up the wages the entrepreneur had to pay for labor without at all improving the standard of living of the worker. As Ricardo saw it: "The interest of the landlord is always opposed to the interest of every other class in the community."

Classical economy depicted the landowner as a parasite who lived in extravagance at the expense of the producing classes. It obscured the harsher struggle between the capitalist entrepreneur and the industrial wage-worker. All that the liberalist economist demanded of the aristocrat was to give up the special privileges conferred on him by tradition and by law—to force him to lower the ground-rents, and to induce him to invest his inherited capital in industrial enterprises. For the working class, however, the classical economy was indeed a "dismal science." It gave them only the short end of the "work and save" prescription for happiness: he could work but not save. His earnings, determined by the iron law of wages, were barely sufficient for subsistence. A few exceptionally capable and industrious individuals who married late and through continence limited the size of their families could hope to rise to the middle class state of redemption. But the mass of the working population were doomed to everlasting misery in accord with the laws of nature and for the benefit of society as a whole.

"The imposing intellectual structure erected by the classical economists," Schapiro observes, "reconciled a new contradiction in human society: progress and poverty."[2] Identified as they were with the interests of the industrial and trading classes, the Benthamites did not see that their central moral principle "the greatest good of the greatest number" was negated by the Ricardian-Malthusian view that the working classes were doomed by nature's laws to misery and squalor. Bertrand Russell has characterized the Benthamites as "a curious set of men . . . arguing carefully from premises that were largely false to conclusions that were in harmony with the interests of the middle class."[3]

2

The practical outlook of English liberalism expressed itself philosophically in the doctrines of utilitarianism. This prudent, rationalistic philosophy abjured supernaturalism and revelation, frowned upon mysticism, looked unfavorably at all that led away from positive science. Like the eighteenth century thinkers, the utilitarians thought

of the universe as a natural order subject to undeviating laws, a knowledge of which could be obtained through reason and inquiry. The
French thinkers of the Enlightenment, however, retained a high
regard for general principles as a basis for reasoning and for mathematical demonstration as a method of proof. English thought in the
liberalist era went much further in opposition to the scholastic
emphasis on the reality of universals and on the significance of eternal
truths. It developed in an extreme nominalistic direction, stressing
the importance of the individual observed facts as the basis of
generalization; it espoused induction from sense experience as the
only true scientific method. It repudiated all *a priori* thinking and
refrained, so it thought, from the use of speculation in the construction of hypotheses.

As Halévy says: "What is known as utilitarianism, or Philosophical
Radicalism, can be defined as nothing but an attempt to apply the
principles of Newton to the affairs of politics and of morals."[4] It was
imbued with the belief that a precise scientific conception of the
good society could be derived from an analysis of the simple elements
of human nature in the same way that universal natural laws had
been formulated on the basis of a study of physics. These simple
elements consisted of *pain* and *pleasure*. Happiness, the goal of life,
meant a maximum of satisfactions and a minimum of pains—both
of a concrete measurable sort. Bentham attempted to work out a
"felicific calculus"—a quantified scale as "clean as mathematics"—
by which the individual would be aided in estimating the amount of
happiness to be attained by any line of conduct. General ethical
concepts such as duty, right, justice, were for him abstractions which
had neither force as drives nor value as goals. Those who urged
men to self-sacrifice for the good of the state were serving neither
the benefit of the individual nor the welfare of society. The interest
of the whole could be nothing but the sum of the interests of each.
Men were moved only by self-interest; all that men could or should
do was to use intelligence in their self-interest. John Stuart Mill,
more sensitive than the angular Jeremy Bentham, would judge the
quality as well as the quantity of the pleasures. But he, too, in
principle maintained the creed of utility as the foundation of morals
and conceived of happiness in terms of the pain-pleasure principle.

Despite their insistent individualism and their self-conscious materialism, the utilitarians were far from encouraging self-indulgence. They renounced the pleasures of passion and embraced the delights of the intellect, they discountenanced the rich living of the aristocrat leisure class and urged the middle-class regimen of work and save as the way to happiness. Their high evaluation of concrete goods was a reaction against the preachment of ethical generalities which had no effect on life, and so often served as a means of buttressing the old regime of clerical authority and aristocratic privilege. Their insistence that men were selfish arose not out of cynicism but from their desire to build their social theory on realistic and sure foundations. There was, perhaps, a bit of pose about it: the honest Bentham gave the case away when he declared, "I am a selfish man as selfish as any man can be. But in me, somehow or other, so it happens, selfishness has taken the shape of benevolence." John Stuart Mill granted to all men "an innate feeling of unity with his fellows," as one of the basic human wants which led men to seek satisfactions as would not interfere with the satisfaction of the needs of others. Despite much descanting on individual self-interest, it may be said that the welfare of the many was in their minds. Their belief in "the greatest good of the greatest number" was sincere although the number who could achieve it was limited, they thought, by natural economic laws.

Some ambiguity and doubt persisted. While they believed that the average man was reasonable enough to follow the line of enlightened self-interest which implied an equal regard for the other fellow's interest, they did not depend on nature alone to preserve the good social order. They had a high estimate of the part that ownership of property had in making men rational and responsible. They recognized the value of education in developing an enlightened social self-interest. But they placed the greatest emphasis on legislation and with Bentham, the key to securing social behavior was the "scientific" dispensing of pleasure and pain, in such a way that private interest should be made to coincide with the public good. Despite their advocacy of a natural identity of interests in the economic sphere, in politics and morals the utilitarians followed the Benthamite doctrine of "the artificial identity of interests" through legislation. The civil law formulates obligations; the penal law imposes punishment when obligations are violated. "Law alone has accomplished what all the natural feelings were not able to do."[5]

In line with its practicalist tendency, utilitarianism rejected the concept of natural rights as a basis for social and political organization. Jeremy Bentham decried the doctrines of the "state of nature" and the "social compact" as nonsensical fiction, as a "sandy foundation" on which to erect a government; he ridiculed the Declaration of the Rights of Man as a "hodge-podge of confusion and absurdity." Much as he contemned the aristocratic tradition of England, he hated the French egalitarian movement even more. In general, he had no faith in abstractions and broad moral sentiments. He was mainly concerned with achieving concrete reforms in law and in the administration of government. The question was not, in his view, what general rights mankind had before government was instituted, but what tangible benefits they derived from it after it had been formed. The practical and utilitarian attitude of the Benthamites, as Carl Becker has pointed out, was greatly influenced by the anti-revolutionary mood of an age "that looked back to the Reign of Terror and forward to the socialist menace." "The very word 'utilitarianism' had a pacific and practical sound; it enabled men to be democratic without being visionary—above all without being thought by others to be pro-French and revolutionary."[6]

The principle of equality, though not absent in the liberalist philosophy, was made secondary. Liberalism held that all men of whatever race, class, or religion should be equal before the law and on this it stood firm. But it never assumed that men were born with equal faculties or that they should enjoy equal economic status. Equality of opportunity was its thesis not equality in material rewards: it justified differences of property and of social position when these were the result of competition. On no point was Bentham more insistent than on the superiority of the principle of property over that of equality: "When security and equality are in conflict, it will not do to hesitate for a moment. Equality must yield."[7] When the Benthamites agreed to extend the suffrage to the working class, they did so as a means of counteracting the power of the aristocracy not on the principle that all men were created equal.

In the question of equality among the nations there was, likewise, a divergence between the broad doctrines of the eighteenth century revolutionary era and the nineteenth century English liberalist theory. Liberalism theoretically favored freedom for nationalities as it advocated independence for individuals. International cooperation, it was believed, could be achieved through the limitation of armaments, the arbitration of disputes, the interchange of thought—above all through the promotion of free trade. The Benthamites were opposed to colonialism, but they were motivated not by the idea that each nation was entitled to equal status among the powers of the earth but by the belief that free trade between the colonies and the mother country would be mutually beneficial. They gave the impression that they were anti-imperialists, but they did not, when it came down to cases, advocate the dissolution of the British empire. Their readiness to allow self-government to the colonies was no more than an application of the laissez-faire principle to imperial affairs. It seems, moreover, that their advocacy of colonial emancipation was limited to dependencies which were of the same race and to nations which were "civilized"—that is, heirs to European culture. Even John Stuart Mill allowed himself to say in the essay *On Liberty*: "Despotism is a legitimate mode of government in dealing with barbarians provided the end be their improvement and the means justified by actually affecting that end."

The eighteenth-century revolutionary doctrine had made equality paramount with liberty. Liberalism erected the social structure on the cornerstone of freedom. Among the intellectual leaders of the liberalist philosophy, freedom meant first of all freedom of thought as a positive factor in social and cultural life. Freedom of inquiry and of discussion was not conceived as a wilful assertion of the relativity of truth but as means to achieving a firmer hold on truth. As Mills' essay testifies, liberalism wished to defend truth against the tyranny of mass public opinion as well as against the suppressive forces of church and state. However, under the influence of laissez-faire, there developed a strong tendency to interpret liberty, in the negative sense, as meaning freedom from external control. In America particularly, intellectual freedom became tinged with rebellion against authority and with the assertion of the will of the individual against that of society.

Liberalism as a social philosophy was formulated by intellectuals in the name of reason and science. It was inspired by a genuine concern for the abolition of abuses and for social reform. But these positive features were qualified by a close affiliation with the material

interests of the middle class. Liberalism became as Laski termed it,
"The Philosophy of a Business Civilization."[8] It raised the striving
for financial success to the plane of a high virtue and identified the
advance of capitalism with the progress of mankind. It rationalized
low wages and periodic unemployment as unavoidable consequences
of unchangeable economic laws. The main support of measures
designed to ameliorate the conditions of life for the factory worker,
e.g., protection against unhygienic conditions, limitation of working
hours, came not from Liberalists but from Tories and Conservatives.
The more fundamental political changes, e.g., manhood suffrage, the
secret ballot, abolition of property qualifications for members of
Parliament were promoted by the Chartists, the first organized class-
conscious movement of English workers.

3

In the last quarter of the nineteenth century, liberalism branched
into two opposite directions—one in line with extreme individualism,
the other inclining toward an emphasis on social control. Herbert
Spencer represented the utilitarian view in an extreme form, carrying
the idea of laissez-faire in politics and competition in economics to
bitter logical conclusions. He made the Darwinian conception of
natural selection the basis of sociological theory. Evolution was the
result of the struggle for existence which eliminated the weaker members of the species and led to the "survival of the fittest," a phrase
which he coined before Darwin's conception was elaborated. The
struggle for existence, Spencer taught, was nature's way of bringing
about continuous progress which led from homogeneity to heterogeneity, to the emergence of ever greater and mightier individuals
whose leadership brought society forward. Any action on the part of
society to extend help to the weak in body or mind—to those who
had fallen by the wayside in the economic struggle, was an obstruction
to the natural advance of society to ever higher levels. He was opposed to all legislation that interfered with "industrial freedom."
Though he believed in widespread education as a means of preparation for social life and for vocations, he was against any public support
of it.

The beginnings of a contrary trend are evidenced in the later
writings of John Stuart Mill. The Report of the Royal Commission
of 1841 on conditions in the mining industry and similar investiga-

tions revealed back-breaking hours of work, for women and children
as well as for men, the complete lack of attention to sanitary provisions, the generally degrading moral situation. Mill was led to modify
his views on laissez-faire and acknowledged that government might
abridge freedom of contract when the general social interest demanded. He recognized the trend toward socialism as an important
movement in the political life of Europe.[9] He does not seem to have
heard of Karl Marx despite the fact that the latter lived in London
and there is no echo in his writings of a class struggle between the
proletariat and the bourgeoisie. He was, however, well acquainted
with the ideas of the utopian Socialists, Saint-Simon and Robert
Owen. His own conception of socialism, if so it may be called, implied
a system of cooperative associations of workers which would retain
the benefits of capitalism without the evils. He made some proposals
for limiting inheritance of large properties which characteristically
were directed not against capitalists but against landlords whom he
would deprive of excess land and unearned increment.[10]

John Stuart Mill never wholly emancipated himself from the influence of the classical economists and of the utilitarians who believed
in the sacredness of the rights of property. It was Thomas Hill Green
who broke with the principles of laissez-faire and individualism. His
conception is reminiscent of the classic Greek view that citizenship
implies membership in a community. He puts forward the idea of
"positive freedom" as an alternative to laissez-faire. Freedom was not
an absolute end in itself: it was a means to the achievement of welfare
for the individual and the community together, and when freedom,
as in the case of freedom of contract, operated against the general
good it ought to be restrained. Thus Green's revision of liberalism,
as Sabine has pointed out, "closed up the gap which laissez-faire
had placed between economics and politics and put on government
the duty of regulating the economic system when it fails to produce
humanly satisfying results."[11] Although reflecting "the rediscovery of
the community" as a corporate body, an idea strongly developed in
the Hegelian philosophy by which he was influenced, Green did not
embrace the latter's exaltation of the state. In harmony with the
British tradition he regarded the liberation of the capacities of the
individual within the framework of community life as the purpose
of government.

The new liberalism provided philosophical support for the "reform state" which came into being in the new century as a result of a combination of forces—of religious humanitarianism, the extension of the suffrage, and the pressure of organized labor. In the years preceding the First World War, the Liberal Party in England sponsored social legislation which made incursions on the freedom of enterprise: regulation of minimum wages, child welfare measures, old-age pensions, unemployment insurance. Trade union organization was encouraged; public support for education was recognized as essential. The business classes accepted the new social legislation with the extra burden of taxation which it entailed as a practical necessity. They saw in it a means of avoiding labor unrest; the more enlightened realized that minimal decent living conditions and a modicum of education and literacy made for a more efficient worker. The reforms touched only the grosser evils of poverty; they did not affect any basic changes in the social order. The greater part of the land remained in the hands of a relatively small number of landlords; the mines and factories were still owned by the well-to-do capitalists. The mass of farmers and factory workers continued to live on what was little better than a subsistence level.

Nevertheless, on the eve of the First World War, liberalism was still confident that its major doctrines offered a sound basis for policy and would lead to continuous social improvement. Progressives urged a greater degree of social control over industry and advocated co-operatives as a means of counteracting the "evils of the profit system." In the main, however, attacks against capitalism were directed against its predatory aspects and monopolistic practices; small-scale free enterprise was accepted by the intellectual elite as well as by the public at large as the major premise of the democratic order. Socialists, a small minority in any case, welcomed the new social legislation as the augury of a new era when government would take over the major industries, operate them for use and not for profit, and secure for every worker by hand or brain a fair return for his labor. It was generally believed that the forces of social liberalism would soon overthrow Russian czardom and convert the German autocracy into a constitutional monarchy.

In its central trend, liberalism continued to rely on the ideas of maximum freedom for the individual and a minimum interference on the part of government. Through enlightened self-interest and freedom of enterprise, through freedom of speech and discussion, of inquiry and scientific research, the spread of popular education, through philanthropy and moderate measures of social reform, through the promotion of international amity by means of commerce and arbitration of disputes—by measures that avoided coercion, the liberal believed that an uninterrupted era of peace and of progress would soon be initiated in the world. In a little book entitled *Liberalism*, published a year or two before the outbreak of the First World War, L. T. Hobhouse, one of its progressive representatives, proclaimed, "You cannot fight against the future, time is on our side."

NOTES

1. Élie Halévy, *The Growth of Philosophic Radicalism* (Augustus M. Kelley, 1949), pp. 318ff.
2. J. Salwyn Schapiro, *Liberalism and the Challenge of Fascism* (McGraw-Hill Book Co., 1949), p. 109.
3. Bertrand Russell, *Freedom versus Organization, 1814-1914* (W. W. Norton Co., 1934), p. 75.
4. Halévy, *op. cit.*, p. 6.
5. *Ibid.*, pp. 35ff, and pp. 486ff.
6. *The Declaration of Independence* (Alfred A. Knopf, 1948), p. 237.
7. Quoted by Schapiro, *op. cit.*, p. 55.
8. Harold J. Laski, *The Rise of Liberalism: The Philosophy of a Business Civilization* (Harper & Brothers, 1936).
9. Schapiro, *op. cit.*, pp. 276-278.
10. Michael St. John Pache, *The Life of John Stuart Mill* (The Macmillan Co., 1954), pp. 488-491.
11. George H. Sabine, *A History of Political Theory* (Henry Holt and Co., 1937), p. 676.

8

THE COMMUNIST AND FASCIST
CHALLENGES TO LIBERALISM

THE decade after the First World War witnessed the beginning of the Great Disillusionment—the disenchantment with the liberalist beliefs that popular education, the promotion of science, the exchange of thought would gradually and inevitably bring about continuous social progress and lead to the elimination of war between the nations. Doubt came soon with the failure to implement Woodrow Wilson's Fourteen Points in the post-war settlements. The United States abandoned the League of Nations of which the American president had been one of the prime movers. The League proved ineffective as an agency for international peace and degenerated into an instrument for securing the supremacy of Great Britain and France in Europe and for maintaining their domination in the Middle East through the control of the mandated territories carved out of the defeated Turkish Empire. The Russian Revolution, hailed as opening up a new era of justice and freedom in the world, early began to show its true totalitarian colors. Side by side with the establishment of communism in Russia, fascism raised its head in Italy, its viciousness partly hidden by the *opera bouffe* character of the "Sawdust Caesar." Then came the collapse of the Weimar Republic, overthrown by the diabolical forces of Nazism.

A total eclipse of liberalism was marked by the West's capitulation to Hitler in the Munich Pact of September 1938. The irony of history would have it that the betrayal of the cause of democracy in the hours of decision was fated to come under the guidance of England, the land where political liberty had first been established and freedom of opinion long encouraged. There was in the Munich appeasement something more than the usual—often necessary—expediency of international diplomacy. The ready assent to the Four-Power Conference with Hitler suggested by Mussolini—from which Czechoslovakia as well as Russia was excluded—laid bare the preference of the leaders of Britain and France for the Fascist as against the Communist dictators. The indifference to democratic principles was revealed in the whole procedure of cynical disregard for the fate of the Czechoslovakian people.

The fear of Russian communism was certainly a central factor in the emergence of fascism and in the support it received from western countries. But that is only one aspect of the matter. Fascism's hatred of British liberalism was at least as strong as—and at heart more bitter than—its opposition to communism, with which in its totalitarian aspect it had in part a common element. The dark forces which expressed themselves in Italian and German fascism, moreover, were not confined to any particular race or nationality. Fascism with its anti-semitic inlay found a sympathetic response throughout the Western world—in the Nordic as well as in the Mediterranean countries, in the British Isles as well as on the continent. In the United States, fascoid agitation during the Hitler period gave evidence that the principles of tolerance and good will were far from securely rooted in the American mores. There can be hardly any doubt as between communism and fascism, the popular choice would have been the latter.

To dismiss communism and fascism as two varieties of the same totalitarian plague, as is most often done in books on education, is no service to democracy. With the defeat of the Axis powers, fascism has suffered a setback, but its seeds have been by no means extirpated, as is evidenced particularly in the rise of violent nationalism in recent years among some of the Arab countries of the Middle East. The power of communism has immeasurably grown since the end of the Second World War, and its readiness to ally itself with fascist powers as against democratic forces has become indubitably patent. It is futile to pretend that its victories have been due to military superiority alone or that its ideology has, in all instances, been imposed on the people without their consent.

However erroneous or pathological we judge the communist and fascist ideologies to be, they are responses to the challenge of an era of crisis. The inadequate attention given to the study of the totalitarian movements in our colleges—in many instances the complete taboo on such study—has been a great defect in college education. The neglect has been particularly serious in the field of teacher training and educational philosophy. All our major educational issues are in some way related to the contemporary attack against democracy. Some analysis of communism and fascism is indispensable as a means of bringing into relief the lines along which liberalism must be revised if it is to regain leadership in world affairs. Our enemies, as George Kennan quoting Shakespeare observes:[1]

> . . . are our outward consciences
> And preachers to us all, admonishing
> That we should dress us fairly for our end.

1

What here concerns us is not contemporary communism but its underlying Marxist philosophy. The character of the regime in Soviet Russia has no doubt been influenced by cultural background and historical factors and the course of events has played an important part in determining its policies at various times. But the driving force in Russia's endeavor to build a socialist state as a step toward the establishment of communism throughout the world derives from the Marxist ideology. There might have been a revolution in Russia against the czarist regime after the First World War in any case, but it would have taken a very different course if its leaders had not been imbued with the doctrines which Karl Marx in collaboration with Friedrich Engels formulated a century ago. The same may be said of China which has followed the Russian revolutionary pattern.

To understand Marxism—its failings as well as its power—it must be viewed as a critique of liberalism, of its philosophic presuppositions as well as of its economic principles. A fundamental difference is the Marxian attitude toward nature. As contrasted with the liberalist view which made nature the ultimate determining factor in human relations and institutions, Marxism magnified the role of historical and social forces. It recognized that man's wants were rooted in nature but maintained that the manner and the means of fulfilment were conditioned and molded by social organization.

In his emphasis on the social and historical factors, Marx followed the Hegelian philosophy which was oriented against the individualistic attitude and the laissez-faire doctrine of English liberalism. He admired the Hegelian dialectic because "it regards every historically developed social form as in fluid moving" and because "it is in essence critical and revolutionary." But in the ideationally dominated Hegel, Marx declared, the dialectic was "standing on its head" and lent itself to mystical implications. The rational kernel could be recovered by turning the Hegelian dialectic "right side up again"—by reversing the relationship between ideational and material. The ideal, Marx asserted, was nothing but the material world as reflected in the human mind.

Marx' conception was broader than usually implied in the term "materialism." It meant first of all that the causes for historical change were to be sought not in any inferred transcendental realm but in discernible factors operating within the social process itself. His view differed from other materialist conceptions of his day, which attributed social causation to climate, food supply and technological inventions. He regarded such factors as significant only insofar as they influenced the total pattern of the economic system—not only the machinery of production but also and particularly the human relations in production, e.g., the customs and laws which regulate the mutual obligations of workers and employers. The Marxian view may be regarded as an extension of the Aristotelian conception exemplified in English thought by Harrington and Locke, namely that economics and class interests are basic to politics. Marx made economics fundamental to the whole range of culture: in the Marxian view, feudalism, capitalism, and socialism represented value-systems as well as forms of economic organization.

In later years Engels was at pains to explain that the Marxian conception never meant that economics was the *sole* determining factor. Other factors, e.g., legal forms, philosophical theories, religious doctrines, interacted with the economic substratum in any given stage of development. The economic factor was decisive only "in the last instance." Despite this strong demurrer, the economic factor—the problem of producing the basic necessities of life—remains the determining force in the history of civilization in accordance with the Marx-Engels version as well as in subsequent Marxist ideology. In the Marxian exposition, determinism was not to be identified with fatalism. On the contrary, it was designed to combat the Ricardian-

Malthusian doctrine which consigned the masses of mankind to poverty as the result of the working of nature's forces. It was likewise opposed to Hegelian determinism which saw history as the automatic evolution of an Absolute Idea not subject to man's will.

In the Marxian view, social forces like natural forces act blindly only when men do not understand them. Once we grasp the real nature of the forces at work in society they can be transformed into powerful instruments for the attainment of desired ends. Men make their own history, though they make it within the framework of given social and economic conditions. The moral of the Marxian analysis consisted in the programmatic conclusion: to achieve the good society, the basic economic structure must be changed. The causes of social advance, Engels wrote "are to be sought not in the minds of men in their increasing insight into eternal truth and justice but in changes of the mode of production and exchange; they are not to be sought in *philosophy* but in the *economics* of the epoch concerned."

This brings us to the critique of the capitalist system, the main target of the Marxian attack. Marx maintained that capitalism which had worked admirably in its early stages when it replaced feudalism had, in the later complex industrial stage, become subject to inner contradictions which would inexorably drive it to ruin. Profit which the classical economist regarded as the spur of industrial advance would lead to the self-destruction of the capitalist system. Profit was "surplus value," a concealed form of exploitation of the worker. It resulted from an appropriation by the class of owners of the value of commodities produced by extra hours of labor which the system of competition enabled the employer to exact. The exploitation of labor under capitalism, Marx averred, was as harsh as under the previous slave and serf system. It was more insidious because it was indirect and impersonal, the result of the ruthless working of the competitive system, little subject to amelioration by benevolent consideration of individual entrepreneurs.

The moral evil of exploitation was, however, not the main point of the Marxist critique; the appropriation of surplus value was bound to have an economic nemesis. It led to technical "overproduction," not to genuine abundance, but to the production of more goods than the mass of the people, the underpaid workers, could buy back. Production for profit was the ultimate cause of the business cycle; competition would lead to the decrease of the number of entrepreneurs; business would enter a monopoly stage. Society would be "polarized," divided into a tiny group of great capitalists and a mass of proletarians struggling for bare subsistence. These developments in the domestic economy would be accompanied by a competitive struggle for sources of raw materials and for markets in colonial lands. The struggle among the great capitalists would lead to economic domination of a few great imperialist nations who would destroy each other through devastating wars.

The root difficulty, the Marxian analysis maintained, lay in the contradiction between the interdependent character of modern production, which demanded planning and coordination, and the private ownership of the means of production which involved dispersed, divisive controls. The potentialities of modern technology for human welfare could be released only if the control and direction of the national economy would be socialized. Moreover, only within the framework of an internationally regulated system could the economic problem be resolved. The radical change from capitalism to socialism could not in ordinary circumstances be made by peaceful parliamentary processes.* The governments of the capitalist countries for all their show of democracy were representatives of the middle classes and would resist by strategem and by force any real shift in the balance of political power. The workers of the world, internationally organized, were the suitable agents of the coming revolution. They had suffered the most from the contradictions of capitalism, they had been reduced to factory hands, items in booking, alienated from the products of their labor, depersonalized. Their struggle was not only for themselves: it was for the whole of humanity. The class struggle was part of a historical process; the workers were protagonists in a

---

* The climate of the age was undoubtedly a factor in the Marxist revolutionary formulation. The memory of the French Revolution was still very much alive in the days of his youth. The *Communist Manifesto* was drafted on the eve of the turbulent year of 1848 when movements of rebellion were widespread on the continent. In the often quoted address delivered in Amsterdam in 1872, however, Marx conceded that in Western countries where the suffrage had been extended and trade unions well developed, the workers might gain their ends by peaceful means. Lenin reverted to the primary Marxist doctrine of unavoidable violent revolution.

world drama of battle between a decaying civilization and a new era of justice and equality.

In the new era, science emancipated from its subservience to capitalist interests would increasingly be applied to production, labor would no longer be onerous; the problem of distribution would no longer be the cause of strife. When scarcity—the ultimate cause of social conflict—should have been substituted by abundance, the dictatorship of the working class would end, and the state as a coercive force would "wither away." The end of the dictatorship would not be followed by a restoration of political democracy in the liberalist sense. "Without representation," Lenin affirmed, "we cannot imagine democracy, not even proletarian democracy; but we must think of democracy without parliamentarianism." The disappearance of the state would not mean the government organs would disappear; they would continue, as the managerial staff of the new society. Society would carry on much as the well-ordered family does without the force of coercion. The ideal of the family "from everyone in accordance with his abilities, and to everyone in accordance with his needs" would at last prevail. The individual would become a free personality again each following the bent of his interests. To the Marxist this is not utopianism, since the material conditions necessary for the good life for all shall have been established.

2

It is not difficult today to point out the errors, distortions, and excesses of the Marxist doctrines. The principles by which the present-day free enterprise economy is governed have been so changed that the Marxist critique of the classical economy is largely, if not wholly, inapplicable. The prophecies of the inevitable breakdown of capitalism, of the impoverishment of the worker, of the polarization of classes have not been verified by events. The Marxist overemphasis on class consciousness has had its counteraction in the fascist regression to tribalism. The Marxist lack of faith in political democracy, its contempt for parliamentary procedures, its suppression of freedom of thought, and its antagonism to religion have been a veritable misfortune for mankind.

It would be futile, however, and less than intelligent to deny the power of the Marxist program—the force of its intellectual analysis as well as its appeal to the felt needs of men. Volumes have been written to attack and also to defend Marx's subtle and erudite critique of the workings of laissez-faire capitalism. John M. Keynes, the brilliant economist whose name identifies an influential contemporary school of economic thought, goes as far as to say: "Marxian socialism must always remain a portent to historians of opinion—how a doctrine so illogical and so dull can have exercised so powerful and enduring an influence over the minds of men and through them, the events of history."[2] Bertrand Russell, has a more generous appraisal of Marx's economic argument on the "surplus value" theory.[3] He judges it to be "partly valid and partly fallacious," and the late Joseph A. Schumpeter, one of the ablest economists of our day, in his meticulous critical analysis, seems partially to agree with this verdict.[4] The deficiencies in the argument are due apparently to the inadequacy of the foundation principle of the labor theory of value formulated by the political economists as much as to the biased interpretations given to it by Marx himself.

While Marx may have failed to prove his own position, he succeeded in overthrowing the major assumption of the classical economy, namely, that prices and wages are controlled by unchangeable natural laws. For all its propagandist bias, the Marxist ideology represented a less disingenuous social analysis than the liberalist compound of natural law and laissez-faire. Marx tore the mask from the liberalist rationalizations and revealed the emptiness of "the greatest good of the greatest number" principle alongside of the iron law of wages which *a priori* doomed the majority of the nation to poverty. The charge of the exploitation of labor under capitalism was essentially true in his time when a working day of sixteen hours was not uncommon. Marx's prediction of the age of Big Business was a notable achievement considering the stage of capitalist development a hundred years ago. His understanding of the relation of large-scale production to mass consumption may be considered even a greater accomplishment. That war is inherent in the competitive struggle for markets and sources of raw material would today be regarded as a truism. If Marx's prophecy of the decay of capitalism has proven incorrect, this is due to the transformation of its character induced by criticism to which his own analysis was not the least contribution. Although the changes did not in the western countries necessitate revolutionary action, they were accompanied by economic depression, by violent labor struggles and by a modification of the balance of political power as between the working and owning classes.

Marxism exemplifies the power of ideas when these are related to human needs and to actual social conditions. It proposes a direct and unqualified attack on poverty and inequality. It has had an appeal not only to the masses of men throughout the world who feel themselves deprived and oppressed; it has evoked a response in the humanitarian conscience. It is the ethical-social factor in communism that has permitted ministers of religion to see an element of Christian teaching in Russian communism despite its antagonism to the traditional churches and its avowed atheism. Karl Barth, outstanding Protestant theologian who recognizes the Russian regime as aggressive and brutal, as "coldly non-Christian" nevertheless has allowed himself to say: "What has been tackled in Russia—albeit with very dirty and bloody hands and in a way which shocks us—is, after all, a constructive idea, the solution of a problem which is a serious and burning problem for us as well, and which we with our clean hands have not yet tackled anything like energetically enough: the social problem."[5]

With its appeal to human needs and humanitarian sympathies, Marxism joined a keen analysis designed to persuade the rationalist and realist. It provided an impressive logical structure, supported by plausible philosophical and scientific arguments. As Schumpeter has pointed out, the combination of emotional appeal and intellectual persuasion has given to the Marxist a conviction that what he stands for can never be defeated. "Preaching the goal would have been ineffectual; analyzing a social process would have interested only a few specialists. But preaching in the garb of analysis and analyzing with a view to heartfelt needs, this is what conquered passionate allegiance . . ."[6] It is to the quasi-religious elements in Marxism that this acute economist partly attributes the success of the communist movement. The spiritual craving left unsatisfied by the decline of traditional religious belief found in Marxism a rationalist version of the ancient longing for paradise. In an age dominated by mechanistic materialism, by secularist scientism and by cultural banality, Marx as a prophet of the socialist utopia, Schumpeter believes, brought a new meaning to life.

This judgment which recognizes the emotional appeal as well as the intellectually persuasive aspects of communism contains no doubt an element of truth. But it should not obscure the ethical impulse that pervades it in the original formulation by Marx and Engels: the emphasis on human equality and on the unity of the human race. The paramount contribution of Marxism—and this, too, reflects an ethical purpose—is the recognition of the significance of the economic factor, not only in and of itself as basic to human welfare, but as an indispensable prerequisite for the freedom of the person, and for the advance of the cultural and spiritual life.

3

Fascism, unlike communism, was not an intellectually supported theory worked out through years of patient study. Its ideological pronouncements were motivated by considerations of expediency designed to win over mass public opinion. This has led some writers to the conclusion that it was no more than an opportunistic attack on the problems that faced Italy and Germany in the period of insecurity which followed the First World War. Nazism has been described as lacking in any defined purpose whatsoever, as no more than a blind drive for domination by power-crazed men leading the world toward a "revolution of nihilism." But the lack of a clear political theory in the academic sense does not mean that the fascist leaders were devoid of an orientation toward life, a conception of human nature, and of values. Certainly it does not mean that they had no political and economic objectives. Of fascism it might well be said, "If this be madness, yet there is method in it." Despite important differences between the German and Italian versions, and notwithstanding the contrast in the temperaments of the Fuehrer and Il Duce, the leading ideas and the stated political purposes of the two fascisms were strikingly similar.

Fascism which offered itself as an alternative to communism arose, like communism, as an antithesis to liberalism. There was a profound difference, however, between the nature of the two contrasting denials of the liberalist doctrines. Communism's drastic critique was designed to further human equality and human dignity. Fascism rejected liberalism in toto, its ethical aims as well as its political structure. It went further: it repudiated the Western ethic in its classical as well as in its Christian form. The cardinal point in this repudiation was a denial of human equality. The official Nazi handbook for the training of youth states as its first principle: "The foundation of the National-ist Socialist outlook on life is the perception of the unlikeness of men." The Christian Church, particularly the Roman Catholic, is condemned because it asserts, "before God, all men are equal." Free Masons and Marxists are denounced for joining with the Christian Church in denying the German racial concept. The international order of Free Masons, it asserts, "conceals its Jewish plans for ruling the world behind the catchword 'Mankind' or 'Humanity.'" Marxism is no better than Free Masonry: "Under Jewish leadership Marxism intends to bring together everyone 'who bears the face of man.'"[7] The principle that men were born equal was contrary to nature. Some men were predestined to lead, others to follow; some races were created to rule, others, ordained to accept subjection.

Fascism deliberately denied the fundamental principles that under-lay the religious and philosophic traditions of Western civilization. But this is not all: it fanatically proposed a contrary set of principles. On no matter was Hitler more insistent than on the assertion that ideas cannot be crushed by force alone, that along with the ruthless use of force to exterminate the old ideal, a contrary ideal had to be set up. "Every attempt at fighting a view of life by means of force will finally fail, unless the fight against it represents the form of an attack for the sake of a new spiritual direction. Only in the struggle of two views of life with each other can the weapon of brute force, used continuously and ruthlessly, bring about the decision in favor of the side it supports."[8]

Fascism was a positive creed. Its repudiation of the idea of equality was accompanied by an affirmation of the principle of inequality. The classic conception of natural law based on an ideal of right was re-placed by "nature's law" of the survival of the fittest. For the Western belief in a universal ethics with its two-fold regard for the sanctity of the individual and the unity of all mankind, is substituted the apoth-eosis of the nation-state, and the complete merging of the individual into the community of blood-brothers and countrymen. In place of the ideal of self-realization, the fascist offered a glorious *nostrism*, a rapturous "we experience" of self-identification with the "community of blood and soil."* [9]

Liberalism's failure to understand human nature, the fascist maintained, had made it a deceptive and equivocal doctrine. It had robbed men of the basic need of union with the community, made of them unsatisfied "atomized" fragments. Men did not desire individual independence: they wanted well-being, security, a sense of devotion to a group cause. The greatest error of all was liberalism's belief that people wanted to govern themselves. "No," said Hermann Goering, "the people want to be led and governed." The liberal nations did not practice their avowed ethics; they violated the principle of equality in both domestic affairs and in international relations. The real motivation behind liberalism was an inordinate drive for private profit without regard to the welfare of the state as a whole. Liberalism was a shrewd device concocted by the English for weakening the will to live of other nations.

Parliamentary democracy, the fascists declared, taking a clue from Marxism, was a sham. The ordinary citizen had no real voice in government; he had to wait patiently for what came out of the confused councils of a leadership bereft of a realistic political philosophy. Under the fascist regime, the leader was in harmony with the will of his people; and all questions in the national life had been made so clear and simple that every comrade could understand them and cooperate in their solution. The "understanding" was, of course, of a policy laid down from above, and "cooperation" was a compelled duty. But the fascists' desire to obtain psychological consent of the people was

* It is in the light of the conception of the unconditional supremacy of the nationalist conception that we can understand Hitler's hatred of the Jews. Antisemitism is a logical concomitant of fascism, if not its absolutely necessary corollary. It is true that Nazism's persecution and spoliation of the Jews netted it many practical gains: ousting Jews from positions gave jobs to party members; fines, expropriation, forced emigration, brought substantial sums into the treasury; the use of Jews as scapegoats for the defeat of Germany and for exploitive aspects of capitalism turned attention away from the true causes. But above and beyond all these purposes was a psychological purpose. Hitler regarded the Jews and Judaism as symbolizing all that he hated: the idea of equality, of internationalism, of humanity. Just as he aimed to concentrate the love impulse of the "we feeling" on national selfhood, so he aimed to converge the hate impulse on "them," on "the others." And in the light of a traditional European antagonism not confined to Germany alone, but well developed there, it was easy to pick the Jews for this purpose. Anti-semitism is the psychological negative pole of fascism, just as love of the racial national community is its positive.

genuine. They recognized the need of fostering a sense of emotional participation as a means of obtaining mass support for the achievement of their objectives. *Gleichschaltung*, bringing into line, was the method for achieving unified support for the state policy. But it was recognized that terror alone could not achieve this. While coercion and extermination were the instruments of policy against determined opponents, with respect to the uncommitted and wavering propaganda and welfare measures were the means of conversion.

The liberalist economic system based on laissez faire was decried as incompetent and irresponsible, as perpetuating the anarchy of modern life. The concept of the "corporative" or "organic" state was adopted. The fascist economic system was neither socialist nor capitalist in the usual meaning of these terms but a national economy completely controlled in the interests of the state. The capitalist structure was maintained intact, but the operation of business was subjected to strict regulation on the part of the state. The fascist state crushed the power of labor, but also narrowly limited the business man's independence in the interests of the coordinated economy.

4

In much of the current educational and psychological literature the tendency is to find the cause of fascism in mental and emotional attitudes. A usual view is to attribute its rise to the persistence of traditional authoritarian habits of mind. According to this view, the Italians and Germans, inadequately schooled in the processes of democracy, easily, even gladly, yielded to dictatorships. Another approach places the emphasis on psychological factors—on sadistic and masochistic tendencies, on the lust for power on the part of dominating personalities, on the need of identification with a strong leader on the part of the insecure. Most writers imply or recognize that social factors, economic dislocations, national defeat, threat to class position, affected the psychological reactions. But the total impression conveyed, nevertheless, is that fascism was the bitter fruit of individual character traits rather than the result of objective economic and political factors.*

* Among the psychologists, Erich Fromm comes closest to giving weight to the economic factors. He agrees that "psychological conditions were not the 'cause' of Nazism. They constituted the human basis without which it could not have developed, but any analysis of the whole phenomenon of the rise and victory of

To attribute the development of fascism to mental attitudes and emotional forces is to place the cart before the horse. Psychological factors were fully exploited by the fascists before and after they came to power, but the psychological factors were not the causes of the development of fascism. It is obvious that the roots of the Italian and German movements are to be found in economic conditions of the period after the First World War. Fascism became a dominant and aggressive power at the end of the decade of the twenties during an era of depression throughout the industrialist and capitalist world. The positions of Italy and Germany were particularly unfavorable; these countries could not have solved their economic problems without aid from the Western countries who apart from being their industrial rivals were themselves in a parlous economic condition. The situation in Germany was particularly bad. Inflation had led to bankruptcy of the middle class and to mass unemployment among the workers.

Fascism was an attempt to cut the Gordian knot of the economic problem with the help of military force. There were two aspects. One was the imposition of coordination of the various aspects of the economy, between agriculture and industry, and between capital and labor. The other was the stabilization and further development of the industrial economy through imperialist expansion. The key to the understanding of the fascist state is the recognition that it was a political-economic structure designed for the effective pursuit of aggressive war as a means of resolving problems that were integral to industrial society.

At the opening of the century, Italy and Germany found themselves far behind France and Great Britain in colonial possessions on which access to raw materials and markets on a favorable basis largely depended. The First World War was the result of Germany's drive to penetrate the undeveloped area of the Middle East already known to be rich in oil. But at its conclusion, Germany's position was worse than it had been before. Italy likewise driven by the impulse of expansion had joined with Germany and then gone over to the Allied side in the hope of obtaining a share of the spoils of war—the

Nazism must deal with the strictly economic and political, as well as with the psychological, conditions." Even he, however, does not develop the point adequately. See *Escape from Freedom,* (Rinehart & Co., Inc., 1941), p. 218.

carved-up Ottoman Empire. But it got next to nothing and felt itself cheated by the Allies. The League of Nations, idealists hoped, would assure fair equality to all countries in access to raw materials and markets in colonial countries. In the light of the character of the competing nationalist imperialisms of the era, the conception was naïve. The League became an instrument for maintaining the domination of France and Britain as industrial colonial powers.

There was ground for lack of faith on the part of political realists in Italy and Germany in the possibility of finding a solution to their problems through international agencies, or through the cooperation of the Western powers. A German patriot, in the face of actualities, might have formulated a dilemma: either the nation accepted for all time a subordinate position, crushed between the rising power of the Soviet Union and the old Western democracies, unable to solve its internal problems except on the basis of a lower standard of living; or return to the old Bismarckian policy of "blood and iron," and take the long chance of war, either against the East or West, or possibly against both. A similar though less drastic situation faced Italy consigned to poverty if she did not industrialize. Both of these "have-not" nations were in an intermediate and unstable condition; they were not so weak as submissively to accept economic and political subordination; tradition and history induced them to conceive of themselves as the equals of the Great Powers; there was enough in their position to warrant a bid for equality and for power.

Franz Neumann's detailed study documents the conclusion that the purpose of the Nationalist Socialist movement was to unify the nation behind an immense effort at territorial expansion as a means of resolving the discrepancy between the potentialities of the German industrial apparatus and the actualities that existed at the time.[10] First, there was the problem of uniting in a common policy the two controlling elements of the German economy—the agrarian aristocrats of Eastern Germany whose main competitor was agricultural Russia and the great industrialists of Western Germany who regarded England as their enemy.* This was accomplished by building up the navy and air force as well as the army and planning an offensive against both the West and the East. The other more difficult task was to get

---

* This is the only plausible explanation for Hitler's suicidal policy of simultaneous war against both the Western powers and Soviet Russia.

support for the war policy from the German people who were disillusioned with the result of the First World War and who were
strongly impregnated with socialist ideas.

The key to the problem was to persuade the *Junkers* and the industrialists that the successful pursuit of foreign policy through war
demanded social reforms. Neumann's conclusion is that while Germany's return to imperialism was engineered by the industrialist capitalist leaders in combination with the Prussian agrarians, the Nationalist Socialist Party, which also favored imperialist expansion, served
the essential function of gaining mass support for it. This made it possible for Nazism to appeal to all classes. To the worker it promised all
that Marxism offered, without a class struggle: "National Socialism
offered him a higher form of life, 'the people's community,' and the
rule of labor over money, without compelling him to fight against his
own ruling class."[11] To the uprooted middle class—who hated the
banker, the rich industrialist, the arrogant Junker—National Socialism
offered security in position, support against being driven down into
the class of proletarians. The industrialists got the promise of protection from the threat of communism and also from what they considered inordinate demands of organized labor. Fascism was not a
dictatorship established in opposition to the people. As Stephen
Raushenbush discerned in *The March of Fascism* written shortly
before the Second World War, "Fascism is not simply dictatorship,
it is dictatorship with mass support."[12]

Fascist totalitarianism was not the creation of a few evil men who
drew the doctrine out of the recesses of their own fantasy. At the base
of the problem—and without consideration of this fundamental factor
no explanation holds—it was a response to the far-reaching economic
maladjustment due to the contradictions between nationalist economic control and the international character of modern economy.
This is not to say that the fascist solution was inevitable, that there
was no alternative. Germany and Italy might have satisfied themselves
with the position of second-rate powers dependent on the mercies of
France, Great Britain, and the United States. They might have gone
Communist and related themselves to the Soviet system. They might
have suffered and waited patiently in the hope that the League of
Nations would be strengthened and that an international solution to
the European problem would be found. In the light of history, any

of these solutions would have been better than what actually happened to the fascist countries as well as for the world. But given the situation that confronted Italy and Germany, it must be conceded, the choice of war as a means of industrial expansion was "realistic" rather than irrational. It was a method sanctioned by leading statesmen and philosophers and supported by a large part of the people.

The eruption of fascism in Europe shattered the easy belief in the essential goodness and rationality of original man. It exposed to naked view the brutality of the human species when the directives of historically developed conceptions of right and principles of law are abandoned. It revealed a paradox—how in fanatical devotion to cause and to community men can give vent to their basest instincts and commit the most heinous of crimes against mankind. It demonstrated the impotence of religion and education—in and of themselves—in deterring men from abandoning all moral restraints in the struggle for survival in an existent context of insecurity.

In its most vicious form fascism developed in Germany, land of philosophy and music, where classical and scientific studies of a high order were widely pursued, where universal elementary education combined with compulsory religious instruction had long been in force. Nor may it be forgotten that the ascendance of fascism was aided and abetted by the elected political leaders of Britain and of France, many of whom were the elite products of great secondary schools and universities. Perhaps, as some maintain, the divorce of traditional liberal education from concern with social welfare in the class-riven educational system of Europe contributed to the political ineffectiveness of the intellectual class. But the real trouble lay deeper.

However immoral and hateful we may judge fascism to have been, it was a response to conditions which could not be wished away, and which unresolved are always likely to lead to attempts to cut the Gordian knot by measures of force. Fascism—and the same may be said of communism—remains a tragic commentary on the failure of the Western democracies to find solutions to the problems of modern industrial economy in harmony with the interests of the nation as a whole and in the light of the interdependent international character of production. Central in this failure was the inability to make of the League of Nations an international organ of power.

The failure was not only in technical intelligence, in the lack of knowledge and in deficiency of what is sometimes called social inventiveness. The European debacle was, at a deeper level, due to moral and intellectual inadequacy that was not unrelated to the class structure of European society. Despite the fact that liberalist thought looked toward a progressive solution of economic and social problems, it cannot be exonerated from blame—insofar as blame can be attached to any system of thought. Liberalism, in the broad sense, was overoptimistic and rationalistic: it attributed too much to the effects of science, reason, and education, too little to the need of reform in the institutional structure. It laid emphasis—as it still largely does—on methods and processes, too little on definite aims and on concrete social objectives. In the narrower form of utilitarianism, it was devoid of vision and constricted in human sympathy. Its psychological observations lacked insight, its philosophical views were shallow, its moral code was penurious and lacking in grace. Its interest in practical reforms led it into circumscribed compromises. Its separation of politics from economics was a temporizing expedient in the interest of the middle-class.

Underlying the liberalist position was a divorce of ethics from politics which the declarations of the preceding revolutionary age had attempted to unite.

NOTES

1. *Harper's Magazine*, "Overdue Changes in Our Foreign Policy," August 1956, pp. 28-33.

2. John Maynard Keynes, *The End of Laissez-Faire* (Hogarth Press, 1926), p. 34.

3. Bertrand Russell, *Freedom versus Organization*, 1814-1914 (W. W. Norton and Co., 1934), pp. 201ff.

4. Joseph A. Schumpeter, *Capitalism, Socialism and Democracy* (Harper & Brothers, 1947), pp. 21ff.

5. Karl Barth, *Against the Stream, Shorter Post-War Writings, 1946-1952* (Philosophical Library, 1954), p. 139.

6. Schumpeter, *op. cit.*, p. 6.

7. *The Nazi Primer*, translated by Harwood L. Childs (Harper & Brothers, 1938), pp. 5ff.

8. *Mein Kampf* (Reynolds-Hitchcock, 1940), p. 223.

9. Aurel Kolnai, *The War Against the West* (Viking Press, 1938), pp. 63ff.

10. Franz Neumann, *Behemoth: The Structure and Practice of National Socialism,* 1933-1944 (Oxford University Press, 1944), p. 38.

11. *Ibid.,* p. 189.

12. Stephen Raushenbush, *The March of Fascism* (Yale University Press, 1939), p. 24.

9

THE DEMOCRATIC CONSTITUTION:
LAW, BILL OF RIGHTS, AND EQUALITY

THAT a vast transformation is going on in the world has now become a truism. Most apparent are the scientific-technological changes and the political-economic upheavals. The release of nuclear energy, the expansion of communism, the revolt of Asian, Mideastern, and African nations against colonialism are the major factors emphasized in current discussions of the contemporary world. Ideas and aspirations are involved however, not only as secondary effects of the material factors but as primary impelling forces. Already before the Second World War, the literature of the West was pervaded by a consciousness of a widespread disturbance affecting the moral and spiritual, as well as the material and political aspects of life. Publicists wrote of "the world-shattering transvaluation of values," of "the emergence of a new world order."

The revolution of our times is marked by a challenge to liberalism. The wide appeal of fascism and the spread of communism give countenance to T. S. Eliot's assertion: "The attitudes and beliefs of liberalism are destined to disappear, are already disappearing."[1] The failure of liberalism to win world support, one may contend, had objective economic and political causes. It was the result of a long historical process, brought into being by a commercial and industrial class which had succeeded in throwing off the incubus of autocratic rule. Where the necessary development of commerce and industry was lacking or where it had taken place, as in Germany under the tutelage of feudal lords, the political frame necessary for liberalism was never achieved. But the decline of liberalism has had internal causes as well. It compromised the principles of the revolutionary era which originally gave it vitality; it became complacent in the face of widespread inequalities and injustices; it reconciled itself to the submergence of the working class; in practice it acquiesced in the traditional notions of racial and cultural superiority of the white Nordic peoples. It did not move rapidly enough to readjust its economic conceptions to democratic principles or to technological possibilities. It lagged in revising its mechanistic presuppositions of the nature of social evolution.

A fundamental defect was its failure to emerge from its compromising moral neutralism—a neutralism which as T. S. Eliot has pointed out amounts to negativism in our age "when economic as well as spiritual forces are proving the efficiency of cultures, which, even when pagan, are positive." The exponent of "The Idea of a Christian Society" admits that if liberalism disappears from the philosophy of the West we still have the concept of democracy. He has, however, no faith in democracy with its liberalist connotation of freedom, since neither "Liberalism" nor "Democracy," he observes, has any definite meaning; both could be used by the totalitarian as well as by the pluralistic state. But cannot the same be said of any great idea? Has not Christianity itself, which he proposes, been utilized to support the most autocratic and despotical regimes? T. S. Eliot touches the heart of the matter in saying that democracy undefined is weak, even dangerous; the logical inference should be to proceed to define it.

If democracy is to remain a positive force in the world of thought and action it must be defined in terms of ends as well as in terms of method, in terms of embodiments in the social structure as well as in terms of personal relations. The struggle of democracy with communism remains the momentous conflict of the age. Communism has an advantage in that it has a clear and firmly held ideology, related to the felt needs of great masses of men, buttressed by consistent intellectual supports, interpreted in action by a disciplined group of devotees. The strength of democracy is diminished by a lack of an agreed-upon definition of its meaning, by an absence of a unified commitment to its ideals, and, one might say, by an uncertainty of belief in it as a valid principle of life among large sections of the people who render it lip service. It is of the essence of democracy to encourage diversity of opinion. But diversity must be seen within a framework of unity. There must be a community of ethical aims, an accepted political system, and at least a minimum

consensus on economic implications. The reformulation of social
policy will, in part be a reaffirmation of old principles, in part, a
modification of them and an application of new insights. Some of
the points to be emphasized may seem to be a repetition of truisms,
but this is a time when the "vindication of the obvious" assumes
fundamental importance.

1

The first requirement of a definition of democracy is to assert
the primacy of its ethical end as the directing idea of social organization. Democracy proclaims the infinite worth of each person, the
essential equality of all human beings, the unity of the human race.
In this three-fold definition, democracy reaffirms the triune ethical
principle of the Judeo-Christian heritage even when it discards theological and ontological doctrines. In like spirit, the poet of democracy,
speaking in the naturalistic mode, announces the theme thus:

The quality of BEING, in the object's self, according to its own central
idea and purpose, and of growing therefrom and thereto . . . is the
lesson of Nature. . . . For after the rest is said . . . it remains to bring
forward and modify everything else with the idea of that something a
man is . . . standing apart from all else, divine in his own right, and a
woman in hers. . . .

Not that half only, individualism, which isolates. There is another half,
which is adhesiveness or love, that fuses, ties and aggregates, making the
races comrades, and fraternizing all. . . . The liberalist of today has this
advantage over antique and medieval times, that his doctrine seeks not
only to individualize but to universalize. The great word Solidarity has
risen.

Both are to be vitalized by religion (sole worthiest elevator of man or
state), breathing into the proud material tissues, the breath of life. For I
say at the core of democracy, finally, is the religious element. All the
religions, old and new, are there. Nor may the scheme step forth, clothed
in resplendent beauty and command, till these, bearing the best, the
latest fruit, the spiritual, shall fully appear.[2]

The universal ethical-religious spirit pervades the Declaration which
is the fountainhead of modern democracy: "We hold these truths
to be self-evident, that all men are created equal, that they are
endowed by their Creator with certain unalienable rights; that among

these are life, liberty, and the pursuit of happiness." In his essay on "Democracy and America," Dewey brings out the point that "Jefferson's formulation is moral through and through; in its foundation, its methods, its ends." As Dewey explains, when Jefferson uses the word "natural," he means, "ideal aims and values to be realized—aims which though ideal, are not located in the clouds but are backed by something deep and indestructible in the needs and demands of human kind."[3]

As Dewey is led to admit, although Jefferson insisted that the forms and mechanisms appropriate to their realization were subject to change, the *ends* of democracy, the *rights of man* were in essence unchangeable. Adherence to principle and readiness to modify institutions and laws to embody them more fully are both equally involved in the idea of democracy from the very beginning. Emphasis on the enduring moral ends brings the Bill of Rights into the focus of attention. Although it appears in the form of amendments, it is historically prior and, from the democratic point of view, logically prerequisite to the Constitution. The Bill of Rights is designed to preserve the natural rights of man in its major aspects: the security of the person, the pursuit of economic well-being, the aspiration for freedom of mind and conscience.

These remain the fundamental aims of any genuine democratic order. But the specific terms of the Bill of Rights, as formulated in the first ten amendments of the Constitution, bear the impress of their day. It has been necessary to redefine, modify, and extend them through legislative enactment and through judicial decision. In our own day, the right to bear arms, as Carl L. Becker has pointed out, is of greater benefit to gangsters than to decent citizens. "Freedom from want" and protection of the wage earner are as important for the general welfare of the nation as the protection of property rights. Freedom for political discussion in halls of learning may be more significant than the right of orators—fascoid or communist—to harangue the people on the street corners. The content of the Bill of Rights may change from time to time, but the changes are for the purpose of an ever more perfect realization of the enduring rights of man—whether these are conceived as the endowment by the Creator, the ordination of natural law, or more simply a universal human demand formulated in the course of history. Whatever rationale is given, the democratic constitution must be based on imperishable human rights.

The principle of natural rights which was weakened by nineteenth-century utilitarian thought is to be reasserted as a commitment. In this we go back to the eighteenth-century American and French Declarations with their idealistic imprint and dynamic force. On the other hand, in the question of popular sovereignty and its corollary "majority rule," we are right in retaining, as a central principle, the British liberal interpretation. Again, Carl L. Becker's comment is to the point: ". . . although no nation is more entirely committed than we are to republican government operating by majority vote, we have found more (and more ingenious) ways of moderating, delaying, sidestepping, and hamstringing the will of the majority than any other nation has thought it necessary or desirable to submit to."[4]

The principle of popular sovereignty arose as an antithesis to the divine right of kings and aristocracies, and remains indispensable as a counterweight to any conception of absolutism in government. But if it is itself made an absolute it becomes self-defeating. The idea that democracy means that whatever the people decide is right would lead to a pernicious *reductio ad absurdum*, for it could make democracy equal to fascism or communism, that is, to make it mean nothing at all. The idea of "majority rule" as conceived of in the Anglo-American tradition, has to do with limited objectives, e.g., with the election of representatives in the legislative bodies, with the decision on measures within a constitutional framework, as it is interpreted from time to time in legislation and judicial decisions. The events of recent decades have underscored Lord Acton's famous dictum: "The most certain test by which we judge whether a country is really free is the amount of security enjoyed by minorities."

Constitutional government requires at some point "the consent of the governed," but at the same time places limits on what the governed may or may not do. Progressive liberals have been prone to decry "the idolatry of the Constitution." But there is as much danger in the idolatry of "the people" in the collective sense. There lingers on in our political folklore the notion that our civil liberties are threatened mainly by government when in fact they are to a larger extent obstructed by widespread popular prejudices and misunderstandings. While the Supreme Court has in certain periods been the

bulwark of the *status quo*, it has on the whole done more to defend
civil liberties than any other governmental agency taken alone. Constitutional government implies gradualism and non-violent change.
Here, too, our political folklore retains a vestige of the eighteenth
century situation, in the not infrequent reference in high places to
the revolutionary origin of our own government as justification for
rebellion as a legitimate political method.*

2

The emphasis on constitutional principles and qualification of the
doctrine of popular sovereignty is connected with another modification in outlook. It implies a revision of the estimate placed on the
rationality of the individual and his competence in making good
political judgments. The liberalist view as prevalent among progressives in the United States has placed confidence in the good judgment
of the average man. Decisions arrived at by the interchange of individual opinion, it is thought, are likely to represent rational consensus. This view had some warrant in the simpler conditions of life
in New England townships in previous periods, although even in
earlier times the positive influence of the mores and of religion in
determining judgments has generally been underestimated. In any
case, the character of modern life has reduced the modicum of truth
in this view. The complexity of contemporary issues, the heterogeneity
of the population, the absence of a common cultural background,
the lack of opportunities for daily face-to-face discussion, the sharp
division of interests in our industrial competitive society—these and
similar factors minimize the ability of the average individual not specially trained to make truly intelligent, independent judgments. To
a degree, the instruments of mass communication, the radio and tele-

* Thomas Jefferson's letter in connection with Shays' rebellion wherein he
defends periodic bloodletting as a means of refreshing the tree of liberty is sometimes cited. This *obiter dictum*, however, can hardly be regarded as a considered
opinion on the nature of democratic government. Although Jefferson was critical
of certain aspects of the Constitution while in the process of formulation, after
its adoption with the inclusion of the Bill of Rights he described it as "unquestionably the wisest ever yet presented to men." He made his position clear
beyond cavil: "I do then, with sincere zeal, wish an inviolable preservation of our
federal constitution . . ." and he prefaced the affirmation by the comment that
any imputation of a contrary opinion to him would "bear the mark of falsehood
and calumny."

vision may offset, if one selects the best programs, the disadvantages of distance and the lack of personal contact. But, notoriously, for the most part they bombard the public with propaganda that must leave the average person confused if not conditioned to partisanship. Today, to no small extent, as Schumpeter remarks, "The will of the people is the product and not the motive power of the political process."

If the "will of the people" is to retain an important part in the determination of policy, we must modify our conception as to how it is formed and how it finds expression. We must cease to consider it as the sum of the views of self-contained individuals and think of it in terms of increased group participation—of labor organizations, professional associations, scientific, educational, and religious bodies—in political discussions and actions. Another factor which holds out promise for the increase of rationality in the conduct of public affairs is the greater use of scientific knowledge and scholarship in governmental decisions, through consultation with economists, educators, and physicians and through planning boards, university, and private research bodies. While partison orientations undoubtedly play a part in professional counsels, nevertheless the introduction of the scientific, scholarly, and engineering type of mind constitutes an invaluable countervailing factor to the parliamentary discussion which though indispensable as representing particular concerns and commonsense views is at the same time subject to the pressures of vested interests and of local prejudices.

The comments in the preceding paragraphs are intended to emphasize the idea that democracy does not admit the domination of any single factor in government, not even the domination of the "sovereignty of the people." Democracy depends on the interplay of a variety of factors, of majority and minority opinion, of a division of the legislative, executive, and judicial functions and cooperation among them, of the opinions of voters and the views of their representatives who are not, in the democratic system, mere automatic mouthpieces for their constituencies. Above all, democracy implies a pluralistic state; it rejects totalitarianism—the identity of the state with society—as well as dictatorships. In the nineteenth century the state was considered as the servant of the individual citizen; in reality its significant contribution lay in the support it gave the right of association. The function of the democratic state is to serve the life interests of the people and in so doing it will allow to the agencies which promote these interests—the family, the church, the school, business, professional, or labor organizations—the greatest amount of autonomy compatible with the unity of the whole. The liberalist concept was to allow the individual the greatest amount of freedom compatible with the freedom of other individuals. The democratic idea would be to allow each association the greatest amount of autonomy possible without infringing on the autonomy of other agencies.

Democracy involves an element of voluntarism, the sheer will of the individual to protect his self-interest and to realize his individual capacities to the full. But it includes the indispensable factor of control by law based on principles. Prior and prerequisite to the idea of freedom—if democracy is to maintain continuity with the Western tradition—is the conviction as Sir Ernest Barker says: "that a political community is not swayed by caprice . . . but moves in the orbit of known rules. . . . In brief the rule of law is the origin, and always remains at the heart, of the Western political tradition."[5] Walt Whitman adds his definition: "Democracy too is law. Many suppose (and often in its own ranks the error) that it means a throwing aside of law, and running riot. But briefly it is the superior law . . . Law is the unshakeable order of the universe forever."

Our first point, then, is the need of a reaffirmation of the universal principles which found expression in the Declaration of Independence and in the Bill of Rights. Whatever its immediate causes, the American Revolution—as D. W. Brogan has well emphasized in his *Politics in America*—became in the minds of oppressed peoples all over the world as well as in the United States not merely a war of independence from Great Britain but a struggle which signified "recasting a society." The Constitution with its Bill of Rights was looked upon not merely as a frame of government, but as an instrument for the implementation of the Declaration, "as a means of social and political salvation."[6] If America was hailed, during the nineteenth century, as a land of promise, it was because the idealistic version of the character of its government became a part of the folklore of the world. If the moral leadership of the United States has, now in the middle of the twentieth century, been weakened, it is mainly due to the inadequate fulfillment of the ethical ideals underlying the Declaration of Independence and the Bill of Rights.

This is true, despite the fact that on a rough and all-around judgment a greater degree of social equality and individual freedom has been achieved in the United States than anywhere on earth at any time. But in the circumstances that we face today this comparative manner of judgment will not satisfy. The contrast between promise and performance is still too great, in moral attitudes as well as in material conditions. The high principles which have found expression in our literature and in public pronouncement have not been without effect on the lives of many individuals and on the development of American life generally. Nevertheless, the democratic ideals can hardly be said to have won the hearts of our people taken as a whole; they have not penetrated the climate of public opinion, nor become significant factors in legislative enactments.

Toleration of religious differences has been forced upon us by the diversity of creeds rather than by generosity of spirit. Ethnic and racial minorities are taken into account in political decisions but this is due to calculations of expediency rather than to genuine consideration of human rights. Freedom of speech in public places is as often used to preach hatred as to discuss governmental policies; the fascist agitator will find less opposition in the crowd than the advocate of communism. Academic freedom is much qualified when it comes to the discussion of religious, moral, or political issues, and this was true long before the fear of communism aggravated the situation. In some quarters advocacy of civil liberties is likely to be considered the mark of radicalism, however firmly it is based on American tradition, and a reputation for the use of intelligence, as Elmer Davis notes, may put one in the category of a security risk.[7]

A certain distance between ideals enunciated by the leaders of any society and the actual beliefs and practices of the people at large is to be expected. But the gap between the promise of American life and the performance has become too great to allow honest men to be at ease in their consciences. The dualism of theory and practice, moreover, has now become an important factor undermining the integrity of Western civilization. The ambiguity of our position has greatly weakened, if it has not already destroyed, the prestige of the Western form of democracy in the rising countries of Asia and Africa. Material prosperity and efficient technology may for a period of time maintain our power in the world, but moral leadership of the West will in the long run, as Eugene Staley says, depend on "the degree to which we in the United States and other free countries will make democracy work well and live up to the precept of democratic ideals. . . ."[8]

3

It is in the matter of equality, in opportunity and in social position, that the democratic principle is disturbingly compromised. In a series of studies of typical middle-sized cities throughout the United States W. Lloyd Warner of the University of Chicago has described a well-intrenched class status system of "lowers," "middles," and "uppers," the Negroes representing a separate caste with a social status inferior to the lowest caste whites. Perhaps the picture of hierarchical organization would not be so dark if the situation in the large cosmoplitan areas were taken into consideration. But it is undeniable that American society is marked by relatively stable social stratifications, accompanied by deep-seated attitudes of superiority and inferiority. The principle of inequality is accepted and tacitly approved in the mores.

In *Who Shall Be Educated?* Professor Warner in collaboration with Robert T. Havighurst and Martin B. Loeb applies his social analysis to education.[9] Here he underscores a contradiction between theory and fact. The American educational myth, he says, is that all one needs to get to the top are "brains, a will to do, hard work, and plenty of ambition." But in practice, our educational system has a double function: to help the few exceptional individuals to rise in the social scale, but at the same time to keep the main body of pupils in their social place. Professor Warner approves of this policy as properly realistic on the ground that class structure is necessary for all social organization and condemns as well-meaning but dangerous propaganda the educational views which make equality the directive principle.

Economic status plays a primary part in social class stratification but it is not the only, and at times not the most important, factor. Race, ethnic origin, generations of residence, church affiliation combine with occupational status and the source as well as the amount of wealth to determine one's place in American society. At the top of the American social scale are those of "Anglo-Saxon" stock and other members of Nordic Protestant groups. At the lower end of the scale are those marked with color, of South American or Asian origin. The sort of discrimination practiced against the so-called "minority groups"—who in some regions are no longer minorities—are not equally severe or of the same nature. The antagonism on the part of Protestant, English-speaking citizens of Maine toward French Catholics in which political, cultural as well as religious factors play a part differs greatly from their prejudice toward the Jews, characterized as the latter is by the covert insidiousness of anti-semitism. The sense of distance that marks the attitude of New Englanders toward their neighbors of Italian or Polish descent is something quite different from the strong racial feeling harbored by the average Southerner toward the Negro. Economic, political, and legal factors operate differently in each type of discrimination, as is obvious in the case of the two outstanding and yet quite diverse forms of prejudice, that against the Negroes and the Jews.

Discrimination against the Negroes represents the most serious denial of human rights on the basis of membership in a specific group that still exists in the civilized world. In the southern states, Negroes remain, almost a century after emancipation, deprived of political influence through poll tax laws and intimidation at the voting places. They have inadequate protection in the courts; they suffer violence inflicted at times with the collusion of officers of the law. Jim Crow arrangements in public transportation systems give them the status of a low caste. In the northern states the situation is by comparison vastly better, but the prevalence of residential segregation, exclusion from many hotels, restaurants, and theatres, and discrimination in social life generally, still decisively handicap all but a small minority who by reason of wealth or professional accomplishment have achieved relative equality with whites. The situation has improved in the last score of years. The number of lynchings have been greatly decreased in recent decades and there have been none in the last few years. Poll tax restrictions have been somewhat ameliorated by the Supreme Court rulings. In some states legislation has been enacted against discrimination in public housing. The decision of the Supreme Court of May, 1954, against segregation in public schools augurs a revolutionary change in American life. But the delaying and obstructive tactics accompanied by considerable violence in the states of the deep south indicate that it will be years, perhaps decades, before the gross external inequities will be eliminated. The change in attitude, the achievement of equality in a human psychosocial sense is a deeper problem.

Anti-semitism is a far less serious evil than the discrimination against the Negro, if judged by the deprivations with which it is associated. One important difference is that practially all vestiges of legally supported inequalities have been eliminated. But anti-semitism is not less evil in its psychological and moral effects. The seeds of Jew-hatred lie deep in the Anglo-Saxon psyche as well as in the Teutonic soul, and evidences of it are all too frequent among Americans of English as well as of German descent. It persists in vulgar forms, of gibes, of insinuations of dishonesty, of charges of promotion of vice. It finds expression in personal abuse when anger or intoxication break down the bonds of conventional restraint. Worst of all are the vestiges of anti-semitism in the universities and professional schools which still practice the quota system for admission of students and in staff appointments. Apart from the injustices to individuals of merit, anti-semitism in our universities, as formerly in Germany, gives the support of the intellectual class to the prejudices of the backward rural communities and of the provincial small towns. In the last decade the situation has improved, perhaps in some measure due to the excesses of Nazism. Anti-semitism, however, is a strongly rooted weed in Western culture. Its persistence reveals the nodules of unresolved irrationalities and equivocations in Christian thought.

The issue of racial and religious discrimination goes far deeper than the liberalist patronizing advocacy of "tolerance." The democratic philosophy has hitherto made the idea of liberty the keystone of its conception of social life and of government. But true liberty cannot continue to exist in an atmosphere of inequality. Material equality can perhaps be achieved without liberty, but liberty without equality is a contradiction and leads to a perversion of the idea of liberty. The demand for equality is the ferment which is stirring the world to unrest and rebellion. A crucial problem in our era is to abolish the pattern of inequality that has dominated civilization since primitive times. The elimination of racial and religious discrimination is a many-sided task involving educational and legal measures. Any fundamental change requires the abolition of the status system which, whatever other factors it includes, rests on an economic substratum.

NOTES

1. T. S. Eliot, *The Idea of a Christian Society* (Harcourt, Brace and Co., 1940), p. 16.

2. Adapted from *Democratic Vistas*.

3. John Dewey, *Freedom and Culture* (G. P. Putnam's Sons, 1939), pp. 156-157.

4. Carl L. Becker, *Freedom and Responsibility in the American Way of Life* (Alfred A. Knopf, 1946), p. 67.

5. "The Nature and Origins of the Western Political Tradition," in *The Western Tradition* (The Beacon Press, 1951), p. 30.

6. *Politics in America* (Harper & Brothers, 1954), pp. 10ff.

7. Elmer Davis, *But We Were Born Free* (Bobbs-Merrill, 1954), p. 22.

8. Eugene Staley, *The Future of Undeveloped Countries* (Harper & Brothers, 1954), p. 315.

9. W. Lloyd Warner, Robert T. Havighurst, and Martin Loeb, *Who Shall Be Educated?* (Harper & Brothers, 1944).

10

ECONOMIC WELFARE
AND WORLD COMMUNITY

THE acceptance of democracy as a guiding social philosophy requires a recommitment to the moral ends of the Declaration of Independence and of the Bill of Rights and a consistent and unconditional application of racial and religious equality. But such a reaffirmation of the ideals underlying the Constitution and of the need of their better realization in practice is not enough. While the ultimate aims and the political instrumentalities of liberalism remain basic for the emerging democratic philosophy, the circumstances of the age demand a reconstruction of its preconceptions in two interrelated spheres— in the economic field and in international affairs. Any discussion of democracy which does not include a statement on these issues is tantamount to an evasion of the central issues of our age and as such also an evasion of a crucial problem in educational policy.

The attitude of the school toward controversial social issues goes to the very heart of democracy in its moral aspect. The views of teachers on the economic questions and toward international organization are decisive in the teaching of the social studies and may affect the general orientation of the student in all social relations. The conception that educational policy must be erected on the foundation of an ethical-political philosophy of life implies two corollaries: "a charter for the social sciences," that is, giving social studies an adequate place in the course of studies; and, no less important, investing the teaching with a democratic moral purpose.

Two extremes are to be avoided. The first is the pretense of neutralism—which generally means evasion of issues, support of the status quo, or blind following of uncritical public opinion. The other policy to be avoided might be called "social evangelism," the advocacy of ideological blueprints unrelated to existing economic and political organization. The teaching of economics and contemporary affairs must go beyond the conveying of factual information. But the ideals that the school promotes must be rooted in American history and conceptions, and must take into account competent technical knowledge.

1

It is essential to move in the direction of a general equality of condition which was a basic factor in the development of social democracy in agrarian America. The growth of industrial society tended to accentuate class divisions in the United States as well as elsewhere. In previous periods when men perforce adjusted themselves to a scarcity economy, class divisions seemed unavoidable. Today, objective conditions as well as moral principle no longer warrant a system which allows a considerable part of the population to live in poverty or on a bare subsistence level and permits a minority the luxury and power that go with great wealth.

The situation is hopeful in that the demand for greater equality in the distribution of income coincides with the technological possibilities. Indeed, the wide distribution of purchasing power is a necessity if the highly productive power of modern industry is to be fully utilized. Economists agree that if we are to avoid a return to the old routine of the business cycle with an eventual breakdown of the free-enterprise system altogether, then we must continually expand the power of consumption along with our continuously expanding productive power. Enlightened business men have increasingly recognized the importance of high wages in maintaining the dynamic character of the American economy. As compared with the conceptions and practices of nineteenth-century capitalism, things have been turned upside down. In that period the good business man was the one who could manage to pay the lowest wages and to get his employees to work the longest hours. Today, the good business man is the one who realizes that his own success is connected with the economic health of the country as a whole.

In line with the new technical possibilities as these interplay with the ethical aims of the democratic society and with the political system inherited from liberalism, a new economic order is taking shape in the Western world, in the United States as well as in Europe in countries outside the Communist bloc. Developing out of capitalism and retaining some of its features, it includes cooperative associations and various types of publicly directed and nonprofit undertakings. Whether the emerging economic system should be called capitalist or socialist is partly a question of the preponderance of one or another element in the economy, partly a matter of definition. In total pattern, however, the new economy differs so greatly from capitalism or socialism as those economic views were conceived a half century ago that neither is fitting designation for it. Despite differences in various countries, the new systems have several common characteristics: they operate within the framework of a democratic political order; they comprise mixed economic forms—private, cooperative, and corporative free enterprise along with governmentally directed or controlled economic operations; the character and degree of each type of economic operation is worked out empirically and not determined beforehand in accordance with an ideological blueprint.

The emerging democratic economy is fittingly called "the economics of welfare." Ordway Tead has stated its primary proposition: "The purpose of economic effort is the well-being of all the people. We do not live to work. Economically, consumption is the aim. And until the interests of *all* the people as consumers are taken adequate account of, the economic system is at odds with democratic professions."[1] The welfare conception implies concern for the whole person as well as for all the people: health, education, security. It means taking into consideration conditions under which the individual lives and works as well as insuring steady employment. It is committed to the achievement of genuine equality of opportunity in the economic and cultural spheres. It involves reduction of the great disparity in the distribution of personal income. Democracy does not require a leveling of income to a single mean standard, but it does connote a gradation of income that will prevent the continuation of the status system.

The presuppositions underlying the new welfare conception differ radically from the assumptions of the classical economy not only in social outlook but also in what makes for the effectiveness of the system as an apparatus of production. In the nineteenth-century capitalist view, profit was the main drive wheel: the goods required by the nation would be produced as by-products of a system designed primarily for yielding a profit to the owners of enterprise; the automatic working of the market would provide controls to insure the production of the kinds and amounts of the commodities needed. The new economic policy recognizes private profit as a legitimate stimulus and counts on the market as a controlling factor. But it makes consumption the key to the ordering of the economic system from the point of view of effective working as well as from the viewpoint of life objectives. It sees need as the source of economic energy and recognizes that purchasing power limits the amount of this energy that can be utilized. The economic problem is now conceived in terms of reciprocal action between production and consumption. Profit loses its pivotal function while remaining normally an important factor. In some areas, particularly in agriculture and housing, government subsidies are recognized as necessary either to limit or to stimulate production. The economic system cannot be left to the working of natural law; coordination and planning become essential. Ordering the economic system begins to assume the aspect of social engineering.

Technological development has all but destroyed the possibility of genuine competition among individual entrepreneurs as a means of advancing and stabilizing the economy. Although the establishment of absolute monopoly has been avoided, legislation has not prevented the growth of what A. A. Berle has called "oligopoly," the concentration of control in the major national industries, e.g., steel, automobiles, oil, electrical equipment, by a relatively small number of giant corporations. A few "concentrates" in an industry may set the conditions of operation for the so-called "independents." The great corporations can eliminate marginal operators; their power of control extends to suppliers of materials and sales agencies. The decision of a large corporation to move its plant from one locality to another may influence the fate of a whole region. Several concentrates acting together might initiate a chain reaction affecting the national economy as a whole. As Mr. Berle points out, "The corporation is now essentially a non-statist political institution."[2]

The large corporation is becoming the characteristic and necessary form of modern industrial order within the democratic political frame. There is no going back, in the major industries, to the nineteenth-century small-scale enterprise. Its ability to marshall huge capital, its

power to coordinate and plan ahead, its readiness to use and to promote scientific research make it an extraordinarily efficient instrument
of economic production and advance. Its acceptance by the public is
due to the realization that it has been the major factor in raising the
standard of material welfare. Because of its enormous power and possibilities, its operations must be subject to controls which will prevent
it destroying the balance of the economy and destroying itself in the
process.

There are, of course, some checks on the arbitrary use of power by
corporations derived from intelligent self-interest—the fixing of a
"fair price," recognition of the value of good public relations, realization of the desirability wherever possible of settling differences by
negotiation, regard for the health and convenience of the worker as
an element in efficient production. These are minor though important
factors of control. The foremost check on the ambitious use of power
by the great corporations today is that of the well-organized trade
unions now consolidated into a powerful force by the joint organization of the C.I.O. and A.F.L. The trade unions taken as a whole represent an outlook more in accord with the general welfare of the
nation than that of big business. But the concentration of power in
the hands of labor presents, if uncontrolled and undirected, a potential danger not less serious than that represented by "management,"
the new euphemism for the executive power of large-scale industry.

Only the national government has the power and the authority to
serve as the coordinating and directing agent of economic policy in
its domestic and in its international relations. The welfare economy
requires regulation, coordination, and planning within each industry
and sector of the economy at the local and regional level. But it unavoidably involves national direction under governmental agencies
over a wide and expanding area of activities, the extension of functions already initiated and the assumption of new responsibilities. The
furtherance of a welfare economy necessitates the coordination of
agricultural and industrial production, the maintenance of a balance
between the great power groups of Business and Labor, the support
of uniform minimum wage standards throughout the country, the
protection of small-scale enterprise in fields where it is still viable. It
involves currency and credit control to expand or contract consumption or production and to prevent extreme inflationary movements

which economists rank with unemployment as the twin dangers of the free-enterprise economy. Periodic unemployment still remains the Achilles' heel. Though only a palliative, the introduction in the automobile and other industries of partial payment for unemployment is an important step toward a guaranteed annual wage based on continuous work with regular vacations.

On the constructive as well as on the regulative side, the government has an increasing series of obligations to supplement and direct private enterprise. This includes conservation and development of natural resources in the public interest, the improvement of highways and waterways, the development of hydroelectric power and, in the near future, of atomic energy for civilian uses. In the area of the conservation of human resources, there is need of a planned public health program on a large scale to supplement private medicine and philanthropy. The program of social security requires further extension to safeguard completely against the disabilities due to accident, ill health, and old age. Of basic importance to the welfare of the nation is the problem of slum clearance and the construction of low-cost housing. Progress has been made throughout the country in the development of educational opportunities. But an extreme disparity still exists as among the various states, between rural and urban communities, and in opportunities afforded to whites and Negroes. The high schools have now been opened to a very large proportion of the population of all classes. But without additional support from government funds, colleges and universities remain—despite the opportunities afforded by scholarships and the GI bill—institutions for the middle class and wealthy.

2

We have still far to go before we attain a reasonable embodiment of democratic principles in our economic system. Despite some reduction of extremes in the distribution of wealth, the status system remains a characteristic feature of American society. Monetary rewards from business operations are disproportionately large as compared with earnings from intellectual occupations and from public service. Commercialization pervades the mass communication media, the moving pictures and the television offerings. Too much survives of the unsavory aspects of capitalism which John Maynard Keynes, not a moralist but an economist, has described as "absolutely irreligious, without internal union, without much public spirit, often, though not always, a mere congeries of possessors and pursuers."[3]

We have moved a considerable distance in the direction of a welfare economy in response to the lessons of the depression of the 1930's, the urgencies of World War II, and the fear of possible conflict with communist states. Despite the efforts of the Eisenhower Administration to delimit the participation of government in the economic area, the major measures of the New Deal have been preserved. But we are far from having accepted the principles of the welfare economy as a clear basis of policy. The huge defense budget and federal participation in promotion of aircraft production and the development of atomic energy conceal the large part that government plays in maintaining the national income on a high level.

The experience of the last score of years should have taught us that government participation in the national economic effort is a means of releasing potentialities, not curtailing them, and that its efforts are directed toward the protection of genuine free enterprise against the encroachment of gigantic corporationalism. Nevertheless, our preconceptions are still weighted by nineteenth-century economic views. Our liberal economists are led to publish their proposals under such titles as "Saving American Capitalism" when their real purpose is to advance the welfare economy; and conservatives score a point when they decry as "creeping socialism" any nonprofit public project, however reasonable in conception and democratic in method of execution.

The welfare state could indeed become a "road to serfdom" if it were not developed under the democratic constitution which requires ratification of each step by freely elected representatives who respond to the varied interests of the different sections of the population. In the context of a democratic frame of reference, every element in "planning" assumes a different form than in totalitarian states. As Mary P. Follett has observed, "planning" as the opposite of laissez faire is coordination not coercion. In totalitarian societies control is mainly associated with penalties for failures to perform in accordance with the plan imposed from above. In the democratic procedure, acceptance of government control, as in the case of the parity payments to agriculture, is achieved primarily by the inducement of a benefit, a choice of alternatives is present, and a large area of action is left to local and regional planning. The emphasis is not on the power of government to enforce decisions but on its ability to attack problems on a large scale and to bring to bear expert knowledge and scientific research in their solution.

The democratic welfare state operates under a mixed constitution in the economic as well as in the political area. What is envisaged is a pluralistic economy in which a large scope is left to free enterprise. Freedom of the person is related to freedom in the economic field, freedom to choose one's occupation and freedom of initiative. The freedom of the individual depends, moreover, on his ability to organize voluntary associations and this implies freedom to use savings for other than state purposes. A point that needs emphasis is the part that free enterprise plays in maintaining free research and academic freedom in higher education. While private endowments may be used to limit academic freedom, the dangers are less than in a completely state-controlled system. A state-dominated educational system, at the higher levels of education, at least, would mean the end of academic freedom in the political field.

Democracy and the welfare state are in the profoundest sense complementary to each other, since both rest on a high regard for practical intelligence and a deep concern for the common welfare. The school cannot alone counteract the competitive attitudes encouraged by existing institutions or itself greatly modify the social order. But it can, in times of transition, when social forces are already in movement, aid, through study and analysis, in directing them toward the fulfillment of democratic ends. Participation of the educational profession in formulating economic goals is requisite today as a matter of social responsibility and as a demand of non-evasive honest thinking about contemporary issues.

3

In two major aspects, in the areas of racial equality and economic welfare, important progress can be recorded since the end of World War I, even though the achievement still falls short of a reasonable fulfillment. In the task of the organization of an international agency for the prevention of war, the high hopes of a generation ago have been bitterly disappointed. The League of Nations has a historical significance in the fact that it was the first institutional attempt to embody the idea of a political world authority. Through its various commissions, bureaus, and institutes, it accomplished something in the way of promoting international cooperation in the fields of health, education, agriculture, and technology. In the main purpose for which it was conceived, however, the abolition of war as a means of settling international disputes, it failed utterly as we know only too well.

The weakness of the League consisted in its inability to bring effective sanctions to bear on nations which refused to abide by its decisions. The principle of unanimity on which it was based and which made coercive action impossible reflected liberalism's dependence on man's rationality and good will, its belief that war so obviously destructive to both victor and vanquished could be eliminated through proper education, through cultural exchange, through the promotion of international commerce, that is by measures that did not involve resort to coercive force. The liberal made a false antithesis between "force and reason": he did not face the fact that civilization has advanced not by the abandonment of force but by the organization of force under law. The real opposition is between the disciplined use of police and military power, when this becomes necessary, under the direction of constituted authority, on the one hand, and the use of violence, the arbitrary use of force by individuals or nations in defiance of accepted principles of an established community. In the organization of the United Nations, the futility of dependence on reason and persuasion alone has been recognized. At the same time, the immense difficulties, in this stage of the world development, that stand in the way of erecting an effective supra-national authority and the creation of a collective force operating under international law have become abundantly clear.

Another fallacy which sometimes attaches to the liberalist-humanitarian mentality is that national sovereignty is the major obstruction to international peace and welfare. Abstract cosmopolitanism fails to reckon with the fact that the nation is still, in our day, the basic social-cultural unit as well as the essential political entity. For any nation to yield its right of decision on issues which affect its survival or its unique cultural character would in the present stage of world development mean submitting its fate to a more powerful nation or to an imperial power. It was the consciousness of nationality which enabled Yugoslavia to exercise a measure of independence from Soviet domination with decisive consequences in the modification of communist policy. It is the difference in culture and tradition that gives hope that China will, despite its communist ideology, refrain from merging with Russia into a single colossal monster to bestride the world. It is the impulse to national survival as in France and Germany which compels international agreements in which each nation protects the interests essential to its own preservation within the regional plans for European unity. The international world organization that we look forward to will be directed by the democratic principle of a federal authority which will leave a wide range of autonomy to each nation. As Dag Hammarskjold, United Nations Secretary General has formulated it, the task of the United Nations is "to provide us with a framework inside which it is possible to serve the world by serving our nation and to serve our nation by serving the world."[4]

The valid principle of nationality may become perverted and turn into an aggressive nationalism just as the democratic principle of individuality may become distorted and turn into an anti-social individualism. In the integration of the individual into the national community we have the advantage of common conditions and interests, of the influence of schools, and of the ordering force of law backed by police power. The international idea, on the other hand, is still supported only by intangibles, by aspirations, and by voluntary agreements. A genuine international community cannot be created by fiat or quickly fabricated by conceptual blueprints any more than a nation can be. It will require the extension of cultural and economic interchange, the organization of regional bodies and alliances, and above all, the gradual strengthening of the powers of the United Nations as an instrument of collective security. But before any real world organization can be brought into being—there are two complementary spheres in which a far greater degree of unity must be achieved than now exists: first, the sphere of the material conditions of life, and second, the area of common beliefs.

4

Underlying the many factors that obstruct one-world unity is the radical disparity in levels of civilization clearly correlated with huge differences in standards of living. Two-thirds of the world's population live in underdeveloped countries where the masses of the people struggle daily for subsistence while a tiny minority are wealthy. In regional terms, a shocking contrast exists between the economic conditions in the industrialized countries (United States, Canada, Great Britain and the northwest countries of Europe generally) and the countries based on a still primitive agriculture (nearly all of Asia and Africa and a large part of South America). The countries on the shores of the Mediterranean represent an intermediate but still low condition. The threat of communism in the underprivileged areas of the world grows in the soil of "hunger, poverty, disease and illiteracy," as all writers agree.[5]

The United Nations has given recognition to the importance of the economic factor in the promotion of world peace. Significant as its efforts are as tokens of international cooperation, the amounts available represent only a drop in the bucket in face of the vast problem of raising the standards of living throughout the world. The same may be said of bilateral and regional plans through loans and technical assistance, such as the British Colombo Plan and our own Point Four. Though Point Four represents the largest expenditure, it touches only the fringes of the problem; confined as it is to teaching "know-how" its immediate effect on the general development is hardly noticeable except by those closely concerned with the experimental programs. Moreover, as our political leaders make plain, our aid is given in line with the policy of containment of communism. The nationalist leaders of Asia and the Middle East resent this as an attempt to subordinate their countries to foreign domination. In lands still smarting under the wounds of colonialism, the aid we give may be regarded as a step toward a new imperialistic penetration or at best a well-meaning but mistaken attempt to impose our own economic and social ideas upon them. As Eugene Staley says in *The Future of Undeveloped Countries*, in the absence of drastic reforms, our technical and economic assistance may "actually contribute to widening the gap between the haves and the have-nots, with the result that the country would be more susceptible to communism than before."[6]

The establishment of a façade of political democracy in the background of illiteracy and poverty may in effect support the continued domination of a privileged class. Democracy has been built up on the basis of a substantial middle class and at best works slowly. Its successful operation depends on a balancing of fairly equal political forces and requires an atmosphere of security favorable to discussion, negotiation, and compromise—a willingness to take less than the full loaf since half a loaf is already assured. Moreover, democracy once revolutionary is today a force of conservation. In the underprivileged countries, the United States, its announced exponent, has as often as not thrown its support to reactionary groups, and by abstention if not by positive action helped to maintain the vestiges of colonial policies of our allies. The Asian intellectual, though not at heart unfriendly to America, is likely to regard us with less than full confidence; he "sees the bad in us and not the good in us," as Paul H. Douglas has phrased it.[7] The Asian world suspects us of imperialism, thinks us not fully committed to peace, and is convinced that we are a prey to racialism. A fourth charge is that our civilization is superficial—characterized by addiction to "chewing gum, hot dogs, and comic strips"—and that it is materialistic, as George F. Kennan terms it, that it has "no higher social goal than the self-enrichment of the individual, and where self-enrichment takes place primarily in material goals and gadgets that are of doubtful utility in the achievement of the deeper satisfactions of life. . . ."[8] These one-sided views of American policy and caricatures of American life do no credit to the insight of the critics. But certainly there is enough truth in the distorted picture as many others see us to disturb us in our complacency.

In the areas which hold the balance of power between the Western democracies and the Russian-Chinese bloc, communism has certain advantages as seen from the point of view of the nationalist leader. It promises a quicker solution to the social and economic problems; it does not hesitate to use ruthless measures to confiscate land and destroy the ruling minority of privilege. It joins its attack against poverty and illiteracy with support of the national aspirations in each country for freedom from colonial rule. It promotes its revolutionary program through native leaders, and wherever successful communist regimes open opportunities to youth for personal advancement and for service to their country. Always, along with their promises of material prosperity, communist propaganda lays the emphasis, as Eugene Staley says, on "the human desire for status, equality, freedom from domination or oppression." The Asian intellectual, who plays a leading part in the insurgent nationalist movements, not too sure of the disinterestedness of the Western powers, may be inclined to give communism the benefit of the doubt—to hope that the period of violence and regimentation inevitable in revolutionary change will be moderated by native leaders and that it will be temporary.

Despite the extraordinary difficulties of the problem, Eugene Staley concludes: "*If the resources of the West are really brought to bear on the development of the problem,* then the Communist challenge can be met successfully."[9] In the light of his own analysis—his emphasis on the importance of living up to our democratic ideals in our own affairs as well as on the need of very great sums for foreign aid—there would appear to be a large grain of wishful thinking in this optimistic resolution of the world problem, achieved with the aid of an "if."* Raising the standard of living throughout the world is a long-range problem that must be accomplished by the backward nations and regions in terms of their own conditions and in the light of their own counsels. Aid from the outside can at best be supplementary; the more of it the better, the more of it channelled through the United Nations the wiser. It should be given, as Hamilton Fish Armstrong suggests, on an objective practical basis, on a judgment of what each country can absorb in consideration of all factors, of available personnel, of political conditions, of financial stability.[10]

Above all, foreign aid must be granted strictly as a means of economic development, not as an inducement for political or military alliance. The relation of a country to the Soviet orbit cannot realistically be disregarded. But we need not go on the assumption that nations not completely committed to us or to our way of life are necessarily against us. Much in the next period of history depends on the bloc of Asian and Mideastern nations—whether their neutrality will turn into a negative pacifism, be betrayed into a tacit collusion with communism or evolve into a true internationalism in a loyal adherence to the United Nations in its principles and in its spirit. We must do all we can through moral influence and through material aid to keep the neutral nations on the road to democracy; but we cannot whatever we do coerce or buy integrity.

* A more realistic analysis is presented by Gunnar Myrdal, *An International Economy, Problems and Prospects,* (Harper & Brothers), 1956.

5

All that can be expected in the foreseeable future is a gradual emergence out of the stalemate characteristic of the post-Korean era into a less hostile coexistence, eventuating in the course of time in some form of cooperation between East and West. A secure and enduring peace in the world awaits—in addition to an appreciable reduction in the differential between the living standards in various parts of the world—the development of a basic unity of belief and a sense of community with all mankind. "International war," A. N. Feller has told us in what has proved to be his testament, "cannot be eliminated without strong international institutions and . . . such institutions cannot be created without a growing sense among different peoples sharing common beliefs and aspirations and a common desire to live together in a community with others."[11] This cannot be metaphysical principle, however universal, or a religious conception, however catholic, or a monistic political system described by an ism. It can rest only on an ethical idea—a charter of human rights— embodied in a structure of law and supported by political power.

For such a charter we have an outline in the United Nations' *Universal Declaration of Human Rights*. It was drafted by a special Commission appointed for the purpose under the chairmanship of Mrs. Eleanor Roosevelt, and adopted after a full discussion on December 16, 1948, during the third session of the General Assembly convened at Paris. There were forty-eight affirmative votes, none in opposition, but eight states of the Soviet bloc abstained. As it stands, it is, as its title says, a Declaration: it has no legally binding power. It was to be followed by two covenants, one containing civil and political rights, and the other economic and social rights. Differences of opinion have arisen both as to content and procedures, the United States as well as the Soviet Union offering objections. But the Declaration has not been without some influence: it has been cited by national courts and legislatures and been embodied in the constitution of a number of new governments.

Despite the fact that the Declaration at present has mainly a moral and educational value, it represents an epochal development significant in the large measure of agreement on fundamentals and in the cleavages it dramatizes. "The Declaration stands as an entity."[12] Its

Preamble and thirty paragraphs cover the whole range of human rights: *Individual and Personal Rights*—e.g., slavery, equality before the law, public trial, freedom of movement; *Right of Relationship*—e.g., family, property, freedom of expression and association, participation in government; *Economic, Social and Cultural Rights*—e.g., right to work, to rest and leisure, standard of living, universal education. The human rights included two major areas: the classic civil and political rights which we associate with liberal democracy in its broadest sense, and the economic and social rights which have been more clearly advanced in socialist trends of thought. The Western powers would have been satisfied with the former but "the under-privileged peoples of the world," as Dr. Eichelberger reports, "argued that the right to eat was as important as the right to vote."[13] It is due to their insistence that the economic clauses dealing with the right to work—to free choice of employment, to protection against unemployment, to assurance of social security—were introduced along with the right to own property, guaranteed in the traditional Bill of Rights.

It is a matter of extraordinary significance that the representatives of the two views, that which emphasized economic rights as well as that which laid the stress on civil liberties, came together in a united statement. Outside the communist states in the Soviet orbit, a broad consensus on fundamentals was in evidence despite variations in estimate of importance of different sections and differences of opinion as to how far to go in detailing provisions. The division between the commonalty of nations who voted for the Declaration and the abstaining communist minority, on the other hand, revealed the gulf between two world-views of the relation of human rights to social organization.

The Preamble of the U.N. Declaration following our own Declaration of Independence recognizes that: "the inherent dignity and . . . the equal and inalienable rights of all members of the human family is the foundation of freedom, justice and peace in the world." Thus, as in the religious and the classic tradition of the Western world, it makes human rights "anterior and superior" to the state. It repudiates the view that the state is superior to the person, that it can deny the individual the declared rights of man. The tenor of the communist arguments was in the opposite direction. In the final debate, Andrei Y. Vishinsky, the Deputy Foreign Minister of the

U.S.S.R. declared "the rights of human beings cannot be considered outside the prerogatives of governments."[14] Another representative of the Soviet group, A. P. Pavlov, wanted to amend the right of religious freedom and the right of movement by adding the clause: "in accordance with the laws of the state."[15] In all cases, the Communist representatives rejected the general view if it failed to harmonize with Marxist doctrines.

The Universal Declaration of Human Rights points the way to a new era. Before its articles are fully realized in practice, it will require embodiment in law, implementation in institutions, and enforcement through collective security. All this will not happen quickly in our day. But the movement is forward and there is ground for faith in ultimate victory—not only because the more perfect democracy which it represents "is better attuned to the real nature of man" as Kennan has phrased it, but because it represents the fruit of a long historical experience, rooted in prophecy and sanctioned by enduring religious belief.

NOTES

1. Ordway Tead, *New Adventures in Democracy* (Whittlesey House, McGraw-Hill Book Co., 1939), p. 149.

2. A. A. Berle, Jr., *The Twentieth Century Capitalist Revolution* (Harcourt, Brace and Co., 1954).

3. As quoted by R. H. Tawney, in *Religion and the Rise of Capitalism* (Harcourt, Brace and Co., 1926), p. 286.

4. *The New York Times,* June 20, 1955.

5. Isidor Lubin and Forrest D. Murden, Jr., *Our Stake in World Trade,* Headline Series, No. 106 (Foreign Policy Association, 1954), p. 42.

6. Eugene Staley, *The Future of Undeveloped Countries* (Harper & Brothers, 1954), pp. 185-6.

7. *Foreign Affairs,* July, 1955, pp. 535ff.

8. George F. Kennan, *Realities of American Foreign Policy* (Princeton University Press, 1954), p. 115.

9. Staley, *op. cit.,* p. 169.

10. *Foreign Affairs,* July 1956, pp. 616ff.

11. *United Nations and World Community* (Little, Brown and Co., 1952), p. 111.

12. O. Frederick Nolde, *Freedom's Charter*, Headline Series, July 1949 (Foreign Policy Association), pp. 43ff.

13. Clark M. Eichelberger. *U.N. The First Ten Years* (Harper & Brothers, 1955), p. 72.

14. Nolde, *op. cit.*, p. 72.

15. *Ibid.*, p. 40.

11

TRENDS OF THOUGHT IN SCIENCE,
IN THE STUDY OF MAN, AND IN RELIGION

THE social changes discussed in the foregoing chapter—
directed as they are by the ideas of racial equality, of the welfare
state, and of an international order—imply modifications in mental
and moral attitudes from those which were central in the age of
Liberalism. There are signs, also, that a new pattern of intellectual
and spiritual beliefs is taking shape in the world of science and
scholarship differing significantly from that which dominated the
thought life of the previous century. In some respects the new
orientation represents a continuation of trends characteristic of the
modern age; in other respects it is reminiscent of medieval and
classical conceptions. Contemporary thought attempts to give consideration to the aspects of order and permanence as well as to the
ideas of progress and of change. It emphasizes the significance of
general ideas as a means of understanding empirical observations. It
reflects a concern with guiding ethical principles in the control of
conduct without denying the import of the individual's experience and
judgment. There is renewed interest in religion on the part of the
intellectual class and a search for a genuine rapprochement with
science that goes beyond the previous truce of mutual toleration.

A distinctive feature of the contemporary intellectual outlook is a
reaction against the individualistic emphasis of nineteenth century
empirical thought. Stress is laid on the factor of association, on the
significance of groupings, on the effect of whole on the elements
which compose it. Character is defined not primarily by a delineation
of an object of observation seen as an isolated entity but by its
behavior in a context of conditions. This "social" analysis has invaded
the natural sciences; the concepts of field and structure, of organism

183

and *gestalt*, evidence the wide influence of the holistic idea. The new approach which implies the interplay of multiple factors runs counter to the deterministic and mechanistic interpretations dominant in the previous scientific era.

There is some danger today that the emphasis on the organic and on the collective will crowd out consideration of the specific and the individual. In the more careful formulations, attention is given to the dialectic principle—to the need of considering terms in relation to their opposites, of bearing in mind the tensional force of antinomies. Monistic views which make idealism or materialism, freedom or determinism, the single controlling factor are yielding to conceptions which invoke the deliberate consideration of multiple aspects in all areas of investigation—particularly in the fields of history and social affairs. In a fine passage, S. Robert Oppenheimer strikes the new key: ". . . only a malignant end can follow the systematic belief that all communities are one community; that all truth is one truth; that all experience is compatible with all others; that total knowledge is possible; that all that is potential can exist as actual."[1]

1

The new way of thinking finds striking exemplification in the novel views held by physicists today. The Newtonian cosmos of the prerelativity age was made up of individual particles—each one, "solid, massy, hard, impenetrable . . . so very hard as never to wear or break in pieces." These moving bits of matter combined in multitudinous ways in accordance with definite laws to form the diverse things and creatures of the world. Accordingly, everything that happened was predetermined; if we knew enough we could explain all in terms of prior causes; if we knew the present fully, we could prophesy the future. Contingency was eliminated; the universe was a gargantuan mechanism which acted in predetermined ways by rigorous laws of motion on the basis of fixed properties of material particles.

From the new physics we get a different picture. The idea of a predetermined universe governed by precise laws has been replaced by the view that we live in a world of probable happenings. The rigid idea of causation has been supplanted by the notion of mathematically definable correlations between series of events. The classic doctrine of laws as embedded in nature which hold with equal accuracy for the tiny atom and the immense cluster of stars has yielded to the concept of statistical constants which vary in relation to the area of inquiry. In some areas it is possible to predict what will happen with a great degree of probability; in others, as in the world of electrons, neutrons, protons, things appear to happen at random. The isolated atom seems to behave anarchistically, eternally changing in a veritable Heraclitian flux. It takes on character from its relationship to its surroundings.

In accordance with one view, the visible uniformity of the Newtonian laws, as Poincaré first suggested, may be the result of the averaging of the movements of large numbers of phenomena which taken by themselves would exhibit the indeterminate behavior of minute particles. The apparent accuracy of the laws of the physical world, in harmony with this conception, might be compared to mortality tables by which we can prophesy with great accuracy the number of people who will die in a given region at a given period, though we can never tell when a particular individual will suffer the inevitable fate.[2] Einstein, however, still retained the conviction that causal laws are operative in all realms of physics, in the sphere of minute events as well as in the large-scale world open to ordinary observation. He held to the belief that there is a rational order in the universe, a faith which he sometimes expressed metaphorically in his refusal to believe "that God plays dice with the world."

The term "relativity" has been misunderstood to mean that chance and indetermination are universal principles ruling the world in all areas of human experience. "Relationatism" would, perhaps, be a better designation for the idea that the character of a phenomenon is dependent—not on its own properties, whatever that could mean— but on the context of events and of things in which it has its being. In accordance with prevailing views among physicists, indetermination reigns in situations where the object is infinitesimally small or extraordinarily large in relation to the rate of movement. In the happenings of nature as observed by denizens of the earth where things move with the velocities to which we are ordinarily accustomed, the principles of regularity and uniformity hold quite well. As Dr. Oppenheimer assures us: "Newton's law of gravitation and his equations of motion apply to and underlie immense realms of physical experience and are not made wrong by the fact that in other and still vaster spheres they must be replaced by the broader laws of Einstein."[3] Whatever the ultimate explanation, the total effect of the new conceptions in physics, increases rather than decreases "the objectivity, firmness, and consonance to law" of observed phenomena in the world of nature.

The principles operative in any sphere, however, cannot be deduced from a single rigid law; they cannot be ascertained for an area without study of that particular area of human experience. The new physics does not pretend to offer a final, decisive, conclusion as to the *metaphysical* nature of the universe—on the question whether change or constancy is fundamental. For one thing, the findings on the nature of the atom may again be reversed as they have been in the past. In another age, physicists may come back to the ancient view that the atom is really an atom—an indivisible unit of matter. The new physics does not compel us to believe that ultimate reality is ever-changing any more than it forces us to hold that only the unchanging is devoid of illusion. It tends rather to confirm the age-long common-sense view of the dualistic character of all existence: "These two ways of thinking, the way of time and history and the way of eternity and timelessness, are both part of the effort to comprehend the world in which he lives."[4] Ceaseless change and creative novelty on the one hand, symmetrical order and balanced stability on the other hand, are necessary complements of understanding. The main point is that in the observation of phenomena, the changing must be seen in relation to the unchanging.

2

In repudiating absolute determinism, the new physics emancipates from the metaphysical dogma that discourages man's effort to build a better world. It does not support the view that the universe is automatically evolving toward human welfare. But neither does it condemn us to the conception of the world-machine running down. When men of science warn against the possible destruction of the human race by the release of nuclear energy, they mean to urge us to use our intelligence to avoid catastrophe, not to predict an inevitable fate. The theory of probability underlying the contemporary conception of the character of nature does not mean that everything is possible, or possible at all times. Events are not pre-determined but they are not unconditioned. Any happening in the world depends on numerous factors operating in a dynamic context of conditions. What is possible or probable is always an estimate, but the more we know and the better instruments we have, the surer are we of controlling outcomes. If the new view deprives us of absolute certainty, it allows scope—always within limits—to man's possible control of his destiny. The new physics supports the common belief that ideas have power, that devotion to set purposes can shape the world in which man lives.

An important corollary of the "relationist" principle is a denial that all phenomena are governed by or can be reduced to physical laws or defined in naturalistic terms. It suggests that every plane of existence —the physical, the biological, the psychological, the social—has its own distinctive principles and involves a particular language. When a term is taken from one field of investigation and applied to another field—when, for instance, "organism," a biological term, is used in the description of social behavior—this needs to be done with the greatest care, with the conscious realization that it may possibly mislead. The language of two sciences, though similar as in the case of physics and chemistry, will never be identical: in complex chemical forms of biological character, the language of physics might not be applicable. When we attempt to deal with ethical, political, philosophic, and religious questions, the use of physical and biological conceptions is likely to lead us astray. What we learn from one field of knowledge may suggest fruitful ideas or methods of approach for other fields. But in final analysis, each area of investigation requires consideration in terms of its own unique type of phenomena.

The relevance of one field to another is not in the nature of compelling truth but, as Oppenheimer suggests, partakes of the character of an analogy. The validity of the analogy will depend on the insight of the one who makes it, on the liberality and depth of the knowledge employed. The "unity of science" is not to be conceived in terms of a few basic truths that can be universally applied: "It is not global, or total, or hierarchical." The unity of science implies commitment to diversity as well as to homogeneity. The various areas of knowledge cross-fertilize each other: creative thought is stimulated when ideas developed in different contexts are brought in touch with each other. The pursuit of science involves interchange and intercommunication, not only between individuals working in the same fields, and not only between scientist and scientist, but of scientist with students of society, and of philosophy and religion.

The conception of the distinctiveness of various areas of human knowledge and the fruitfulness of interaction among them suggests the lines along which the century-long conflict between science and religion is being resolved. It makes both areas of experience irreplaceable as resources for intellectual and spiritual development, each unique but not self-sufficient, both invaluable, but neither primary. It supports the view that knowledge of the cosmos as the physicist sees it can never provide us with the ends of human action; nor can scientific methods, however broadly conceived, give us any idea of human values. With all his high appreciation of the great achievements of science, Einstein agrees with this common judgment of mankind: science can provide us with objective knowledge which aids in the fulfillment of definite purposes, but it can not give us the ethical aims that characterize the human being. The "ultimate and fundamental ends" must be sought in the great traditions of mankind. "To make clear these fundamental ends and valuations, and to set them fast in the emotional life of the individual, seems to me precisely the most important function which religion has to perform in the social life of man."[5]

The scientific attitude, on the other hand, as the contemporary scientist sees it, can have a beneficent influence on religion, in freeing man's mind from the fetters of fundamentalist literalism and contributing to the spiritualization of our religious attitudes. The pursuit of science liberates men from bondage to narrow egocentric interests, inspires consecration to ideas that have a supra-personal dimension, and fosters a reverence for the rationality manifest in the universe. The true scientist "achieves a far-reaching emancipation from the shackles of personal hopes and desires, and thereby attains that humble attitude of mind toward the grandeur of reason incarnate in existence, and which, in its profoundest depths, is inaccessible to man."[6] The influence is reciprocal: the religious outlook liberates science from enslavement to the individual observed fact, from the crude trial and error procedure, from the subordination of reason to practical utility. The genuinely great achievements in the history of science have been due to the quest for unity and universality, in the urge to find a stable reality behind temporal phenomena, to the pursuit of the ideal for its own sake—for the sake of Heaven, as the Hebrew expression goes.

3

In the study of human nature, trends of thought similar to those observable in the field of physics appear to be operative. Emphasis is placed on the multiplicity and on the interaction of the factors at work in the formation of character. Full recognition is given to the element of association as a necessary condition of human behavior and of the importance of particular social environments—of prevailing conceptions as well as institutional structures—in determining individual and group responses. Like the entities that compose the atom, the human individual taken alone is seen as a locus of undirected impulses not easily harmonized. Matching the notion of the inscrutability of ultimate reality in the cosmos as viewed by the physicists is the conception of the engimatic character of the inner self as analyzed by psychologists.

Under the regime of liberalist philosophy, each individual was regarded as a self-sustaining being. His nature, determined primarily by heredity, could be modified to an extent by social conditions, but society itself was conceived as determined by natural laws. The evolutionary view, with its implication that man is nothing more than "a higher animal," lent support to the idea that human wants were essentially biological needs directed toward self-preservation and reproduction. Political and social arrangements were conceived as means of achieving a generous fulfillment of creaturely wants. Ethics was reduced to giving each individual an equal opportunity to compete in the struggle for existence and in the realization of individual capacities. Cultural values were allowed as leisure-time activities—animals also needed rest.

In the latter decades of the nineteenth century, largely through the influence of German idealism, emphasis began to be laid on the social factors governing human development and on the idea of self-realization of the spiritual personality as a distinct aim in and of itself. In the United States where the idealistic line of thought fused with Darwinism, a biosocial conception eventuated. In this view, man's nature was conceived as continuous with animal nature, but important qualifications were introduced. The repertoire of human instincts and native tendencies was conceived to be larger and more flexible, subject to a high degree of conditioning and modification. The long period of infancy and dependence on the parents characteristic of the human race made possible the process of education by means of which the human animal is transformed into a social being.

From this view, there is a short step to the idea that the human being is a creature of culture and not a creature of nature. John Dewey, pioneer in the elaboration of the biocultural conception represents a transitional position. As he explains in *Logic: The Theory of Inquiry*, his philosophy represents not a pure naturalism but a "cultural naturalism." The characteristic human activities are conceived as growing out of reactions typical of all living organisms in response to environmental situations. The transformation from the animal to the human plane results from a double factor—the element of association interacting with the element of speech. "Man is *naturally* a being that lives in association with others in communities possessing language, and therefore enjoying a transmitted culture."[7] The imprint of the individualistic and biological emphasis, however, remains strong. Human culture and social organization have a primary value as aids for survival in meeting the problems of living and in releasing potentialities which still, somehow, are conceived as being located in an individual self.

Contemporary thought is moving away from the biologically dominated conceptions of the Darwinian era. Ernst Cassirer crosses the frontier into the realm of a consistent cultural conception, equally opposed to a metaphysical and to a biological view of the essential nature of man. "We cannot define man by any inherent principle which constitutes his metaphysical essence—nor can we define him by any inborn faculty or instinct that may be ascertained by empirical observation. Man's outstanding characteristic, his distinguishing mark, is not his metaphysical or physical nature—but his work. It is this work, it is the system of human activities, which defines and determines the circle of 'humanity.' Language, myth, religion, art, science, history are the constituents, the various sectors of this circle."[8] Man's original nature cannot be ascertained from an examination of animal psychology or from the reaction of infants. Native potentialities must be inferred indirectly from a study of man's cultural achievements in literature, in art, in religion, in philosophy and science. Man's nature and needs must be learned from an analysis of the evolution of the institution of law, of the family, of the church, and of the state. The study of man from the biological point of view although indispensable in understanding man's impulsive reactions is bound to mislead if we conceive of it as giving a clue to his true nature. We must begin the other way round and trace back to man's potentialities from considering his distinctive achievements.

As we work back from the cultural achievements to the original nature of the human creature, we find a clue to man's distinctiveness in his power to use symbols. Man is an *"animal symbolicum"*: he lives in a universe created by his mind. To be sure, he makes his universe out of materials which are given; so do the craftsman and the artist. Utilitarian purposes and instinctive impulsions enter into man's productions as creative stimuli as well as disturbing obstructions. But the activating forces in man are not only drives for food and self-preservation and for sex and procreation. In every stage of civilization from the primitive onward we find an aspiration for truth, for goodness, and for beauty—and we may add, for reverence, for holiness, and for adoration of divinity. Such aspirations mingle with and transform the purely animal drives: in the vocations of the artist and the scientist, of the philosopher and of the religious, they become the source of happiness—the very essence of life. It is within man's power to create knowledge-concepts, value-ideas, art-forms by which to measure the validity of his libidinal desires and utilitarian purposes. Language, man's special gift, is not merely a means of communication with other men to facilitate the practical needs of the individual and of society; it is also a means of poetic creation, of prayer, and of communion.

Man's power of imagination and symbolization enables him to extend his living space in time. It makes it possible for him to see the present as the focus of an experience which has a background in past events and a foreground in possible future happenings. Human memory, as Cassirer reminds us, is not a mere recall of past happenings; it involves a selection, re-organization, and evaluation of experience with reference to present and future action. Man's vision of the future, likewise, is not a scientific prediction of what will happen. It is pregnant with hope and expectation; it is not a soothsayer's augury but a prophet's promise. The future that the great prophets of Israel spoke of in the name of God was not the foretelling of an empirical fact but a call to an ethical and religious task. "Here man's symbolic power ventures beyond all the limits of his finite existence"—and this "marks a decisive phase in man's ethical and religious life."[9]

Our abstracting tendency, it may be observed, often confuses the ideal with the actual and makes our hopes visionary. Where the symbolic nature of thought is recognized and the distinction between potentiality and existence is borne in mind, the utopian belief joined with a critical consideration of possibilities may become the means of changing the world. The power of symbolization creates new worlds—a world of contemplation, an enduring universe of values to calm the spirit when action is restrained and a world of ideals by which the actual world may be reshaped in harmony with the spirit.

4

Connected with the emphasis on symbolization which is at the basis of the human capacity to deal in abstract concepts is another divergence from the individualistic and personalistic bias of the biosocial conception—that suggested by the phrase "the rediscovery of the community." The view exemplified in the experimentalist-progressivist philosophy is that society consists of "individuals-in-their relations." This formulation, as noted in previous chapters, misses the point that interactions between persons are rarely direct self-other processes. There are moments, perhaps, when the interchange between persons is a flow of pure spirit: the poet may say, "He aholding my hand has completely satisfied me." But in the usual affairs of life, interpersonal relations are mediated by institutional structures. Man is a social creature insofar as he is a member of associations. The development of the self takes place through participation in many associative activities, not through unrelated individual-with-individual contacts. Man is not only a social creature, he is a *communal* creature. This implies *belonging* as well as associating.

The associations through which self-realization is achieved include a variety of groupings, some casual and temporary, others essential and lifelong. It is of singular importance to make a distinction between the ordinary association and the genuine community. The former is illustrated by the club, the trade union, the political party, the scien-

tific society; the latter by the family, the church, the nation, sometimes the village, the neighborhood, the ethnic group. An association
is organized for a specific purpose, it is joined deliberately, it may
be left at will. The community, on the other hand, sustains a complex
of life values, the individual is generally born into it—leaving it involves an element of emotional struggle. It is, in the first instance,
brought into being by existential factors, by common locale, common descent, common inherited religious affiliation which may carry
little spiritual significance for the individual. What makes it a community as against a mere congregate of individuals is a common
heritage of cultural and spiritual values. Belonging to a community
involves two corresponding responsibilities: the responsibility of securing its survival and physical welfare and the responsibility of devotion to its ideals and aspirations. The former we may term the responsibility of allegiance, the latter, the responsibility of loyalty. Moral
growth involves not only the improvement of person to person relations. It means the transformation of allegiances into loyalties.

This involves the power to envisage abstract ideals and to remain
true to them. Kurt Goldstein has pointed out that the brain-injured
individuals whom he studied learned to do competently such concrete
tasks as were necessary for their own personal life. They could live
in one room with others and carry out accustomed duties, keep their
things in good order and work efficiently by themselves. But they
could only do so when their activities had a utilitarian purpose of benefit to themselves. They could not cooperate with each other for a
common envisaged purpose since this required a power of abstraction
which they completely lacked. Likewise the man in the masses, Dr.
Goldstein notes, who is seemingly working for a group purpose is
merely subordinating himself to others, losing himself in activity as
a means of achieving security for himself and fulfilling individual
concrete wants. He has no true community with his fellows, for this
depends on a conscious realization of a common ideal purpose. "The
differences between individuals in a true community and those in
masses governed by a dictator of any kind," Dr. Goldstein concludes,
"lead back ultimately to differences in the capacity to take the abstract
attitude."[10]

The moral and spiritual problem of the Western world is bound
up with the problem of restoring attachment and belonging to the

basic communities of our society. The experience of loneliness which finds so great an expression in contemporary literature is neither a metaphysical alienation as the existentialists interpret it nor merely an inner soul sickness as some psychologists conceive it. Alienation is connected with estrangement and dissociation from the community life, from its satisfactions and trials and from its opportunities and responsibilities. The conflict within the individual is not merely an inner conflict, it is a conflict among his community allegiances, sometimes between his vision of the ideal universal community and the actual communities of family, of church, and of nation of which he is a part.

Restoration of the sense of meaningfulness requires an active process of reattachment to community life in its double phase, the phase of allegiance—which means concern for its sheer survival and destiny—and the phase of loyalty—which demands commitment to its ideals. The individual needs not only the sense of security that comes from belonging to a community but also the giving of self in its service, not only the warmth of being accepted but the light of devotion to its aspirations. The moral struggle is not only a struggle between the individual and society, it is at the higher level a struggle between an allegiance and a loyalty. The self grows as the allegiances to kith and kin, to country, to religious brotherhood remain strong but at the same time are raised to the plane of loyalty to the beliefs and aspirations implicit in the family, the nation, and the church.

In the past the village and the town represented true communities. They were territorial units, the bases of material interests; their character as communities was determined by a cultural heritage in which a common religion was the inspiriting element. The shift of the center of social life to huge cities with heterogeneous populations has greatly weakened, if not completely destroyed, the part that the small community can play in the formation of the personal character and the achievement of national unity. Today, for self-realization, social unity, and preservation of values, we must rely on the communities of family, church and nation. Each of these represents the two elements necessary for the true community: the bond of tangible, concrete interests and the imponderable ties of belief and value.

Although the family has been weakened by the growth of industrial society, it still has the responsibility of making a living and bringing up the children; it is the center of the most intimate social relations;

it symbolizes the ethics of fatherhood and brotherhood. The church also represents a face-to-face community; in one aspect it grows out of family life and is concerned with the crucial life events of birth, marriage, and death; at the same time it represents a community of belief in universal enduring values. The nation stands between family and church in the balance of tangible interests and imponderable aspirations. It represents a wide area of material concerns. It furnishes a framework of government and law, it mediates between local and sectional interest, on the one hand, and the international organization and invisible world community on the other.

The simple unity of the village and town in which the communities of family, the church, and the nation were well integrated cannot be restored. We must seek the wholeness of life through the separate though interlocking communities of families, church, and nation. Among these there are conflicts—between the family and the national interest, between the needs of the nation and the teachings of the church, between the traditional churches and a truly universal rational and spiritual ideal. But the tensions are also impulses to personal and social development. If, as we struggle in allegiance to preserve the material interests of communities to which we belong and persevere in loyalty to their moral and spiritual aspirations, we may hope to attain an ever-widening spiral of reconciliation.

5

During the last generation, scientists, students of culture and psychologists have shown a more appreciative attitude toward religion than prevailed in the previous era under the influence of positivism and Darwinism. The recognition that the moral-spiritual realm is a distinctive phase of human experience not necessarily subordinate to the domain of natural science and the realization that language always contains a symbolic element have contributed to a more favorable consideration of the values inherent in rituals and doctrines. There is a greater toleration of such terms as mythological and supernatural as conveying valid meanings. The emphasis of the social factor as indispensable to the development of the human being has led to a recognition of church affiliation as a means of attachment to a face-to-face community bound by ties of fellowship and representative of moral-spiritual values.

In estimating the import of this change of attitude, it is necessary to bear in mind the comment made by George Santayana on Bacon's famous epigram: "The God to whom depth in philosophy brings back men's minds is far from being the same from whom a little philosophy estranged them."[11] The major tendency, in the philosophic discussion during the last half century, has been to divorce religion from ontology, to see in it a source of meaning and value, not a source of truth in the scientific sense. Despite his attachment to the moods and insights of Catholicism, Santayana permits himself to say: "Religions will thus be better or worse, never true or false." For him religion is poetry intervening in life, as religion is poetry supervening on life. In American Protestant thought, as illustrated in the writings of Brightman, Hocking, and Wieman, the tendency in the last generation has been to conceive of religion as a form of experience—a form distinct from the scientific, the ethical, and the aesthetic, and yet, in the mature person, not wholly separate from these other forms of high human experience.

In the last decade or two, there have been signs of a change in the climate of opinion toward organized religion among intellectuals, particularly among those who enjoy a position of leadership in literary circles. In some instances, the renewed interest in religion is a rebound from an ardent faith in communism as a way of social-moral redemption. More generally it reflects a reaction against secular liberalism with its optimistic reliance on science and the open mind as sure remedies for all the ills of mankind. In the broadest sense, the "new turn toward religion" is one of the contemporary expressions of the quest for secure values in a complex world of driving pressures and distracting perplexities.

The "return and conversion" among intellectuals reflects negative as well as positive elements. In some phases, it smacks of a tired liberalism, turned obscurantist and conformist. There is point to Meyer Shapiro's comment: "It is good form to 'appreciate' religion without believing in God, or accepting the discipline of a church. Religion now has its fellow travellers."[12] Nor need we place too great an estimate on the highly publicized conversions to orthodoxy of a few prominent personalities, sincere as these may be. As an ancient saying has it: "A few coins in a large jar make a loud noise." The new interest in religion among intellectuals is without doubt of some significance as straws in the wind. But what it adds up to in terms of genuine moral and spiritual advance in our society as a whole is not yet clear. In comparison with the situation a generation ago, the secularization of life has grown apace with the march of industry, the widespread influence of a secular press, the multiplication of commercially sponsored mass entertainment. Insofar as the current religious revival represents a genuine inner development in psychological reorientation it is a movement in literary circles rather than a trend in society at large. In the measure that it reflects primarily a negative attitude toward scientific thought and a withdrawal from social endeavor, its moral significance is open to question.

The turn toward religion on the part of intellectuals is paralleled by a "theological renaissance" among important sections of the Protestant clergy. For a period of time, the "social gospel" was a dominant theme. This was a movement which aimed to apply Christian ethics to public affairs especially to the economic situation. There was opposition from two sides—from theologians who feared that the evangelical message of Christianity was being lost and from lay conservatives who held that ministers were going beyond their proper scope of activity in attempting to interfere in politics and business. In recent years a new opposition has developed which cannot be accused of Biblical fundamentalism or of economic reaction. But the neo-orthodox view, as it is usually designated, joins with the traditionalists in holding that the social gospel movement misses what is distinctive in the Christian theory of salvation. The contention is that the reduction of Christianity to social idealism expressed in terms similar to the pronouncements of secular liberals "leaves them unattached to the driving forces of a religious tradition and a religious cultus, of which the religious community, as such, is custodian."[13]

The neo-orthodox view allows much freedom in the interpretation of traditional doctrines in the light of new intellectual perspectives. But it insists on the use of the distinctive denominational concepts: "The core of faith seems intimately bound up with the original language which expresses it."[14] Neo-orthodoxy seeks an answer to the deeper problems of human life not in individual experience or in metaphysical theory but in history—in the corporate experience of an enduring community. It aims to utilize the insights of the particular church community with which the individual feels himself to be closely identified as a means of strengthening moral determination

and a sense of social responsibility. Its purpose is to utilize creeds and
rituals as educational and disciplinary means to promote universal
ends without exercising pressure on non-members to adopt the same
forms of religious thought or practice, and without setting up bars to
interdenominational communication.

Among the leading exponents of the neo-orthodox theology are
men of great power of thought and of spiritual insight—Karl Barth
from whom the movement stems, Reinhold Niebuhr its outstanding
interpreter in the United States. The genuineness of their religious
attitude has been demonstrated in their unyielding opposition to anything that savored of fascism, and their honest recognition of the
ethical element in communism, despite their own rejection of it as a
theory of salvation and as a political form. They have not hesitated to
speak out when Christian ethical principles were involved in the
political and economic struggles of the day. The emphasis placed on
the need of identification with a historical community, affirming distinctive expressions of universal religious insights, allowing for a continuity of reinterpretation, it may be said, is a significant contribution
not only to religion but to cultural-social concepts.

And yet the impression remains that the theological renascence,
taken as a whole, is in some respects a retreat from the liberal stand-
point of the social gospel. There was not missing from the "social
gospel," as exemplified in the writings of Walter Rauschenbusch and
his followers, a recognition of the tragic involvements of men which
Christian doctrine associates with Adam's fall.[15] At the same time it
reflected a faith—also justified by the Christian tradition—in the ultimate victory of the good, over the evil, inclination in man: it reflected the prophetic vision of an era of justice and peace. It connected
the ethics of Christianity with the theme of democracy and with this
went a friendliness to reason and nature.

Neo-theologism, on the other hand, takes the dark Christian view
of man's nature as eternally corrupt from the beginning. It makes
salvation dependent on the grace of God more than on man's endeavor. It places the emphasis on suffering as a means of religious
understanding rather than on the effort to reduce suffering in the
world. It evidences a distrust of the rational and a preference for the
mystical; it looks to Nietzsche and Dostoevski rather than to Descartes
and Pascal. In the effort to defend old doctrines, interpretations of

history are strained at times to the point of obscurantism. The attack against the modern movements of enlightenment and progress goes beyond bounds in the insinuation that science and secularism are responsible for the cultural crisis of our age. Too quickly has it been forgotten, that the break in the European civilization system was made by Germany where evangelical religion flourished and that communism came first to Russia whose political corruption was joined to a deep religious mysticism.

6

In total effect, the current turn toward religion represents a retreat along two lines—a turning away from reason and science as a means of lightening man's burden of toil and trouble and a withdrawal from societal interest in favor of a preoccupation with the inner self. Its tendency is evidenced by the heavy reliance placed on modern existentialism by lay and theological writers, despite the fact that this doctrine of despair has no common set of principles, no theory of redemption, and that in most of its forms is anti-Christian as it is anti-classic.[16] Existentialism attacks all doctrinal structures, all philosophic *anschauungen*, every church authority, and every definite social order. It is opposed to everything that curtails the will to unhindered freedom of the individual self. Since it acknowledges no ordered society or reasoned conception of the good, it terminates in chaos or in its opposite, in blind conformity; it vacillates between "either-or" or makes an arbitrary decision.

Soren Kierkegaard, suffering from the sickness unto death, presumes to tell the church what it should be and comes to the end of life without spiritual healing. Martin Heidegger, the "great metaphysical genius," who reduces all European philosophies to nothingness, affirming only the "resolute decision" of the will, found it possible to follow the lead of the Nazi chiefs and to accommodate himself to the Fascist regimentation.[17] The courageous Jean-Paul Sartre had the inner strength to fight in the underground against the Nazi tyranny. He urges upon us to become involved, to take responsibility, to make our own lives. But in his neutralism he has no guidance to give and in the final analysis, he cries "No Exit."

Existentialism negates itself. It begins by pointing to the involvements of men in concrete situations conditioned by biological and social factors. It is described as an expression of protest against the dehumanization by the collectivist forces of the contemporary world. But it makes no analysis of the concrete factors that have brought about the contemporary perplexities. It shifts the attention to the "existential anxieties" which it regards as inevitable concomitants of the human predicament—to the "ontic" anxiety of the fear of death, to the anxiety of the sense of guilt, to man's alienation from the world, to the despairing apprehension of life's meaninglessness. Granted that such anxieties are rooted in the nature of man, it should be obvious that in their disturbing forms they arise in connection with the events of life, that they can be diminished or intensified by external conditions.

The existentialist shift of emphasis from the anxieties which men experience in the daily life—in the caring for health, in making a living, in sexual relations in and out of marriage, in bringing up our children, in the catastrophe of war—to the inner anxieties of the alienated self to which no doubt sensitive persons are at times subject—is a method of evading the difficult task of ameliorating conditions through political and economic reconstruction. Existentialism is not mainly a mirror of the doubt and frustration of the twentieth century, it is a defense mechanism—a means of avoiding responsibility. The failures of European civilization are converted into the inevitable failures of man, instead of seeing them as they really are— failures in politics, in philosophies, and in religious thought of particular regions, especially of German thinkers and statesmen in a critical historical period.

The contemporary theological renaissance shares with existentialism a tendency to avoid a realistic analysis of the historical and social causes for the crisis in modern life. It attributes our failures primarily to the original weaknesses and corruptions of man's nature. Emphasis is laid on man's inadequacies as a means of demonstrating the indispensability of religious faith as the only true way to salvation. It reflects the age-long endeavor to resolve the perplexities of life through transporting man into an extra-temporal psychic realm of being outside the sphere of history and social life. The present-day theological literature abounds in mystical expressions, e.g., the Lutheran concept of "a personal encounter with God," Martin Buber's "I and Thou" confrontation, Paul Tillich's "being grasped by the power of being-itself."

In the *Courage to Be* the eminent Protestant theologian defends existentialism—whose negations he realizes—as an indispensable step in the conquest of despair and in the rise to a plane of transcendence.[18] It represents "the courage to be as oneself," to "ex-ist" in the literal sense of standing out in spite of, to assert the self in the face of life's utter meaninglessness. This phenomenon of individuation *in extremis* is a counterforce, Professor Tillich believes, to the equally necessary "courage to be as a part," to relate oneself to the whole, to participate in the common life which though essential to the fulfillment of the self tends in the press of contemporary forces to lead toward collectivist conformity. The reconciliation between the polarities of individualization and participation—of standing apart from and of being a part of—are to be reconciled and transcended in Professor Tillich's mystical idea through absolute faith in "the God above the God of theism."

7

Whatever these mystical conceptions may offer to individuals in relieving personal anxiety, they present no solution for the moral and spiritual perplexities of modern society. The contemporary theological renaissance, it would appear, misses the import of what is distinctive in the Western contribution to the religious development of mankind. In Judaism and in Christianity, in their most significant exemplifications two religious strains are joined together. One aspect reflects a quest common to all the religions of mankind, of the East as well as of the West—the quest for a direct relation to the sustaining Power of the unity of the universe which may be conceived personally or impersonally, in an attitude of adoration or of communion. This is the Psalmist's orientation in his joyous praise of God and in his prayerful supplication for salvation. The other aspect uniquely characteristic of Western religion reflects man's need of fellowship for other men, of a fellowship invested with the spirit of the family virtues, of fatherhood and of brotherhood, of filial and fraternal love. It involves giving help as well as receiving help. It leads to seeking communion with God through the life of the congregation. It seeks identification with God through the attributes of justice and mercy and of incorporation in His unity through unity with all mankind. It finds its culmination in the prophets' pronouncement of an era of peace and good will on earth.

It is only in the measure that these two aspects of religion, the communal as well as the personal, are well balanced against each other, that Western religion remains true to its original foundations in the Biblical source and in the congregational mode of organization. In the contemporary theological renaissance and in the new turn toward religion among the intellectuals there is the regressive tendency of the reduction of religion to an instrument of personal salvation. It is a turning of the self back on the self in a subjective construction of the nature of the self. The classic tradition, in its Christian and Hellenic forms, supports quite another view of the release and the enlargement—of the transcendence of the self. There are two broad avenues for the emancipation from the sense of alienation. One way is through self-identification with a system of universal ideas, through participation in the rational and moral world of the Idea of the Good. The other way is through participation in the life of the family and the civic community, sharing responsibilities with others in meeting life's problems as best we may. These two modes of self-transcendence are interactive: it is through community life that we may achieve an intimation of the divine attributes of justice, of mercy, and of human unity, the identification of selfhood with a pattern of universal values works toward the reconstruction of the community in the direction of its own ideal.

There is truth in the idea that the self retains a sense of its own uniqueness. It remains a center of protest and self-assertion against the confinements of formulations however ideal, and against the regularities of institutional living, however convenient. But even so, it is not always lonely—feeling itself alien. The self is a source of vitality and many-sidedness: it loves to wander over its imaginative world as well as to be closeted with itself in solitary communion. The self is by nature polytheistic and pagan; it cannot, perhaps, in its uncircumcized, pre-Platonic, and pre-Christian state, experience the sublime unity of the universe inherent in all high religion. But it can derive joy from communion with the lesser divinities of the hearth and the countryside as Walter Pater has charmingly related. The self contains a sprite as well as a demon, an elf as well as an imp. It may find salvation in the humbler occupations of the daily life, in art and in artisanship, as well as in the great world of ideas and of public affairs.

The church is one of the pivotal institutions of Western democratic society. It has much to offer toward liberation of the self through leading to identification with the universe of enduring values and toward emancipation from self-centeredness through encouraging works of charity and good will. It serves at once as a spiritual fraternity and as a fellowship of personal friendships. The experiences of which it is custodian is conveyed through many sources—through its literature and its music, through its history and its legends, as well as through its rituals and doctrines. Each of the great religions of the West, Catholicism, Protestantism, Judaism, embraces a rich variety of conceptions and styles of life—rational, mystic, personal, social—within a common frame of reference and spiritual orientation. This diversity of experiential resources within a unity of principles marks their greatness. What the religions of the churches have to give is an enrichment and elevation of the spirit and a deepening of humane understanding—not a certitude of truth or a monopoly of moral values. Although religious experience represents a distinct aspect of experience, its validity cannot escape a judgment in the light of other forms of human experience in science, philosophy, in secular literature. And the mode of organization of the churches, their political tendencies and economic affiliations, cannot be disregarded in estimating their impact on social welfare.

Organized religion has always furthered works of charity, often been on the side of the underprivileged, and at various times supported, even provided leadership for, progressive social movements; but its record is far from consistent—it has as frequently been associated with the forces of reaction as it has engaged in the suppression of freedom of thought. In recent centuries organized religion has trailed behind secular forces in the furtherance of liberal causes. The decline of religion in modern times is probably due to its failure to take an active part in advancing tangible human welfare rather than to its intellectual lag which has also been a serious factor. In placing the major emphasis on the message of consolation and redemption through mystical and emotional measures, organized religion has lent color to the accusation that it offers an opiate, rather than a remedy, for human ills.

The belief at the heart of all religion that our adjustment to life involves a psychic orientation suggested by the terms acceptance and faith is an indispensable idea. However favorable the natural conditions and the social organization, there will always remain a distance between man's wants and visions, on the one hand, and the ability of the social order to provide for full satisfaction and for the happiness that comes from living in accordance with an ideal, on the other. But it is sheer obscurantism to divert attention from the part that social conditions play in the development of selfhood. The release of the self from anxiety and insecurity so that the soul may be invited and the spirit uplifted is, in the first instance, a liberation from economic restriction and political coercion.

In the light of the pressures of our era, those who are not with the forces of social advance must be accounted against them; by default they aid and abet the powers and dominations of violence. Insofar as the new turn toward religion is a withdrawal from active participation in social concerns, it represents a *fin de siècle* phenomenon—not by any means a sign of spiritual renaissance. The "social gospel" is certainly not all there is in the profound message of the great religions of the Western world; but without it, their significance for modern life remains marginal and parochial. To be true to their full mission, the churches joining with secular forces must contribute actively by deed as well as by word to advance the great causes of our era, the promotion of racial equality and international organization, and what is indispensable to both, of the just state erected on the economic welfare of the whole people.

NOTES

1. S. Robert Oppenheimer, *Science and the Common Understanding* (Simon and Schuster, 1953), p. 95.

2. Morris R. Cohen, *Reason and Nature* (Harcourt, Brace and Co., 1931), p. 222.

3. *op. cit.*, p. 21.

4. *Ibid.*, p. 68.

5. Albert Einstein, *Out of My Later Years* (Philosophical Library, 1950), p. 22.

6. *Ibid.*, p. 24.

7. John Dewey, *Logic: The Theory of Inquiry* (Henry Holt and Co., 1938), p. 19.

8. Ernst Cassirer, *An Essay on Man* (Yale University Press, 1944), p. 68.

9. *Ibid.*, p. 55.

10. Kurt Goldstein, *Human Nature in the Light of Psychopathology* (Harvard University Press, 1940), p. 118.

11. George Santayana, *The Life of Reason* (Charles Scribner's Sons, 1913), Vol. III, p. 4.

12. "Religion and the Intellectuals," *Partisan Review Series,* Number 3 (1950), p. 126.

13. F. Ernest Johnson, *The Social Gospel Reexamined* (Harper & Brothers, 1940), p. 4.

14. Daniel Day Williams, *What Present Day Theologians are Thinking* (Harper & Brothers, 1952), p. 13.

15. Johnson, *op. cit.*, pp. 53ff.

16. F. H. Heinemann, *Existentialism and the Modern Predicament* (Harper & Brothers, 1953), pp. 109-133.

17. Jean Wahl, *A Short History of Existentialism* (Philosophical Library, 1949), p. 27.

18. Paul Tillich, *The Courage To Be* (Yale University Press, 1952), pp. 123ff:

PART THREE

PROFILE OF AN EDUCATIONAL POLICY

We who now live are parts of a humanity
that extends into the remote past, a humanity that has interacted with nature. The
things in civilization we most prize are not
of ourselves. They exist by grace of the
doings and sufferings of the continuous
human community of which we are a link.
Ours is the responsibility of conserving, transmitting, rectifying and expanding the heritage of values we have received that those
who come after us may receive it more solid
and secure, more widely accessible and more
generously shared than we have received it.
—John Dewey
A Common Faith

12

EDUCATION AND THE
PROVINCE OF THE SCHOOL

I𝙽 𝚃𝙷𝙸𝚂 final section, attention will be focused on the educational implications of the view developed in the preceding chapters. The intention is not to propose a completely new educational system. An educational policy must be clearly formulated and firmly held in mind, but the ideals set up must be seen as arising from the inherited institutional structure and from conceptions which have developed over a period of time. The social-historical thesis which directs this study requires viewing needed changes as modifications of existing usages and current proposals. The gradualist approach to educational reconstruction is warranted not only as a cautious measure of practicality and as a means of preserving valid experiences and insights but as a demand of sheer relevancy. Philosophy of education based on general conceptions applied deductively are likely to go wide of the mark and to have only marginal significance for the school teacher or educational administrator. The discussion to follow, although not always making direct reference, will bear in mind the major contemporary issues in educational theory and school practice—particularly of the experimentalist and progressivist types—as the endeavor proceeds to work out the lines of a positive educational philosophy. It may not be superfluous to add that the subject is American education and not education in general.

We may at the outset state the general orientation: education has a double responsibility: one of conservation and one of reconstruction. There is danger in this era of transition as democracy tends to move forward—that the imponderable insights which endow it with spirit will be dissipated and the structure of values on which it rests will be weakened. Education today must emphasize anew the heritage of the humanities, the classic literatures, and the political, philosophic, and religious ideas which exemplify Western civilization. To this traditional and essential work of education another purpose of paramount importance must be added: to aid in bringing the new democratic world order into being. This will involve the study of contemporary social problems in the light of our national ideals. Both aspects of education, the conservationist and the reconstructionist, should contribute to the formation of a philosophy of life which besides aiding in social advance will offer guidance to the individual in meeting the personal problems which men face—in different ways—whatever the social and political framework.

A qualification may be introduced at this point. Despite the emphasis laid on the part that the school ought to play in the reconstruction of the social order, education is not to be regarded as the main instrument of social reform. The crisis in modern life cannot be ascribed in any primary sense to the collapse "of human learning and teaching"; nor can we escape further catastrophe, as Dr. Meiklejohn believes, "only as we succeed in devising better learning and better teaching."[1] The analysis in the preceding chapters has emphasized the political and economic forces at work in social change and in intellectual development. Furthermore, the school is only one element in the educational process: the family, the church, the law, and the life experience at large are far more potent in their total influence. What the school ought to do and what it can do will depend on its relation to the other forces at work, on the legal, political, economic, and religious aspects of culture. Our first task is to indicate the functions of education in the general meaning of the term and to mark off the province of the school within this broad area.

1

No single definition of education is adequate whether stated in terms of imparting universal truths, the self-realization of the individual or the integration of the individual with his society. An educational philosophy cannot be based on metaphysics, e.g., idealism, realism, pragmatism. A conception of man's relation to the cosmos is requisite for a fully consistent outlook but cannot of itself provide a foundation for education. Metaphysics may offer a logical support for the building but it cannot give an adequate idea of the dwelling; or to change the analogy, it may supply the backdrop for the play but cannot give more than a hint of the drama. Even less valid is the view that underlies progressive education in most of its forms, namely, that the aims of education can be derived in the first instance from the needs and wants of the child. The view that offers the most promise is the one that relates the school directly to a society and to a definite system of culture. But here, too, the definition may prove onesided if not related to the other two aspects—to the view which aims to transcend particular societies in pursuit of universal ends and the other which has regard for the individual.

Education may be concretely defined as the art of bringing up a child to live the good life in society. It thus has three irreducible points of reference: a growing individual; a canon of standards, values, and ideals; a definite community. Each aspect of our triune definition—individuality, community, ideality—must receive consideration in the determination of the aim, and of the process, of education. Moreover, these are not separate realms but interrelated phases of every educational situation. A full elucidation of any one of these phases would entail a discussion of the others. But it will help to give balance to our educational policy if we bear in mind each phase and the concerns it represents.

The reference to *individuality* keeps before our minds the living reality of the growing child. It directs attention to the uniqueness of each personality, to the special talents or handicaps, to the diversity of individual reactions. It reflects the parental concern with each child, with his health and physical development, with the problem of his adjustment to life, with his welfare and happiness. In this approach as characteristic of progressive education the school's task is conceived in terms of helping the child—aiding him in the proper fulfillment of his needs, guiding him in the constructive use of his impulses, directing his development toward responsibility and maturity. The social context of individual growth is recognized, a conception of good conduct is implicit, but the center of attention is the realization of the personality of each child or youth.

At the opposite pole is the factor of *ideality*, the element stressed by ethical philosophers and by religious teachers. This approach directs attention to values and ideas that have enduring worth for all men regardless of race or nationality, country or region. It draws attention to the need of abstracting universals from the matrix of particulars in which they subsist and to the importance of formulating clear concepts to guide conduct and thought. This emphasis on the significance of ideas does not deny that personality develops through the "self-other process" of individuals responding to each other. A priceless insight is expressed in Dewey's statement: "What one is as a person is what one is as associated with others, in a free give and take of intercourse." But intercourse between human beings on a level of intelligence involves the mediation of concepts and of values. The development of the individual into a person implies the growth of ideas as well as the multiplication of social contacts. Self-realization may be associated with the decrease in the number of our contacts with actual persons, although it will always require communion with the ideal persons of literature and history.

The concept of *community* is the richest of the three ideas: it represents a fusion of the factors of individuality and ideality with the element of association. The child does not exist as an isolated entity in a world of abstractions; he is born, grows up in, and will in the normal course of events live out his life in a community amid a specific complex of customs, laws, and conceptions of value. The individual is bound to his community by many ties, by material concerns, by multiplicity of organizational affiliations, by a variety of cultural interests. Being a member of a community means accepting conventions, recognizing dependence on others, realizing that each one's welfare is intertwined with the welfare of the community as a whole. In the course of socialization, the individual while making adjustments learns also to recognize standards of conduct and to evaluate his behavior in terms of principles. And in varying measures in accordance with his sensitivities as they interplay with his particular cultural background, he may learn to rise above the conventional manners and mores of his immediate social environment and endeavor to live in accordance with a humane, universal, transcendent ideal.

These three factors—the individual, the communal, the ideal—play a part in all educational situations. Development is not from the individual, to the social, to the abstract idea; well-rounded growth means a deepening and broadening of the three aspects in relation to each other. Not every aspect, however, will be equally emphasized in every type of educational activity at all levels; one rather than another aspect will be in the focus of attention. In early childhood the biological needs and native tendencies of the individual will receive central consideration; but even here, how these should be expressed and developed cannot be determined except in terms of the social setting of customs and ideals. In the higher stages of learning, logical organization, principles and theories will have the primary place, but ideas however abstract must be seen in relation to the situations that gave rise to them and to their possible significance in application to the personal and social life.

The weakness in much of the current educational theories lies in inadequate consideration of one or another of these indispensable concepts. The absolutists and transcendentalists tend to neglect the factors of individuality and community. The progressivists and experimentalists undervalue form and idea. Their attempt to counteract individualism by calling attention to the social nature of true individuality is largely vitiated by their failure to stress the institutional forms by which character is shaped. Their distrust of ideas unrelated to immediate action is likely to lead to weakening their force; ideals may become so dissolved in action as to lose their savor.

2

The concept of growth as used in the experimentalist philosophy obscures the fact that all development requires periodic change in form. This is true in the realm of social development as well as in biological growth. Whether the changes in attitudes and behavior which we term "educational" are the result of the indirect action of the environment or effected by the teacher through the process of instruction, a new *mode* of action or *pattern* of thought ensues which has definite character and an element of permanence. All education involves a change from one *way* of doing, feeling, or thinking to another *way*—it means changing from one form to another. Once we introduce the idea of formation, moreover, it becomes clear that all education requires the restraint of natural potentialities as well as their release, so that the concept of development must simultaneously be associated with the concept of discipline—whether the discipline is achieved by injunction or persuasion, whether intelligently self-imposed or results from the obedient following of the rule.

Inevitably the "formation" principle of education implies adjustment to existing social norms, involving both acquiescence and conformity. But acquiescence need not mean slavish acceptance, nor does conformity require a suppression of individuality. We may accept a socially approved form of serving dinner; still a wide range is left to ability and taste. True individuality represents a degree of variation and excellence of performance within an accepted pattern or style. Acquisition of the approved manners and mores in any society is not an easy matter of copying: it represents a raising up from the usual widespread actual practices in the use of language, in the conduct of business and family life, and in human relations generally, so that the conformation that education aims at is at the same time a "reformation" of abilities and of character.

Education as formation includes also the task of idealization, the classic Hellenic conception of education as "deliberately moulding human character in accordance with an ideal."[2] The analogy of the potter shaping clay suggested in the phrase "moulding human character" is repugnant to our conception of human development but this should not make us lose sight of the positive conception—the Greeks used other less mechanical analogies, such as the art of the farmer in cultivation of the soil, and of the physician in nurturing good health. The essential point is that the educator, like craftsman and artist, must use his technical skill as a means of transforming his material to accord with an ideal held in mind.

This ideal of "educating man into his true form" as Werner Jaeger points out, was never an abstract pattern existing outside time and space. "It was the living ideal which had grown up in the very soil of Greece, and changed with the changing fortunes of the race, assimilating every stage of its history and development." A purpose of education—and here the school must play the central part—is to identify the individual with the ideals, historical and emerging, of the community as expressed in the highest cultural productions, in its literature, the work of artists, the pronouncements of statesmen, the teachings of its philosophers and religious leaders. It is through the interaction of the conceived ideals with the normal standards of the community that the life of the individual and society is continuously brought forward.

The task of education does not end here—with the adoption of ideals as means to social betterment. Education includes another function: to enable the individual to transcend his particular community while living in it, and to create for himself a life in the world of spirit. Parallel to our secular life—the life in the world of affairs—flows our inner life indissolubly a part of the self. A stream of consciousness accompanies our course of activities, sometimes crossing it, contributing to it and nourished by it, at other times meandering at a distance, working its way through new fields of imaginative experience. Through literature and history, art and science, philosophy and religion, we become liberated from the distractions and disappointments, the crudities and compromises, of the life in the world of actualities. We broaden the range of imaginative life and deepen its insights; we come to live in a realm where we can hold converse with the immortals; our emotional responses are chastened so that our aesthetic appreciations become more sensitive; our fantasies and superstitions are held in check by knowledge; our minds are disciplined so that we are better able to judge of truth. And, if grace be given, we may with the help of the saints and the poets catch a glimpse of the Ineffable Essence which is the Unity of truth and beauty, of reason and love, of justice and kindness. Thus we may at some moments achieve in this life the true felicity which the religious call beatitude.

The achievement of an ethical disposition involves not only a continuous growth in understanding and control through cooperation with others; it requires a transfer of the self from one plane of sanctions to another. At the lowest level is the morality of common practice and of discretion: living in accordance with the usual code actually followed in the community to which one belongs—e.g., in sex relations, in business operations, in professional competition—keeping close enough to the line of legality so as not to be detected, justifying oneself by the plea that "everybody does it," even priding oneself that one does not consider oneself holier than the next fellow. A second level of morality is achieved when an earnest attempt is made to live up to the publicly approved conventions, and when the flesh is weak, offering confession to oneself or to the priest and performing some penance to make amends before one begins sinning again.

A genuine ethical position is attained in the measure that the individual is guided by a consciously conceived system of values approved by religion or philosophy. All systems of morality require some sanction external to the self; moral development means not only the inner acceptance of the sanction, but a change in the character of the sanction. The experimentalist conception of moral growth as a continuous reconstruction of the self fails to make clear that education to be morally effective must lift one from one plane of sanctions and insights to another—from the plane of tangible, experiential, personal judgment to that of the invisible, imponderable, and impersonal sanction of commitment to the ideal.

3

Thus far the discussion has dealt not primarily with the function of the school but with education in its broadest sense of all cultural influences. The vagueness of much in current educational proposals arises from the failure to make a clear distinction between schooling and education, accompanied often by the implied assumption that the school represents the major instrument of education. The progressivist educator to whom "education is life" is prone to this error. The process of education may properly be considered as falling under three categories: the spontaneous influence of incidental experience, the effects of institutional life, and the work of the school as a specialized educational agency. These three educational modes overlap; nevertheless, each has its special area of operation and its special strength and weakness.

The most effective educational forces in shaping character are outside the school and exercise their influence indirectly and continuously in the course of just living. Education through experience in the genuine sense of the term "experience" falls into the category of incidental education rather than in the activities of the school. The development of character goes on in play, in relations between the sexes, in occasional personal contacts as well as in the organized activities of family and business life, of politics and religion. Books, newspapers and periodicals, radio and television, theatre and moving pictures, all play their part. In both types, whether casual or institutional, the influences operate within a definite social context of beliefs, sentiments, and conventions. It is in the main through incidental education that the individual as he grows up learns to know and, most often to practice, the ethics tacitly approved by the in-group of village, class or club as against the publicly sanctioned code of morals. Life experience provides very effective but not always desirable educational results. Its strength lies in its relevancy and practicality; its weakness lies in its nonselective character, in the small part that principles and ideas play in it. What we learn from life experience reflects common knowledge, the corruptions of ordinary practice, as well as acceptable manners and prudential wisdom. Ordinary life experience is likely to be limited and biased by the region, the denomination, and the class in which one grows up.

Institutional life in the family, the church, and the state combines the furtherance of life functions with regulatory standards which direct experience into social channels and toward spiritual goals. Every institution fulfills a need, embodies a norm of practice, and expresses an ideal. Institutional participation is real education in effect though not in original purpose. Institutions, it is true, tend to resist modification and often violate the purpose and distort the spirit that brought them into existence. Every institution has the possibility of achieving more as well as less than its major purpose implies. The family, originating in the need of mating and caring for offspring, may have as a rich by-product the nourishment of a life-long companionship; it may advance a craft, build a business organization, establish a foundation for educational and charitable purposes, or it may fail of its elementary purpose. The church, established in a spirit of human brotherhood, may become an agency of intolerance and persecution. The state whose function is to provide security and furnish a framework of law may turn into an instrument of exploitation of its people in defiance of men's inalienable rights. But the significance of institutions for the promotion of life and education must be judged by their possibilities, not by their failures.

Despite the attenuation of the place of the family in modern Western civilization, it still retains its central importance as an educational force as well as a nucleus of social life. It must retain this position as long as parents have the responsibility for supporting and rearing the child—a right and a duty which is the very basis of the democratic social order. The influence of the family is pervasive, operating as it does in waking and sleeping hours, and throughout many years; its decisions with reference to religious affiliation and the type and length of schooling are fateful for the child and youth. In our highly specialized life, the family remains the one institution which can integrate the various aspects of life, the economic, the cultural, the vocational, the religious. The life of the family revolves around the most intimate and difficult moral relations—between husband and wife, parents and children, sisters and brothers, between kith and kin. It represents still a social unit where the strict rules of achievement and reward are not observed: the old father is supported even though he be a rascal, the prodigal son is received with open arms; not the strongest but the weakest gets the chicken broth. The life of the family is the root of the ethics of mutual responsibility and still preserves the ideal of conjugal and fraternal love basic to the Western ethical and religious system.

The family arises out of a biological need, humanized by the intermingling of love and a sense of obligation. The church originates from the opposite pole of life, from an idealized conception of fatherhood and brotherhood, from a spiritualized view of personality and human unity. Like the family, the church is parental and fraternal in its interest; it is concerned with the development of each of its members. It blesses the newborn infant, it sanctifies marriage, it consoles the mourner, it invites to its haven all that are heavy-laden with sorrow. It brings individuals and families together in a true community, as it affords a meeting place under spiritual auspices. From the coming together of neighbors, it establishes a congregation for good works of charity, and creates a community of believers in the values of kindness and justice. In its activities and teachings, the church leads toward the invisible unities that bind the generations of man together, and thus, paradoxically, brings men closer to their innermost selves. When it is true to its mission, the church can be of exceptional educational significance: it supports the family, socializes its interests, spiritualizes its values. It sustains the moral virtues of the common life and preserves the transcendent, universal, humane ideals.

The nation, as cultural unit and as political state, represents a third institutionalized community of prime educational significance. Language, law, and customs, family, religious, and public life are all marked with the national imprint in varying ways and degrees. Character is formed by respect for, and observance of, the laws of the state, by participation in the political life; it is shaped by the mores, the styles of life, by public opinion. Our school system, though administratively decentralized, represents a common pattern reflecting the national heritage of literature and history, of cultural values and political ideals. There are local variations of the national pattern and universal elements in it. American civilization is historically linked with European civilization and is today part of an emerging international society. At the same time it represents a community of destiny: for Americans, the widest tangible unity of material problems, cultural concerns, and ideal values.

The institutions of family, church, and nation are particularly significant for moral education because they constitute true communities, membership in which involves the obligation of loyalty. Loyalty does not mean blind adherence. On the contrary since it implies devotion to the principles and ideals of a community as well as concern for its survival, loyalty in the valid sense of the word will always involve opposition to prevailing policies, at some points. As soon as we think of principles and ideals, we have transcended the limitations of the narrow group affiliation—of sectarianism and chauvinism—and have entered the sphere of the humane and the universal. The tragic mistake of the cosmopolitan social utopian lies in his failure to understand that a loyalty to humanity cannot be built on a disloyalty to one's own people and one's own country—or on the basis of any disloyalty to the ideal of loyalty, as Josiah Royce profoundly understood.[3] Nor, considering the opposite extreme, can moral character be nurtured through the type of religion which maintains that the life of the spirit is inward only—that it can be developed apart from concern with the political and economic aspects of life in the family and the civic community.

The very heart of moral education is the fostering of loyalty in the twofold sense—of identification with a community and the simultaneous conversion of the given communal connection into an allegiance to the ideals implicit in it. The development of moral character requires more than social participation; it demands involvement in the problems of the community, and identification with its destiny. The ethical character is developed not only by assumption of responsibility for the intelligent guidance of one's own life, but by recognizing one's responsibility for the maintenance and advance of the institutions that are basic to the life of the community. Through the attempt at reconciling the partly conflicting loyalties to family, church, and state, the moral life is deepened and elevated. Through the realization that no perfect harmony can be achieved between the

actual institutional life and the ideals they symbolize, and that, nevertheless, the striving for advance must never be yielded—that a mature
ethical conception can be achieved.

4

In contradistinction to the incidental and institutional educational
processes, the school represents an agency deliberately set up for educational purposes. Back of it is always a community—a group of families, a public association, a church, or a state. The rise of the school
and of the profession of teaching accompanies the growing complexity of society and the division of labor. In primitive society there are
no schools; the young acquire the necessary skills and absorb the traditional wisdom through participation in the life activities of the tribe.
In childhood the parents are the teachers, the father for the boy, the
mother for the girl; in the initiation ceremonies of puberty a more
distant relative, representative of the clan, the wider community, plays
a leading part. In primitive life, in a sense, the whole community of
elders are the teachers.

Organized education as against incidental education began with
apprenticeship, the half-way house between education through life
experience and the deliberate education of the school. It is illustrated
in the training of novitiates for the priesthood and of artisans for the
crafts. Traces of early schools are found in Babylon and Egypt where
written records were widely used in government and business. These
schools, probably for scribes, were for specialized training and not for
membership in the community. Induction into community life still
was achieved indirectly as in primitive times through participation,
through the institutional life, through ceremonies, customs, legends,
and oral instruction of parents and elders.

It is in Attica and Judea that the genuine school develops. The
distinctive character of the Athenian and the Jewish school is in-
separable from their function in making the young good members of
a definite community, in the former as citizens, in the latter as members of a religious society. In both instances, membership in the
community is associated with an ideal way of life. The communal
element in Athenian education is well illustrated in the ephebic oath,
in which the youth pledged loyalty to his comrades in arms in the
defense of the city and devotion to the laws as enacted by the assem-

bly, and in which he vowed to leave the city "not less but greater and better than he found it." Jewish school education, which developed in the century before the Christian era, arose out of the idea that all Israel—not only the priests—had the right and the duty to know the scriptures as the basis of a way of life divinely sanctioned. The boys' entry into the community at the age of thirteen is marked by being called up to read the scroll of the Law in the synagogue.

Stating the matter broadly, the school has a *raison d'être* when there is a gap between what needs to be learned in any society and what can usually be learned incidentally through ordinary experience—between what can be learned casually and what the elders of the community believe ought to be known. This situation exists when there are socially necessary skills that require training, when a society possesses a heritage of literature considered significant for maintaining a high level of culture and character, when the experience of a wider community than the tribe or the nation can be called upon, when universal ethical and religious ideals receive the approval of teachers and public leaders. The superior knowledge and the higher ideals are accessible through symbolic representation; it is not an accident or an irrelevance that schools have concentrated on language, literature and mathematics, and that books have become central in the curriculum. There is ever the danger that education in schools will get lost in the maze of symbols, becomes formal and verbal. It is a perennial problem, as Dewey notes, to keep "a proper balance between the formal and the informal, the incidental and the intentional, modes of education." But intrinsically the school's function is in the realm of the deliberate, the formal, the symbolic.

The scope and content of school education will vary with the stage of civilization, with the political and economic condition, with the ethical and religious conceptions, and with the school clientele, whether a caste, a class, or the whole people. The school has always at some level included a professional purpose: in Greece to develop the orator as public leader, in Judea to educate the religious jurist, in Rome to prepare for the civil service, in the Middle Ages, to train the clergy for civil and ecclesiastic posts, for knowledge of the law and to some extent for medicine. But these professions were taught and exercised within a framework of a community life and a system of ideals. Along with its professional purpose, the school of Western

Europe always had the broader purpose of advancing communal, cultural, spiritual values. The essential purpose of the school is to raise the level of thought and character through bringing to bear the experience of a wider community—of other generations or of other peoples—on the social life.

It is a natural consequence of the modern development that the school should assume new functions. Until recently schooling was confined to a small segment of the population, mainly in the cities; and even in the West where universal education was established, most children went to school only during the elementary period. With the adoption of compulsory education and the opening up of higher education to a considerable part of the population and with the growing need of skilled technicians in countless fields, new tasks come into the scope of the school's function. Inevitably vocational education for youth must play a considerable part at the appropriate level in the work of the school. In view of the fact that the child and youth spend the major hours of the day away from home, the custodial responsibility of the school is properly enlarged. The transitional character of our culture and the general weakening of standards warrants, to an extent, the assumption of a "life guidance" function on the part of the school. But there is serious danger that in multiplying its responsibilities, the school's function in maintaining a high state of culture may be neglected, and that in assuming to take a major obligation for the development of character, it may actually be weakening the influence of the family and the church, the main resources of character development. In attempting "to educate the whole child for life," it may become superficial and fail in its elementary and essential tasks.

The major function of the school is to transmit the essentials of culture, to widen the sense of community, to advance the good society, to leave the nation "better than we found it." The school represents a scientific, a normative, and an idealizing purpose. In the field of knowledge, its obligation is to present the most accurate, the most comprehensive, the most advanced achievement as agreed upon by competent students in each field. In the area of personal behavior, it should represent the approved manners and the good taste of the community as against actual practices when these fall short. In the field of ethics, which involves belief as well as action, its mission is to cultivate the ideal—the ideal of the society of which it is a part but at the same time transcends—the ideal as expressed in the writings and pronouncements of its leaders and its statesmen. In many matters, it must conform to the local community and to the state authorities, but it should never be blindly subordinate to either.

Where democracy is alive, the school will have a range of autonomy. The school speaks with authority when it represents competent knowledge in the scientific field, when it follows the avowed ideal of the larger community as against local prejudice, and when it conducts its work in harmony with principle as against the requirements of political expediency. *In all its activities, the school aims to emancipate the individual from the domination of direct personal and local experience and to lead him to accept the authority of the objective and rational experience of the race in its historical and ecumenical dimension.*

NOTES

1. Alexander Meiklejohn, *Education Between Two Worlds* (Harper & Brothers, 1942), Preface.

2. Werner Jaeger, *Paideia, The Ideals of Greek Culture* (Oxford University Press, 1939), Vol. I, p. xxii.

3. Josiah Royce, *The Sources of Religious Insight* (Charles Scribner's Sons, 1914), pp. 201ff.

13

EXPERIENCE, NEEDS,
AND THE SCHOOL CURRICULUM

THE view that the school has a limited function and that its aims are to be derived from the organized life and the cultural ideals of the community of which it is a part stands in contrast to prevailing pedagogical theory. In many texts on the principles of education, particularly in the elementary and junior high school field, the progressivist theme that "education is guided living" gives the keynote. The aims of education, it is said, "are lines of growth, not subject-matter to be mastered." The modification of behavior rather than the acquisition of knowledge and skills is recommended as the major objective. Character development is to be achieved not primarily by the formation of good habits but by stimulating the pupil to use the method of intelligence. The curriculum is to be based on the present needs and interests of the learner—on "effective living now"—not on a preparation for future living. The theory of learning is strongly influenced by the current organismic psychology: the learner is "a goal seeking organism reacting as an integrated whole to whole situations."

1

The concepts of the new pedagogy have value in calling attention to aspects of the educative process neglected or not adequately recognized in the conventional schools. In isolation from the cultural aims of the school, the interpretation of the new concepts is likely to be misleading, loose, even at times absurd. Some of the worst excesses are committed in the name of the doctrine that "all learning is a process of experiencing."

A standard text informs us: "The child who has never seen a cow milked and who has never experienced the thrill of actually making butter from cream can never quite gain the understanding of dairying and its importance for life that is possible for a child who has had direct experiences with cows and dairies." Perhaps so, but then nearly the whole human race must be deprived, henceforth, of an adequate knowledge of dairying, including the dairymen themselves. On the farm which the first graders duly visited, the cows were milked by machine, and it was necessary to call in the manager to give a demonstration of milking by hand for the benefit of the class. Although they did not, it seems, get to making butter, the children evidently did obtain a thrill "by hearing the 'swish, swish' of the milk as it entered the pail," and this experiencing presumably contributed to the understanding of dairying, and other problems of our times. The visit to the farm was part of a unit of teaching on home life, and no doubt going out to the country had value for these city children. But the author's belief that as a result of the visit the six-year-olds gained "a growing realization of Father's responsibility in providing a living for members of the family" might be questioned not only by those who are sceptical about the all-sufficient importance of the doctrine of experience but by its authoritive exponents.

In *Experience and Education*, Dewey attempted to correct some of the misinterpretations made by the progressive educators who thought that the doctrine of experience meant the abandonment of all that the traditional school represented. He points out that this negative approach provides us with no real solutions; it only presents us with problems. When the older conceptions of organized subject matter, of authority, and discipline are rejected, new formulations must be elaborated. "The belief that all genuine education comes through experience does not mean that all experiences are equally educative." The trouble with the old school was not that it failed to provide experiences, but that the experiences were of the wrong kind. Too often, Dewey alleges, they deadened native curiosity, made pupils callous to ideas, led them to associate books with dull drudgery.

The newer type of education can lead to equally evil results: an experience may be lively, vivid, and "interesting" and yet may generate loose habits of thought; it may be exciting and yet dissipate energy and contribute to making the pupil scatterbrained; it may be enjoyable and still not lead to growth. If the term "experience" is to serve as guide, two principles Dewey explains must be respected, namely, "continuity" and "interaction."

The principle of continuity demands that we ask, on every occasion, what effect the present experience provided is likely to have on future experience: Does it lead to greater understanding and control of future situations in which the learner will find himself? Every genuine experience is a moving force the value of which is to be judged "only on the ground of what it moves toward and into." This critical judgment, Dewey emphasizes, cannot be made by the young themselves: it needs to be made by the educator who represents a greater maturity of experience, a richer knowledge of subject matter, and a better understanding of psychology. Moreover, the principle of continuity requires that a link must be preserved with the past as well as with the future: the principle that the present must be used to guide the future is sound "only in the degree that present experience is stretched, as it were, backward. It can expand into the future only as it is enlarged to take in the past."

The other term, "interaction," likewise involves a denial of the view that basing education on experience means giving way to children's momentary impulses or to their needs in their "natural" form. Human experience does not go on in a vacuum; it takes place in a social environment which cannot be left out of account. We live in a world which has definite character because of what we have inherited from previous generations; the difference between savagery and civilization consists in the measure in which past experience has changed the conditions in which subsequent experiences take place. To neglect this fact amounts to treating experience as a purely internal affair taking place in each individual. This is what happens when the teacher, books, and apparatus—all of which represent "the mature experience of the elders"—are subordinated to the immediate inclination of child or youth.

Adult guidance, then, is essential. But—here is the main point—it should, as far as is possible, be given by indirect control, not by personal injunction. There always will be exceptional occasions in the best situations when the adult must step in and exercise authority in an arbitrary manner, but the effort must be to arrange experiences which will lead to the development of knowledge and character as a result of activities in which the learner engages. The teacher must have a clear idea of the facts and ideas to be developed, but the learning should begin with activities drawn from everyday living that are within the experience and capacity of the child.

Much as Dewey emphasizes the importance of initiating learning with concrete experiences on the learner's level, in no lesser degree does he insist on arranging the learnings in an increasingly organized form in which knowledge is presented to the mature person. Although organized subject matter cannot provide a starting point, it represents "the goal toward which it is to move." The movement should be from a social and human center toward a more intellectual scheme of organization, always bearing in mind, however, that intellectual organization is not an end in itself, but is "the means by which social relations, distinctively human ties and bonds, may be understood and more intelligently ordered." The organization of knowledge in traditional educational systems failed to take the living experience of the learner into consideration, the modern progressivist, according to Dewey, neglects the need of intellectual organization of facts and ideas. This fundamental weakness, Dewey prophesied, if not corrected would lead to a reaction against progressive education.

With all this insistence on the importance of intellectual organization, Dewey makes no concessions to the traditional conception of logical or systematized subject matter. He reiterates his conviction that the method of intelligence—which he identifies with the experimental method of science—is the key to the solution. The method of intelligence involves the co-relating of ideas, actions, and consequences; it requires reflection on experience, discrimination and judgment, reviewing and summarizing the significant features of any experience in the course of its development. Such building of intelligence for dealing with future experiences he regards as the very core of mental discipline. Thus, in the end, Dewey comes back to his main idea that teaching and learning, to be educative, must be viewed as a continuing process in the reconstruction of experience. In a final sum-up Dewey affirms: "the soundness of the principle" advanced by progressive education "that education in order to accomplish its ends both for the individual and for society must be based on experience— which is always the life experience of the individual."[1]

2

Many of the loose statements in current pedagogical literature which offer easy targets for attack would be eliminated if regard were paid to Dewey's careful analysis of the concept of experience as he employs it as an educational means; if attention were given to his emphasis on relating the present to the past as well as to the future, on the need of adult guidance in the selection of subject matter, on the significance of the intellectual organization of knowledge as the outcome of the learning process. However, in final analysis, he offers only a suggestion of a new approach to the construction of the curriculum, failing to indicate to what extent the present-day subject matter organization is to be retained or modified.

Incidental references indicate a strong bias against the traditional conceptions. In one of the rare instances where he allows himself to become rhetorical, Dewey asks: "What avail is it . . . to win ability to read and write if in the process the individual loses his own soul: loses his appreciation of things worth while, of the values to which these things are relative . . . ?"[2] But why make the gratuitous assumption that learning to read and write leads to the loss of one's soul? It would seem rather that reading is one of the most important means for the expansion of one's experience, and that writing, besides being a basic utilitarian need, is also one of the chief means of self-expression. In another place he says, "It is not an invidious reflection upon trigonometry that we do not teach it in the first or fifth grade of school." But since no one suggests that we should, this is somewhat in the nature of flogging dead asses. The question is whether we should teach trigonometry at all—whether we should have a "systematic and sequential" course in mathematics, as the essentialists urge, or whether elements of mathematics should be introduced only incidentally in the course of experiential learnings. As a result of his diffidence with respect to the existing method of subject-matter organization combined with the inadequate elaboration of his positive proposals, may it not be said that, in the end, Dewey aids and abets the negative attitude of the progressives which he set out to counteract?

While misunderstandings have contributed to some of the vagaries in current pedagogical writings, the real difficulty, it would seem, lies in the doctrine of experience itself. In the first place the term is ambiguous. Dewey gives the case away when he points out that the traditional schools also provided experiences, although they were of the wrong kind. The concepts continuity and interaction proposed as criteria of the right sort of experiential learning are also vague; they could be applied to the traditional curriculum of sequential learnings as well as to the regime of learning by experience. Further, the idea that education is to be "based" on experience—"on the experience of the individual"—is misleading. What Dewey means is that the method of learning particularly in the earlier stages should utilize children's experiences as a starting point. The *content* of education should be selected by the teachers on the basis of its significance. In final analysis, Dewey agrees that education is to be "based" on the cultural heritage and on social interests not on individual impulses or childish desires.

These comments on the vagueness and ambiguity of the term experience, however, are marginal. At the root of the one-sided conception of the educative process characteristic of contemporary pedagogy is the behavioristic bias which regards knowledge and intelligence as arising in overt response of the individual to problematic life-situations. There are serious defects in this view. It misjudges the nature of mind in the assumption that it is derivative from the biological activities of survival and adjustment. It underestimates the part that ideas not immediately related to active experience play in the determination of responses. It fails to give due weight to accumulated knowledge and to the products of previous thought in stimulating thought and in advancing valid knowledge.

Dewey's behaviorism, it is true, is qualified. He recognizes, in his more careful statements, that experience may be internal—the response of consciousness to a reminiscence, to a wish, or to an idea—as well as a reaction to outward events. In application, however, he regards genuine experience of value for education as arising out of some form of activity, the internal emotional and intellectual concomitants being valued in the measure that they lead to desirable action. Dewey never tires of explaining that experience is an active-passive affair, that it involves doing something to things and undergoing the consequences of our doings. More than others who follow the organismic approach in its behavioral interpretation, he gives place to imagination as a factor in thought and education. But he sees its function mainly as furthering "expansion of existing experience" through "outward and active manifestation."[3] Careful reading of Dewey would reveal that he realizes that thought deals with the interrelationships between symbolic events in the mind as well as with symbolic manipulation of actual events.[4] There are passages in Dewey which are eloquent in their affirmation of the indebtedness of the present to the cultural heritage derived from the past. But these aspects—the inner life, imagination, the racial experience—are recessive. The dominant emphasis is biological, behaviorist, and individualist.

As against the experimentalist view that mind is a cleverer way of dealing with the problems of human survival and of the satisfaction of creaturely wants, there is warrant for regarding it as in a degree autonomous. It is a mutation from, not an extension of, the faculties possessed by the lower animals. Emancipation from slavery to sense and instinct not indenture to their service is the distinctive mark of thought. Mind has a creative as well as a reconstructive function: it can design new worlds as well as repair the old. The stream of thought may at times run parallel to experience—a mere epiphenomenon; or interact with it in a process of mutual influence; it may be completely dominated by bodily concerns and emotional involvements. But mind may be properly conceived as a sixth sense, a distinct organ, which can serve as a controlling and creative factor, balanced in importance and power as against all the other senses.

Imagination rather than experience is the protean source of the human mind. It may receive a stimulus from sense impressions, from observation or activity, it may have an origin in a memory of a past experience, but it also is revealed in fantasy and vision. Children are interested in practical activities, but they also characteristically exhibit mental play, self-dramatization and speculation about the nature of things. There is no simple or necessary relation between the stimulus to thought or imagination and the creative product of thought or imagination. A piece of paper variously shaped may represent a shoe, a stick may serve as a hobby horse, a row of chairs may represent a train. In free drawing a child may or may not copy. A four-year-old child, described by William Stern, on request to picture a camel, begins to draw, makes some lines that no one but he would recognize as a camel, proceeds to convert it into a butterfly, and ends up by making the man in the moon.[5] Free imagination in interaction with animal energies and active experiences has been the force at work in creating the cultural systems within which human beings live. Human thought is not directed primarily to survival, or to the satisfaction of the needs of self-preservation, food, and sex, although it may serve these purposes. Even in the satisfaction of the animal wants, thought functions to fulfill such wants in humanly desirable ways not merely to satisfy them.

The essential function of mind on the human level is to transform the quality of life. Its distinctive value lies in its power to direct activity in accordance with a conceived ideal, to stimulate creative activity of a high order in the arts, in the sciences, in philosophy and religion. In its unique sense, human mind is nurtured not mainly by the ordinary experience of casual activity, but by "experience" with the highest cultural expression of this and other ages, by reliving "vicarious" experience. Individuals may occasionally discover for themselves what others have learned from books and in some matters here or there, although untutored, make an original contribution. But it is evident that in major achievements we must rely on absorbing the accumulated heritage of ideas and knowledge. The gist of the matter is that the source of significant education comes from outside of the individual and from products of past experience embodied in records. Books, the wide range of literature, history, and science are sources of intellectual and spiritual experience not only, as the experimentalist holds, a means for broadening and deepening the experience of everyday living.

Words, which are symbols of facts and ideas, may in the process of teaching, as the experimentalists emphasize, become verbalisms—mere counters devoid of significance for the learner. But there is danger also in the opposite method—that teaching through activities may lead to superficiality. Some progressive schools believe that they are helping the children to understand Greek culture by dressing up the children in Greek costumes. There is no harm in this, provided it is not intended as a substitute for a study of Greek thought through its literature, the only way we can in some measure understand it. Our cultural heritage is embodied in a complex system of symbols and can only be grasped through a mastery of symbols. The remedy for sterile teaching is not to abandon the use of words and symbols but to make them come alive, clarifying ideas, relating them to the world of thought as well as to the world of action, stirring the minds, and let us not be backward in saying, touching the hearts of our students.

The cultivation of the mind through transmission of organized knowledge, through exercise in abstract thinking, through training in the ability to define terms is as important as checking thought by reference to fact and is as significant as training in the use of intelligence in the conduct of immediate affairs. As soon as we get beyond the lower elementary levels, there are intellectual and formal elements —in the language and creative arts, in mathematics, in the natural sciences, and in social studies—which cannot be derived from individual experience even if each person were to live a thousand years in the various cultures of the world. What one can learn from his own experience will depend upon what he has absorbed from the accumulated cultural experience.

The school has come into being because the experiences of life are not adequate for learning to live on a high cultural level in any complex civilization. Its work is concerned primarily with nonexperiential learning: its singular purpose is to cultivate the mental life which exists in and through symbolic representation, to transmit knowledge embodied in symbols, and to develop skills in the manipulation of symbols. This is an immense task and the degree to which we achieve it conditions the level of civilization we attain. In our day of the supremacy of mathematical and physical sciences, it may determine the very survival of Western civilization. If it were not for the fact that we had the aid of European physicists and mathematicians who had studied in the old type secondary schools and universities where theoretical studies were honored, it is greatly to be questioned whether we would now have the edge in the struggle to preserve the values of a democratic civilization.

3

Apart from relation to definite cultural forms and social aims, the doctrine of experience offers no clear guidance for the content and the organization of the curriculum. A similar criticism may be levelled against the concept of "needs" which along with the doctrine of experience plays an important part in the progressivist pedagogy. The lists of "needs," "wants," or "values" regarded as basic to a reorganization of school curricula covers a wide range: from the need of nourishment, through the wants of sexual expression and economic security, to the values of companionship, of sharing and participation, of artistic creativity, of literary and scientific knowledge. In books on the principles of elementary education, the emphasis is laid on "the basic personality needs of children"—the needs of achieving group status, of giving and receiving affection, of the growing toward independence, of developing a sense of security and ability to face reality. Most statements include a reference to "social needs." The formulation nevertheless remains vague.

We may agree that education in the broad sense is concerned with human needs. The question remains which of the needs are the responsibility of the school, which the obligation of the family, church, or other social agency. Obviously, it is not the major function of the school to satisfy biological needs; it is to make some contribution to the manner in which elementary needs may properly be satisfied. A school may provide luncheons, but its primary educational function does not consist in fulfilling "the want for sufficient nourishment." It is to teach something about the proper preparation and serving of foods, to study the composition of foods as an incident in the teaching of science, or to investigate the relation of food supply to political problems. Is it the function of the school to concern itself with "the value of sexual expression which all men cherish," as one writer has it, and if so, what should the school do or say about it? How the school will deal with needs will depend on the social structure, on the existence of a body of authoritive knowledge, on prevailing ethical judgments as to the difference between a desire, a want, and a value. Without reference to the cultural situation and to a prior conception of values, the term "need" has no definite meaning. The conception of needs as a basis for educational policy would have significance if it were formulated something as follows: What needs of the child or youth *as a member of our society* can the school help to fulfill at a given age or developmental level?

Viewing needs in relation to the cultural and social setting should lead us back to the commonsense conception of the purposes of elementary education. Whatever else is done in school, the children should learn as soon as they can to read and write, to speak and spell, to add, subtract, multiply and divide. They should obtain some idea of the workings of nature, some acquaintance with the geography and history of America and of other lands and peoples; some notions of current events and problems. They should acquire some knowledge of basic literature, well-known stories, poems, and plays; interest, skill, and appreciation in crafts and arts should be fostered; health and physical education should receive attention. Without preparation in fundamental skills and without a common store of knowledge, children would be handicapped for life, in vocation, in enjoyment, in social position—and, not least, in a sense of security.

At the end of the elementary school age, which may be placed at fourteen or fifteen, the probable future career of the various groups of children should receive consideration. We cannot neglect the fact that in our society the majority will go to work between the ages of eighteen and twenty. The core of their education should be related to the type of occupation they are likely to enter, whether agricultural, mechanical, or commercial. Auxiliary studies and activities of a general educational and developmental value should be provided within the scope of the interests and capabilities of the students. Those who go on to college would divide into two main groups: students who have already made definite decisions as to their future careers in the professions or subprofessions and students who are prepared by reason of ability and intellectual interests to continue their general education for the whole college period and who are enabled to do so with the help of their families or through generous scholarships.

For all students at all levels there would be activities and studies directed toward the acquisition of knowledge and skills, toward the development of broad cultural interests and raising of taste above the popular level, for a study of contemporary conditions with an eye to their improvement, for an extension of the social horizon. Above the junior high school level, for secondary school and college students the problem of relating vocational to general education becomes a central problem as it already was, to some extent, in the days of Aristotle who noted the confusion attending the relation of professional training to liberal education. Its solution is not easy, since there is a genuine conflict between the effective practical life—particularly in our competitive society—and the life of culture and the spirit. Some correlation of the two aspects, liberal and professional, is possible and desirable. But we need not strain for complete integration.

The main point is that we cannot decide on the aims of the school apart from the needs of the individual at a certain level of development in relation to the society of which he is a part. The doctrine of experience and needs is faulty in that it leads away from the cultural and sociological orientation. It cannot provide the principles needed for a sound reconstruction of the curriculum. The reconstruction of the course of study should not begin with an inquiry into the biological needs and psychological wants of the individual. The process must be reversed: it should begin with an inquiry into the nature of our culture—its character and ideals, its achievements and its deficiencies, its theoretical issues as well as its practical problems. Before a curriculum is organized, the educator must know what he wants to teach, what beliefs he wishes to foster, and what loyalties he wishes to inspire. To say that "education must contribute to the democratic way of living" means little or nothing until we define democracy in terms of fundamental ends as well as in terms of process.

The doctrines of experience and needs which recognize the importance of relating school work to the life of the child has significance primarily for the problem of method. If used with discretion, the concepts "experience" and "needs" can serve as counterweights to purely verbal modes of teaching, to exclusive emphasis on the intellectual aspects of learning, to the retention of dead subject matter in the school curriculum. Method is always important, but what its significance is can only be gauged in relation to aims. It is only *after* we have decided *what* we want to teach that we may discuss the question of method. In some instances, the unit-of-work, the project method, the core curriculum, the discussion group and the seminar may profitably be used; at other times lecture, recitation, drill may be in place. The real contribution of modern pedagogy is the diversity of methods it makes available in the various areas of learning for different age groups. In any case method should accomplish the primary learning objective as well as produce good incidental effects.

The traditional curriculum needs modification in organization, content, and method. The narrow divisions into subjects may well give way to broad area divisions and new types of activity may be introduced. Personal experience should be used as a resource wherever appropriate; concrete examples have always been employed in good teaching; laboratory exercises in physics and chemistry have long been part of the teaching process in these subjects; dramatic performances, likewise, are already a feature of school work; field trips have for a hundred years been conducted in many school systems. It is essential —at least above the primary grades in the elementary school—to maintain the logical and systematic organization of the traditional school. The distinction between curricular studies and extra-curricular activities should be kept clear. In actual practice, most schools are working along some such moderate plan. In the earlier years of schooling, the behavioral and custodial functions and the experiential approach are becoming predominant. A gradual transition is then effected to the subject matter form of organization in the upper elementary grades; at the same time the subject-matter areas are being broadened and correlated.

The cliches of current pedagogy—"all learning is experiencing," "the learner is a goal-seeking organism," "the child reacts as a whole to whole situations"—are, in their unqualified pronouncements, misleading. Learning of school subjects requires drill, memorization, intellectual analysis. The human being is an aesthetic and contemplative creature as well as an active being. Physical disabilities, emotional disturbances, illiterate social backgrounds must be reckoned with in the learning process. But above the stage of the amoeba, no organism reacts as a whole to whole situations. On the human level, certainly, learning involves selective response and the elimination of irrelevant reactions, motor, emotional, or intellectual as the case may be. How we learn must be determined in each area by psychologists collaborating with experienced teachers.

There are two broad principles of modern pedagogy which are especially significant if properly used—E. L. Thorndike's concept of "readiness," and W. H. Kilpatrick's idea of "concomitant learnings." The former helps us keep in mind that what and how we teach must be relative to capacities of the learners at the time, to the factor of maturation, to the emotional disposition. Here we must remember, however, that the point of readiness is not absolutely fixed—it may be advanced within a range of variation. It is important to emphasize also that the readiness principle cuts two ways: it means that we should not teach first-graders by the same methods that we teach high school students; but it also implies that we ought not to try to teach high-school students by methods appropriate to first-graders.

The principle of concomitant learnings teaches that we must have regard for the general mental and emotional attitudes developed as by-products of the type of learning process followed. The old education, it is said, encouraged blind obedience, led to a dislike for school, suppressed the desire to think, etc. This principle also cuts two ways: there is danger that the new schools lead to emphasis on goal-seeking and fulfillment of wants as against intellectual and spiritual ends, on endless inquiry as against deep conviction, on expedient behavior rather than on ethical principles. Here, also, if we keep clearly in our minds what we want to teach, looseness of thought may be minimized.

The sum of it is that we must abandon the principle of "the supremacy of method."

NOTES

1. John Dewey, *Experience and Education* (The Macmillan Co., 1939), p. 113.
2. *Ibid.*, p. 50.
3. Katherine C. Mayhew and Anna C. Edwards, *The Dewey School* (D. Appleton Century, 1936), p. 472.
4. Charles W. Morris, *Six Theories of Mind* (University of Chicago Press, 1932), pp. 73ff.
5. William Stern, *Psychology of Early Childhood* (Henry Holt and Co., 1924), p. 244.

14

INTELLIGENCE AND CHARACTER: IDEA
AND BELIEF VS. EXPERIENCE AND INQUIRY

The emphasis laid on experience as a basis of learning stems
in part from the belief that the activity methods which engage the
interest of the learner are on psychological grounds more effective
than the traditional formulations for securing genuine knowledge. As
the leaders of the experimentalist philosophy conceive it, the doctrine
of experience and its correlate, the method of intelligence, has a
deeper—a moral—purpose. That the method of intelligence based on
common experience and on experimental procedures is applicable to
ethical judgments is at the heart of Dewey's philosophy. Professor
Kilpatrick would make character building the fundamental goal and
all-inclusive aim of education, and he connects good character with
the disposition to think and to act on thinking. John L. Childs has
made the moral emphasis of experimentalism the basis of his educational philosophy. The development of intelligent self-determination
as the quality of personality essential to democratic living, he maintains, demands a "morality of primary experience" and a "morality of
inquiry."[1]

1

Professor Childs is explicit in his denial of the child-centered
philosophy of some of the older forms of progressive education. He
agrees that education is impregnated with moral values and cannot be
a neutral process. He recognizes the societal and cultural basis of
personality and he sees democracy as a definite system of political
institutions as well as a distinctive mode of associated life. He repudiates the laissez-faire conception of education which avoids placing
responsibility on the parent and teacher for directing the development

of the child. He agrees that education is a deliberate process by which adults nurture—even "mold"—the life and mind of the young and guide their growth to maturity.

With all this emphasis on society-centered and adult-directed education, Professor Childs makes no concessions to the traditional conceptions. He endorses all the experimentalist doctrines including the "supremacy of method." The guidance which the school should give is a nurture of the use of the methods of intelligence in the moral life. The direction is to be given by providing a special environment in the school. Moral sanctions are "internal, not external." Indoctrination is precluded. The democratic proposition that every person should be an end in himself forbids, Professor Childs believes, subordinating the child to any pre-established system of life and thought. Respect for the dignity and the worth of the individual requires directing education to the end that the pupil will grow in ability to make up his own mind as to what he should believe and consider worthy of his allegiance. The nurture of democratic personality requires the cultivation of the mind of the individual as a means of developing moral responsibility which includes the capacity to cooperate and to evaluate consequences of action. The nurture of mind—this is the crux of Professor Child's position—demands "a morality of primary experience."

The emphasis on primary experience is closely associated with a functional conception of mind "that accepts without discount the evidence and the perspectives of organic evolution." The consistent believer in evolution will always bear in mind that man was a creature of action and feeling long before he developed a capacity for reflective thought; he will never resort to the dualistic body-mind conception which regards consciousness as descending into the animal organism from some transcendental realm. Professor Childs recognizes that the transformation of the fixed habits of response of the lower animals to the conscious, purposed activities of the human person is associated with the use of symbols. But symbols have intellectual meaning only in the measure that they represent the values of things and organic acts in the world of natural existence. "Thus, if we accept the evolutionary point of view, we must recognize that *things* are prior to *symbols* or *words,* and that *activities* are prior to *meanings.*"[2] Consciousness and cognition are derived modes of experienc-

ing whose sources are the doings and undergoings of primary experience and whose ultimate controls and tests are also provided by
primary experience.

The principle of the "morality of primary experience" is supple-
mented by the principle of "the morality of inquiry." To support the
latter, Childs refers to Peirce's analysis of the nature of scientific
method. That aspect of Peirce's conception is emphasized which
maintains that an idea—an assertion, hypothesis, or proposition—has
meaning only insofar as it has "a conceivable bearing on the conduct
of life." An idea has a dual function: it prescribes a plan for an action to be performed and makes a prediction of a result which is likely
to follow. The process of making inferences from present existences
to probable future happenings which involves the use of symbols
constitutes thinking. Following the Dewey line, Childs thinks of an
idea as originating in experience as a possible solution of a problem
found in experience; the idea is elaborated and refined in imagination
by use of concepts developed in previous experience and is ultimately
put to the test of overt behavior.

The experimental method is neither random activity nor a self-
enclosed process of ratiocination; it is a controlled procedure in which
the inferences are drawn by use of both reason and observation.
Deduction as well as induction enters into the process, but in the end
it is action which determines meanings and tests results. It is in this
process of experimental inquiry that the seat of intellectual authority
is to be found. No person, institution, tradition or book has authority
over us as against the test of actual practice. And this process must
be continually renewed; the faith of the experimentalist is not in any
particular finding derived from experience, henceforth conceived as
eternally true, but in the empirical method itself. The meaning and
truth of an idea are thus "internal," not, however, as subjective within
the person, but "internal to the operations by which they are subjected
to the test of existence."[3]

To the mind nurtured in experimental procedures, Professor Childs
maintains, there is no sharp gap between judgments of moral values
and judgments of facts. The child who is learning to discriminate
between the better and the worse in the various spheres of human
activity is at the same time growing in moral judgment. All experiential education carried on in the spirit of experimental inquiry is

therefore a form of character education. The child who is learning through participation in experiential activities is not only acquiring new techniques and practical information, he is at the same time developing a changed view of man in his relation to the world—essentially a new moral orientation. He gains a better realization of the necessity and of the possibility of human control of his natural and social environment. He will come to understand that neither nature nor society will take care of him apart from intelligent effort on his own part, that man lives not by passive trust in transcendental forces but by constructive use of conditions to advance his own purposes.

From the twin conception of primary experience and experimental inquiry Professor Childs draws inferences for the method of the schools. Faculty psychology with its correlate of "intellectual discipline" is rejected. No type of subject matter or form of mental training can be effective apart from experience in a variety of life's activities. The manipulation of mathematical and logical symbols is, on the basis of what is known of the transfer of learning, Childs thinks, the least promising of all educational practices. The morality of primary experience, moreover, counsels against overloading school work with printed reports of the experience of others. Books can broaden and deepen understanding derived from life experience but cannot serve as a substitute; knowledge of what the intellectual and moral leaders have taught can nourish imagination and widen our perspectives but the mature mind cannot be developed without resource to direct experience. The program of the school based on primary experience must provide for "rich and varied interactions, with the world of persons and things." From the moral as well as the intellectual point of view, Childs favors the activity programs, especially the problem approach as formulated by Dewey and the project method as proposed by Kilpatrick.

In the final section of the chapter on "The Morality of Inquiry," Childs discusses the social nature of scientific method emphasizing its cooperative and public character. Objectivity and universality of conclusion are secured by the fact that experimental procedures are available to all men of whatever race, religion, or nationality, and the records of experiments and results are open to the scrutiny of the public. An essential feature of experimentalism is its constructive use of doubt—instead of suppressing doubt and discouraging doubtful opinion, it is cherished as a means of arriving at objectivity through further investigation. Professor Childs recognizes that scientific work requires special training and that the results of scientific inquiries can be tested only by expert competence. He believes, nevertheless, that the layman's acceptance of the scientist's results is not a mere blind following of authority, since application to practice continuously proves the validity of scientific conclusions. The principle of scientific inquiry involves also the idea that the conclusions of our own days are never final but may be corrected by the investigation of future generations of men. Experimental inquiry reaches unity of belief through the Peircean idea of universalizing the community of inquirers in space and time.

The morality of experience and inquiry is to be distinguished from the several conventional approaches to the problem of ethical authority. First, it differs from systems which accept current standards and practices without criticism. It rejects the authoritarian view which implies that ordinary human beings are not qualified to construct their own governing principles and must therefore rely on some supernatural or transcendental authority. Along with this it rejects the absolute and abstract conception of "right for right's sake" which fails to consider the condition and consequences of particular situations. But, on the other hand, reflective morality is to be distinguished from voluntarism, from the cult of self-expression which identifies it with impulsive activity unregulated by concern for conditions and consequences. Underlying the democratic conception of experience as the basis of morality must be the recognition "that the good life is the life within a human community, and that the desires of the individual must not only be reconciled with one another, but also with those of his fellows who share a common experience."

2

With many of the broad statements in the course of the experimentalist's analysis, all American educators of whatever school of thought would agree. Certainly we should not indoctrinate by "withholding pertinent knowledge" or allow ourselves to be "enslaved by our ideas" or be satisfied with "blind reliance on tradition or external authority." But the issues are not resolved by the method of adjectival denunciation, by introducing the terms "blind," "external," "enslaved." Is all submission to constituted authority to be deemed blind adherence? Is it possible to be a member of any society without adaptation in major matters to a pre-established system? Is not the democratic form of government a pre-established system? Should the youth be permitted to make up their minds without qualification "about that which is to be considered worthy of his allegiance" as Professor Childs urges? Suppose the individual believes that allegiance to the Communist Party best serves the welfare of mankind? How can the absolute of primary experience be reconciled with another principle that Professor Childs upholds, "the morality of patriotism"?

An unresolved dilemma runs through the experimentalist discussion. Does authority rest in the morality of primary experience which leaves the judgment to the individual; or does the final authority reside in the morality of inquiry, in the competent investigations of an invisible community whose inquiries stretch over a long period from the distant past to the far off future? The answer that there must be an interaction between these two poles of experience begs the question. The problem of authority arises only when there is an unresolved conflict between the opinions of individuals and the conclusions of science and tradition. An ambivalence is in evidence. On the one hand, there is a high regard for the cultural heritage of the community: "Loyalty to whatever in the established environment makes a life of excellence possible is the beginning of progress. The best we can accomplish for prosperity is to transmit unimpaired and with some increment of meanings the environment that makes it possible to maintain the habits of decent and refined life." But then again, this fine quotation from Dewey's *Human Nature and Conduct* is brought in to defend the founders of the new education from the charge of a lack of appreciation of the value of the social heritage. It is not used as a basis for the school program. The true faith lies in the present experience and in judgments of the individual both in moral as well as in intellectual affairs.

The experience of the individual, it should be apparent, cannot give us the validated knowledge and the warranted beliefs which the school has a primary responsibility to provide. The essentials of school learnings are not to be found in the process of the pupil's primary experiences but in bringing ascertained knowledge and acknowledged

244 THE IDEAL AND THE COMMUNITY

values to bear on the experience of the learner. Authority, it should be unequivocally affirmed, rests not in the opinion of the individual based on personal experience but in the consensus of judgment of competent investigators, not in the process of a single mode of inquiry, but in the reliability of the knowledge used and the warrantability of the conclusions arrived at by the methods of reasoning and inquiry appropriate to each great area of human interest—whether science, politics, art, or religion. We cannot achieve the same degree of warranted assertibility in all areas: in some demonstrable truth is possible, in others only a reasonable conclusion based on the weight of evidence is attainable, in some questions two or more positions may be equally defensible. But in all areas, the views of the scientist, the scholar, the political and religious philosopher are those which the school has the obligation to support and foster. As against the experimentalist's reliance on primary experience and scientific inquiry, a morality, to borrow Childs' term, of fundamental principles and warranted beliefs is proposed as prerequisite for education.

The ability to make good judgments does not follow from a rejection of conventional solutions in favor of one's own primary experience. A first task in the development of critical thinking is not to stimulate doubt but to make the student conscious of the principles and assumptions underlying the subject of discussion. In his attack against the fixed assumption, the experimentalist leaves the impression that we can derive conclusions from direct experience without making assumptions. To permit thought to operate fully, it is true, we must emancipate ourselves from rigidly held dogmas. But it is of equal importance to emphasize that whenever we give up one assumption or principle we must postulate another. There can be no thinking without presuppositions. The evil of the fixed assumption lies in its tendency to prevent us from making other assumptions that better correspond with the facts or satisfy more adequately the difficulties encountered. The removal of one presupposition without the substitution of a new one would not lead to freedom of thought but to the degeneration of the thinking process, just as the abandonment of all definite standards of conduct would lead to demoralization and not to moral freedom.

Likewise, thinking to be effective must be directed toward definite ends, to the choice of alternative possibilities. "How odd it is," Charles

Darwin wrote, "that anyone should not see that all observation must be for or against some view, if it is to be of any service." The tendency of experimentalism runs contrary to this in its emphasis on process and on the continuity of inquiry. The maintenance of a state of doubt and the conduct of "systematic and protracted inquiry" are stressed as the essentials of thinking.[4] Dewey also decries confining thinking to a consideration of finished rival systems, which he thinks men are inclined to do because they want the crutch of dogma to relieve them of the responsibility of thinking.[5] But for most of us most of the time the only recourse is a choice of alternative conceptions or proposals. Protracted inquiry, on the contrary, easily becomes a way of avoiding taking responsibility. Once the individual has the freedom of choice among available systems and proposals, he is no longer subordinated to dogma. Not an absence of proposals but a plurality of possible choices is the essence of freedom.

Another weakness of the experimentalist's reliance on primary experience lies in the underestimation of the part played by knowledge in suggesting solutions and in formulating problems. A problem does not necessarily stimulate thought—it may lead to frustration or despair when no knowledgeable solution can be envisaged. Effective thinking depends on having a store of ideas; our ability to suggest hypotheses for solution depends on a combination of imaginative power and abundant knowledge. While thought is often initiated by confronting problems in experience, on the higher levels, particularly in the field of science, the problems themselves arise out of special subject matter and can be grasped and formulated only by those who have accurate and abundant knowledge. The factors involved in good thinking—discriminating perception, fertile imagination, power to recognize relevancy—are immeasurably increased by knowledge. There is point to the conclusion that the most important contribution that the school can make to facilitate thinking is "to teach facts that are relevant to problems which children and adults are likely to need to solve and teach them in such a way that they will come to mind when the concrete problem is faced."[6]

The problem approach with its five steps of the "complete act of thought" which experimentalism identifies with scientific method is only one facet of a complex combination of processes involved in scientific work and in productive thinking. It does not give adequate consideration to such factors as those to which Gestalt psychology has called attention: finding an inner principle in events, gaining a comprehensive insight into observed facts, seeing what the structure of the whole requires for the parts.[7] The implication that experimentalism provides a general method of attack equally valid for all studies is misleading.

The same line of reasoning that denies that general mental training can derive from the study of a single subject denies with equal force that the use of a single method, despite the variety of content, can achieve the result. We may expect that experimentalism as a pattern of inquiry drawn from the field of physics would apply most closely to physics and, with modifications, to the field of the biological sciences. We should suspect that, in the field of psychology where a social framework is involved, experimental method—as against the case method or the personal interview—would have a limited application. In mathematics the element of deduction would predominate; in esthetics the element of imagination, of intuition, appreciation would have relatively greater place. One of the main reasons that the traditional subject-matter approach ought to be retained in its broad divisions and major subdivisions is that a significantly different mode of investigation and of constructive thinking is appropriate to each.

3

The experimentalist's reliance on experience and inquiry as against acceptance of norms and commitment to ideals is particularly open to question in the area of character development. The conception of the school as a miniature community where opportunity is given for the development of social intelligence and a cooperative spirit through life-like activities is an outstanding contribution to education in its moral as well as pedagogical aspects. But, at best, by itself the school's influence on interpersonal relations and on social practices outside the school must remain peripheral. However closely the school attempts to bring its work into harmony with the life activities of society, it can never achieve more than a superficial imitation of the realities of living. The major issues in the moral life revolve around the individual's involvement in the problems of marital relations, vocational life, professional and personal status, situations which in their social and psychological complexity the school can never duplicate. The fundamental principles of experimentalism, the doctrine of primary experience, the idea that it is futile to attempt to prepare for the future, its scepticism of the possibility of transfer, contradict the view that the school can be a central factor in character development. Professor Kilpatrick's celebrated principle, "We learn as we live," negates his other thesis that the school's major function is the development of character.

More is lost than gained when the regime of purposeful activity and critical intelligence is represented as a substitute for, instead of as a supplement to, instilling a devotion to principles and directing toward definite moral ends. The undertone of antagonism to authority, to traditional belief, to doing right for right's sake is likely to lead to loosening of existing standards rather than to raising to a higher mode of conduct. In its lack of confidence in the established order, experimentalism unwittingly casts a shadow of distrust on conventional mores and accepted institutional forms even when these serve valid social purposes. In its emphasis on creativity and initiative, it slurs over the ideals of good craftsmanship and excellence in achievement; in its stress on cooperation for group purposes, it minimizes the concept of obligation, of duty, of kindness, even of courtesy and good manners. The proposal to base morality on the firsthand experience of the individual and on the experimental consideration of conditions and consequences leads, too easily, to an ethics of expediency. The doctrine of internal authority amounts to a denial of authority altogether; placing authority in the process of inquiry is too vague a directive to be of use in any pressing moral issue.

If we are to live civilized lives, we must learn to live in the given institutionalized social structure. Within the frame of the existing order, there is a range of choice—in occupations, in styles of life, in religious and secular affiliations, in philosophic outlooks. Democracy aims to enlarge the range of choice, but choice is always a selection of alternative possibilities always limited. We must listen to the music that has been written although we have a choice among many works of many periods and styles. For nearly all of us, it is high achievement to be able to play what others have created and to express our personalities through individual interpretation. To expect each youth to work out a novel philosophy of life is to expect each one to become composer or master artist. Instead of releasing talent and developing individuality, this may impose an impossible demand resulting in frustration and in a lasting sense of inferiority. Although the school ought to encourage the gifted, its main function is to help the average and the less than average. It should, through its program and activities, convey the assurance that he also is worthy who accomplishes with competence the tasks that society sets and fulfills honorably the obligations it requires. The school should help the youth utilize existing possibilities, and even, as Erich Fromm counsels—although this is certainly not the whole function of the school—to mold the character structure so that ". . . *they want to do what they have to do*" as members of the society of which they are a part.[8]

A primary function of education in the sphere of morals, as in the area of science, is acculturation. A first task of the school is to endeavor to raise conduct from the level of local usage and average practice to the plane approved by the larger community which the school represents. This involves a conservationist and, in a measure, a conformist element, a "reproduction of the type" as the essentialist maintains. But the preservation of the cultural heritage, in an enlightened and a liberal sense, signifies the transmission of the heritage of ideals as well as adjustment to the traditional mores. And this, if consistently carried out, necessarily brings in its train criticism of existing embodiments and participation on the part of the school in the reconstruction of the social order. But social criticism and social reform cannot be based on individual judgments which rely mainly on primary experience and scientific inquiry.

The program of social reform which the school may properly support must be derived from bringing to bear the cultural ideal on conventional practice. The directives by which the existing institutions are to be reconstructed as well as the established forms have their source in history. The ideas of human dignity and equality, of law and justice, of freedom of worship and freedom of thought, lie at the very heart of "the great tradition of the Western world." It is from tradition that we draw the moral strength and authority to contend against the inadequate embodiments in present-day institutions. To obey an "internal authority" does not mean setting up an individual opinion against an established authority; it means a challenge of a particular authority by the higher authority of a fundamental principle; it means identifying the self with a wider community of persons and ideals.

4

The recognition of the import of tradition implies giving a prominent place to history and to the humanities as a means of nurturing the "inner directed" person. Dewey goes far in expressing appreciation of the significance of history as providing in simplified yet integrated form an opportunity for studying the forces at work in any given epoch and in revealing the lines of social advance. Valuable as this approach is, it nevertheless regards history mainly as a means of understanding the present-day society. To see history only in the social dimension narrows its import, to think of it as "the past" misses its real significance.

History is rich with many values for the understanding of life and thought. It is in a true sense philosophy teaching by example, as Lord Bolingbroke wrote, the record of man's successes and follies: "We see men at their whole length in history, and we see them generally there through a medium less partial at least than that of experience." In the genuine sense of the term, history is never a mere record of the dead past. History represents what the present generation remembers as significant in the lives of men from the beginning. It reflects what we regard as distinctive human development, it gives us norms by which the present may be criticized as well as understood. The hope for the future often directs its interpretation: "So everywhere a man's ideal of the future is the fixed point from which his interpretation of history proceeds. It determines the most significant points of the past, and through these points the curve is plotted which describes the course of history."[9]

Although there is a line here or there in Dewey's writings indicating that he recognizes the significance of literature in developing sympathy and responsiveness, he gives but little consideration to its study. In *Democracy and Education* he mentions literature along with the fine arts as having educational value but proceeds to discuss only the latter, his main point being that there is no sharp distinction between the fine and industrial arts. As always, he favors the arts that require the use of the hands rather than the use of words; he rarely refers to poetry. He values literature as well as the arts as a means of enhancing ordinary experience; at times, he refers to aesthetic appreciation as experience at its best. But he underestimates, if he does not neglect, the import of literature as a source of ideas and values of direct significance for building the moral life. In this, the experimentalist view reveals its sharp contrast with the humanist conception. For Jacques Maritain, literature, poetry, drama, historical writings lie at the heart of genuine education: the reading of the great classics "feeds the mind with the sense and knowledge of natural virtues, of honor and pity, of the dignity of man and of the spirit, the greatness of human destiny, the entanglement of good and evil, the *caritas humani generis*."[10] Literature not only enhances ordinary experience; it is itself experience out of which the moral life grows; it sustains the ideal despite experience, nourishes the spirit to withstand the attritions of the daily experience.

There is danger, of course, that concentration on the humanities may serve only to cultivate good taste in literature and have little effect on the moral or social life. Historically, classical education, as the term suggests, was an education for the upper classes. Liberal education is, today, often advocated as a means of drawing attention away from concern with contemporary social issues and with social reform. Experimentalism represents an endeavor to counteract the pure estheticism, the abstract intellectualism, the complacent moralism of the traditional conception of a liberal education. In its emphasis of relating thought to action, experimentalism reflects an impulse toward ethical integrity, toward realizing ideals in social life. But by dissolving mind into intelligently directed activity, experimentalism deprives it of its tensional force in elevating character to a higher integration of moral-aesthetic-spiritual insights. By fusing values with a quality of action, it undervalues the function of historical ideals as norms by which to evaluate existing institutions. By merging ends with processes, it is led to turn away from stating with effective clarity the goals of social reconstruction in which, it rightly holds, the school has a moral responsibility to play a part.

Advocacy of social change in general, without indicating the lines of social change, leads to fruitless debate. The school's responsibility for promoting social change is a corollary of its function in advancing the cultural and communal ideal. The proposals for social betterment which the school is warranted in furthering must satisfy two criteria: they must be designed to realize an avowed social purpose; they must have the support of competent knowledge. In the application of proposals, moreover, the strategy of democracy requires giving consideration to local conditions and permits temporary compromise. But the school has the obligation at all times to favor measures which are calculated to implement professed ideals in the interest of the national welfare. If it fails to do so, it fails in its moral purpose: it tacitly supports existing evils, it reduces its moral teaching to empty verbalisms, it engenders a habit of evasion and equivocation. The test of moral discipline is our readiness to apply our avowed ideals.

In its function of character development the school works in three ways. It supports the existing mores and institutions when these are not opposed to the professed principles of the wider community. It endeavors to raise the cultural level through the superior environment it provides, through the personal relations it encourages, and not least through cultivating ideals and nurturing moral sensitivities by means of the study of history and literature. In the third place, the school should make a deliberate effort to enlist the interest of maturing youth in social issues with a view of promoting economic and political measures calculated to fulfill in ever greater measure the moral ideals of the nation—the principles of freedom and equality and of human brotherhood. In the pursuit of its work in the development of character, the school must avoid the illusion that it alone can have a decisive effect on the moral life of the nation. Its contribution is essential, but character is the result of the operation of many social forces interacting with the nature of each individual. The major influences emanate from the laws, the economic class structure, the mores and current beliefs—forces which operate intensively and continously in the life of the family, in the occupational grouping, in the religious and recreational activities.

The school, working along with other forces in the community, can accomplish something in raising the standards of beauty, of truth, and of goodness above the common level. On some individuals, the school can have a decisive and lasting influence, particularly during adolescence and young adulthood. But we cannot expect the school to accomplish much in changing the general temper of moral life as long as social customs, economic forces, political practices compel or encourage attitudes that are in conflict with the teaching of the school. We cannot teach cooperation effectively if competition is the dominating social motivation: what is learned in school is soon vitiated by the pressures of life. In order that the schools may become more effective in character development than at present, the gap between the ideals represented by the school and the actualities of social life must be reduced. Improvement of character education cannot, in any appreciable measure, be achieved by a change from verbal methods of teaching to an activity program: to a large extent it is a matter of social reconstruction.

NOTES

1. John L. Childs, *Education and Morals* (Appleton-Century-Crofts, 1950), pp. 135-177.

2. *Ibid.*, p. 141.

3. *Ibid.*, p. 166.

4. John Dewey, *How We Think* (D. C. Heath and Co., 1910), p. 13.

5. John Dewey, *Democracy and Education* (The Macmillan Co., 1916), p. 394.

6. E. L. Thorndike and A. I. Gates, *Elementary Principles of Education* (The Macmillan Co., 1929), p. 131.

7. Max Wertheimer, *Productive Thinking* (Harper & Brothers, 1943), pp. 189ff.

8. Erich Fromm, *Man for Himself* (Rinehart and Co., 1947), p. 241.

9. Friederich Paulsen, *Introduction to Philosophy* (Henry Holt and Co., 1906), p. 318.

10. Jacques Maritain, *Education at the Crossroads* (Yale University Press, 1943), pp. 68-69.

15

INDOCTRINATION, ACADEMIC FREEDOM,
AND RELIGIOUS TEACHING

THE view that education implies the nurture of definite beliefs and the promotion of clear social objectives raises a number of issues with references to the relation of the school to the democratic society. The position that the teacher must be neutral on all controversial questions leaving it to the individual to decide is unrealistic and evasive—a source of confusion and equivocation. The opposing view which affirms "as is the state so is the school" is ambiguous. Taken literally it represents the totalitarian position; conceived broadly to mean that the school's function must be limited to the preservation of the accepted culture, it is still indefinite. Should the school support the existing practices and the local mores or should it seek to advance the highest ideal of the national community? The crux of the matter lies in the fact that there is a diversity of opinion and a conflict of authorities *within* the community. The formulation of a positive educational policy necessitates defining a position on several questions—the validity of indoctrination, the nature of controversial issues, the meaning and limitation of academic freedom. Two questions of current importance are the rights of communists to teach and the relation of the public school to religion.

1

Education represents a conscious attempt on the part of the community to form beliefs and develop habits in accord with standards of knowledge and ideals of conduct. Whether this is done indirectly through ordering the school environment or whether it is accomplished through direct instruction and injunction has important psychological and moral consequences. But no matter which of these approaches predominates in the total educational effort, a process of indoctrination is necessarily involved. The terms "fostering" and "nurturing" are more in accord with democratic assumptions and psychological conceptions than the terms "inculcating" and "instilling," but the semantic substitutions do not change the fact that the direction comes from outside the learner, and is "imposition from above." That education involves indoctrination cannot be denied. On the other hand, this does not mean that education is nothing but indoctrination. Nor does it imply that all indoctrination is legitimate from the educational point of view.

Indoctrination has two connotations. It may be properly employed in a neutral sense to designate instruction in basic principles, in the fundamentals of a branch of knowledge, or in generally accepted rationally defensible beliefs. This is the primary dictionary meaning of the term. In liberalist circles, however, "indoctrination" has come to be used in an unfavorable sense to describe biased teaching aimed at producing blind following of authority. Indoctrination becomes an important issue only when there is a genuine difference of opinion among equally competent judges, as in the case of religious beliefs, philosophic positions or economic theories. When there is general agreement, indoctrination need not be regarded as objectionable. Direct instruction in rules of health, training in skills, inculcation of scientific principles would not ordinarily be considered indoctrination in the obnoxious sense. Nor should instilling a loyalty to the Constitution be regarded as opposed to the democratic process.

Indoctrination is not wrong because it involves positive teaching. It is wrong in situations which call for critical analysis of important differences of opinion. Indoctrination of an undesirable kind may be carried on in many ways and need not be conscious or deliberate. A usual form is to present only one view of a controversial issue or to present alternative views only in a deprecatory fashion. Another method is to carry on group discussions on issues far beyond the knowledge or the capacity of the learners who miraculously arrive at a consensus in complete harmony with the views of the teacher. Indoctrination becomes inevitable when insufficient time is allowed for critical analysis, when the process of reasoning is short-circuited in situations where it is important to encourage it. Indoctrination is not avoided by substituting "pupil-centered" for "teacher-dominated" methods. At the high school or college level student participation may be a means of guarding against biased teaching. But where the teacher provides accurate knowledge, supports conclusions by evidence, gives consideration to contrary views, formal presentation may involve less indoctrination of the undesirable sort than the method of discussion when it circles around the raw opinions of unprepared students. Providing the spirit of free inquiry prevails, the presentation of positive views challenges thought.

The nature of knowledge and thought, which always involve presuppositions, and the exigencies of teaching conditions, which rarely permit full discussion, make a large measure of indocrination unavoidable. The more we are conscious of this, the less likely are we to fall prey to its negative aspects. In any case, frank indoctrination is better than the pretense of neutrality. The teacher must recognize and take responsibility for the attitudes and conceptions that he is furthering. An honest relation between teacher and students requires that the teacher indicate his definite view, in order to avoid leaving the impression that he has no convictions or is evading the issue. From a pedagogical point of view, the teacher would often do well not to express his own view at the outset. He may on occasion permit an erroneous conclusion to be maintained and rely on further study to clear up the matter. When competent scholars are divided, he might state though he ought not urge his own opinion. He certainly should not express an opinion if he does not think the evidence warrants it. But there are issues on which a clear position should be asserted.

Neutralism in teaching should not be confused with objectivity; it is the latter which we should try to approximate. Objectivity requires —not the absence of a point of view—but seeing the matter from more than one point of view and by emancipation from a narrower outlook in favor of a wider perspective. Teaching should be as positive as is reasonably warranted by the field of study. The teacher who fails to impart a knowledge of the premises and conclusions generally accepted is as culpable as the one who engages in one-sided instruction when there is a difference concerning central issues.

Good teaching will have two aspects. It will include the communication of positive knowledge and accepted principles along with an analysis of the line of reasoning, or wherever appropriate, the repeti-

tion, or at least the description of the experiments by which the conclusions were reached. The other aspect is the discussion of diverse
views on issues still unsettled. Controversial issues could be profitably
discussed only if there is an accepted frame of reference and agreed
upon subsidiary principles, e.g., in the physical sciences, naturalism
would be assumed and the teacher of physics would not take seriously
a supernatural explanation even if a student "thinking for himself"
offered one.

In the social studies, the problem of positive teaching is more complex. In the study of history, of economics, and of international affairs,
there are wide differences on basic presuppositions as well as in normative conclusions. But the wide divergence of views should not obscure
the fact that the democratic society, as all other forms, must be
erected on a foundation of fundamental principles. Just because there
are wide differences of view, it is necessary to formulate foundation
principles and proximate goals to guide the educational endeavor. The
assumption is that the concept "democracy," the avowed principle of
American life, provides a corpus of ideas and of practices that must
serve as the directive and unifying principle. Its meanings are embodied in our Constitution, have found expression in our literature,
and are continuously being interpreted by leaders of thought. An
indispensable function of educational leadership is to formulate its
directives—its established principles and ideal aspirations—as a basis
of school policy.

A common agreement on democratic fundamentals already in part
exists; in part it is in the making under the pressure of contemporary
conditions and in the light of new possibilities. In preceding chapters,
it has been suggested that the democratic social philosophy of the
new age must include the following: adherence to the principles and
procedures of the Constitution; a renewed emphasis on the Bill of
Rights; a consistent implementation of racial equality; the furtherance
of economic welfare for the nation as a whole; the promotion of a
democratic international order based on the Universal Declaration
of the Rights of Man. These five purposes reflecting current liberal
conceptions, it is submitted, establish criteria for an educational program in the social studies. Such directed teaching is not a matter of
catechetical or doctrinal instruction. It implies rounded study of history and contemporary affairs, of government and economics, of

literature and political theory. It allows for differences of views with references to means and measures designed to achieve the goals set forth. But the teaching would not be neutral; it would be directed toward the realization of stated social purposes.

2

The adoption of an educational policy along the lines projected, however well supported by reference to the American heritage and to contemporary thought, would undoubtedly involve conflict with the views of some sections of the population. The question arises whether the school administration or the teacher has the right to support conceptions of social reform which are opposed by local school authorities or by the parents of the children. What are the responsibilities and limitations of academic freedom in dealing with controversial issues?

One view would give the academician unqualified liberty in the expression of his views and justify this "as simply part and parcel of American freedom." Academic freedom is linked in this conception to the civil rights guaranteed by the First Amendment. This was the line of argument implied in the position taken by Dr. Hutchins, at that time Chancellor of the University of Chicago, in his forthright statement before the Subversive Activities Commission of the Illinois State Legislature. He defended the right of members of the faculty to hold and express unpopular views on economic and political questions as well as on scientific matters.[1] A similar approach to the defense of academic freedom is reflected in coupling it with the right of the individual to follow the dictates of his own conscience. Dr. Meiklejohn made this point central in his contention that teachers should not be dismissed for membership in the Communist Party, since they joined as a result of conviction and at a conscious risk of their material interests.[2]

There is, no doubt, a spiritual kinship, so to speak, between the freedoms affirmed in the Bill of Rights and academic freedom. Reference to the First Amendment is relevant to the question of the rights of teachers as citizens, in extra-mural activities such as membership in radical organizations. But, strictly speaking, the principles of freedom of speech and of the supremacy of conscience are only marginally related to the problem of academic freedom in its major reference to class instruction and the organization of the curriculum.

Freedom of speech is an elementary human right which the individual may or may not exercise but which government may not abridge except under the exigent circumstances of "clear and present danger." It is not limited by any intellectual criteria: a man may use the public forum to talk nonsense, to propound a goldbrick economic theory, or preach the advent of the millenium. Academic freedom has a different basis and character. It is not guaranteed by the Constitution; it applies to a special group—of teachers and students; it is an obligation rather than a right.

Academic freedom confers no personal privilege. The term "freedom" is to a degree misleading. Academic freedom makes demands on self-restraint, on intellectual integrity, on respect for colleagues and students. It abjures dissimulation; it implies the duty of declaring the convictions that the teacher has arrived at as a result of his study in his area of competence. It precludes taking advantage of position to promote personal views through a one-sided presentation. Academic freedom, as Professor Lovejoy has emphasized, rests on the right of the students to hear and discuss alternative views as much as on the teacher's right to expound his own conclusions.[3] It is a corollary of the belief in the value of scholarship and scientific inquiry for the extension of knowledge and the service of human welfare. In substance, it makes the ethics of the profession of scholars and scientists supreme over the arbitrary control of outside forces—of the state, the church, the political party, and, not least, of public opinion.

Academic freedom is not grounded in any special right that the teacher has as individual or as citizen but in his capacity as a member of a profession which enjoys a measure of autonomy requisite for the carrying out of its social function. Like other professions, the educational profession is the custodian of a body of knowledge and is characterized by a corporate conscience. Academic freedom is granted to the teacher in so far as he respects the ethics of his profession. As a member of a profession the teacher is never merely the employee of the educational institution which engages him or of the local board of education. He is a servant of society in the broadest sense, a representative of the cultural heritage, of the community as its highest achievements and aspirations. The loyalty of the educational profession is due to the nation as a whole, to the fundamental principles of the democratic society.

In the nineteenth century, academic freedom had to contend against the claim of the church to authority in science and in religion. During the last half century the pressures exerted by business interests have been the major, although more indirect, deterrents to completely free discussion of economic and social programs in the colleges and universities. Today, the forces of opposition emanate from the public at large, through local educational authorities, through investigating committees established by the national and the state legislatures, and through self-constituted vigilante groups. The danger of these attempts at interference in academic freedom are the more serious because they are made under the plausible argument that parents and teachers have the right to direct the educational endeavor. In the light of the present situation, it is particularly important to make clear that academic freedom means freedom from domination by lay public opinion as well as from domination by church, state, and vested interests. Parents and citizens have the right to subject school work and educational policy to criticism. The school administration and the teacher are in democratic duty bound to consider such criticisms. But when local and sectional views conflict with approved policies of the educational profession, respect for the principle of academic freedom demands that the views of the latter take precedence.

A distinction should be made between two types of controversial issues. There are differences of opinion in all areas of science and scholarship. It is the essence of the teacher's responsibility to present minority views supported by scholarly or scientific evidence. But a difference of opinion between a professional opinion and an individual local or sectional view does not constitute a controversial issue in the genuine academic sense. The theory of evolution is not a controversial issue in the academic sense. Although differences of opinion persist among scientists as to the mode of evolution and a variety of views are maintained by philosophers as to its moral implications, the Darwinian hypothesis is, broadly speaking, accepted in the world of natural science. The fact that local opinion disagrees with the biologists on religious grounds and the fact that the state of Tennessee still forbids its teaching represents a serious political and administrative problem. But the lay and legal opposition does not affect the moral right and duty of the teacher to expound the theory of evolutions as a warranted scientific conclusion. Similarly, equality of treatment for Negroes and whites does not become a debatable issue in the academic world because large sectors of Southern opinion hold fast to the politics of white supremacy. Even before the decision of the Supreme Court in May 1954, the principles of academic freedom gave the American teacher warrant to draw inferences from the principle that all men are created equal, and to oppose racial discrimination and segregation.

The ethics of academic freedom justifies the educator in promoting economic and social measures for which there is professional warrant. This implies also that the proposals have some support by public bodies in the nation at large. Academic freedom does not give the teacher as individual any right to air purely personal views in the classroom and certainly not to use it as a platform for partisan propaganda. The maturity of the students and the level of education must be taken into consideration in the application of the principle. At the college and university level complete freedom of opinion should be encouraged to the point of erring on the libertarian side—providing always that heretical views are based not on emotional protest but on reasoning and evidence recognized in the area under discussion. Below the college level discussion of abstract ideological issues such as capitalism *vs.* communism should be avoided; discussion should be centered on concrete proposals made in legislative bodies, by welfare organizations, by scientific associations. At the elementary grades, teaching the social studies should be predominantly descriptive and exploratory, designed to supply information and develop general attitudes rather than to analyze or discuss proposals. At the lower levels, the problem of academic freedom applies more to organization of the curriculum and the use of textbooks than to problems of the teacher in the classroom.

3

Under the tensions of the cold war between the United States and the Soviet Union, the issue of academic freedom became centered around the question whether Communists—that is, members of the Communist Party or other organizations regarded as subversive—should be permitted to teach. In the sphere of higher education, the problem was widely discussed in connection with an investigation conducted in 1949 at the University of Washington which resulted in the discharge of three professors and the retention of three others on probation. In the field of public education the issue was brought to a head by the Feinberg law of New York State, passed in the same year, aimed at eliminating teachers and others in the employ of the schools of the state who were suspected of disseminating subversive propaganda. It included a provision to the effect that membership in any organization designated as subversive by the Board of Regents would serve as *prima facie* evidence of disqualification. The Supreme Court declared the law constitutional in 1952 with a strongly worded dissenting opinion by Justice Douglas. As a result of this law, teachers in the elementary, secondary, and college grades have been dismissed either for membership in the Communist Party, or more frequently for using the fifth amendment as a means of avoiding possible self-incrimination.

Both sides—those who favor disbarment of communists from teaching and those who are against—base their positions on the doctrine of freedom of thought and inquiry. Both rely on the view that democracy requires the unhampered discussion of ideas, particularly of such—echoing the thought of Justice Holmes—as we hate and regard as dangerous. But those who are opposed to allowing Communists to teach urge that a sharp distinction must be made, as Professor Sidney Hook has epitomized it, between a "heresy" and a "conspiracy."[4] Marxism, as a heretical political and economic *doctrine*, should be given a full hearing; a teacher convinced of its significance should be allowed, even encouraged, to expound his views freely in accordance with the usual democratic procedures. But membership in the Communist Party at the present time is another matter: it leads to a violation of democratic principles in two aspects—intellectual and political.

In the first place, it is argued, membership in the Communist Party contravenes the teacher's obligation under the principle of academic freedom to follow the argument wherever scientific investigation and scholarly research lead. Membership in the party obliges the acceptance of a complete set of beliefs, in religious, philosophic, scientific, and political as well as in economic questions, and imposes undeviating assent to the official interpretation of those beliefs and their application to action by the current party dictatorship. The philosophy of communism denies the principle of academic freedom in theory as well as in practice, and anyone who maintains that the

Communist Party is innocent of hostility to academic freedom, Professor Lovejoy suggests, may be compared to one who would insist that the Nazi's were innocent of anti-semitism. A member of the Communist Party is aiding and abetting "the most aggressive and formidable conspiracy against the freedom of the human mind."[5]

In the second place, it obliges every member when so ordered to participate in subversive activities, to resort, as Lenin instructed, "to all sorts of strategems, manoeuvres, and illegal methods, to evasions and subterfuges. . . . to take advantage of their positions, without exposing themselves, to give to their students to the best of their ability working class education." Membership in the Communist Party, it is argued, is not only divergent belief; it is in essence a conspiratorial act; it constitutes participation in a movement aimed at disrupting the present regime, its political as well as its economic foundations. Since every applicant for membership must sign a pledge to accept party discipline, "it is not," as Professor Lovejoy has put it, "a question of 'guilt by association'; it is a question of guilt by voluntary cooperation." There is little likelihood that any teacher who remained a member of the Party after the Nazi-Soviet pact of August 1939 should have been unaware of the conspiratorial purposes and the meretricious methods of the Communist Party. Because of the violation of academic freedom and disloyalty to the Constitution, membership in the Communist Party constitutes a prima facie ground for dismissal. In any particular instance, the period and circumstances of membership would be taken into consideration, and the decision made by the faculty and officers of the educational institution.

The other view—which may be termed "libertarian"—rejects the doctrine of "guilt by association" as a violation of any enlightened sense of justice, as antithetical to the Anglo-American tradition that a man is innocent until proven guilty, as opposed to a judicial conception of evidence which requires relating a condemned act to specific performance by the individual accused. In fine, the libertarian position maintains that the only criterion by which the teacher should be judged is by his work and actual behavior. If he is competent, if there is no positive evidence that he has engaged in subversive activities, then his right as a citizen or his right to teach should in no way be abridged. As long as the Communist Party is legal, teachers have a right to join it. "To deny a sincere Communist opportunity to expound views held by millions of human beings is as wrong as to deny a sincere democrat the same right."[6]

Any attempt, this view would hold, to subject teachers to special tests or restraints not imposed on other citizens is pregnant with the evils of totalitarianism. Justice Douglas reflected this fear in his scathing attack on the Feinberg law. ". . . what happens in this law is typical of what happens in a police state. Teachers are under constant surveillance; their pasts are combed for signs of disloyalty; their utterances are watched for clues to dangerous thoughts. . . . Where suspicion fills the air and holds scholars in line for fear of their jobs, there can be no exercise of the free intellect . . . A problem can no longer be pursued with impunity to its edges . . . Instruction tends to be sterile; pursuit of knowledge is discouraged; discussion often leaves off where it should begin . . . This system of spying and surveillance cannot go hand in hand with academic freedom. It produces standardized thought, not the pursuit of truth."

There are several questionable assumptions in both contending liberal views connected with the failure to keep clearly in mind the distinction between freedom of speech and academic freedom. Undue reliance is placed on Justice Holmes' celebrated proposition "that the best test of truth is the power of thought to get itself accepted in the market-place." This principle may to some extent be applicable to discussions in the public forum and on the college campus, but can hardly serve as a guide to instruction in the classroom or lecture hall. Acceptance or nonacceptance is not the best test of truth in the scientific sense unless we so reinterpret the term "market" as to radically alter its ordinary meaning. The classroom is not a public forum; it has, to a large extent, the aspect of a captive audience. Discussion is only one aspect of scientific procedure; there is the matter of logic and experimental procedure, of the competence of the discussants.

Even in public affairs the free trade in ideas is questionable as a sufficient criterion for all issues. What is the test of the validity of racial segregation—its acceptance or nonacceptance by a particular community, or its concordance with the moral principle that all men are created equal? The *application* of any law in a democracy must reckon with the state of public opinion but this is a test of practical strategy not a test of validity. The test of *the truth* of any major social issue that the *school* deals with is never, strictly speaking, subject to anything that may be called a "market." The school's obligation is to follow established principles and to uphold warranted knowledge as against the views commonly held in the market-place. The competition is between scientific and critical beliefs, on the one hand, and popular emotional beliefs, on the other.

A second, and related, weakness of the liberalist position in its experimentalist as well as in its absolutist expositions is its one-sided emphasis on the school's function as an agency of free inquiry to the detriment of its responsibility as an agency for the inculcation of basic principles and the promotion of definite aims. Our schools must be committed to democracy not merely in terms of process and interpersonal attitudes but in terms of adherence to a pattern of beliefs and to a system of institutions that have been defined for us, in major exemplifications—although not absolutely, completely, or unchangeably—through a long historical experience. If this were kept in mind, it would not be necessary to engage in tortuous dialectical analysis to prove that members of the Communist Party—or, for that matter, convinced revolutionary Marxists not members of the party but merely fellow-travellers—lack the qualifications to teach in public schools.

An indispensable purpose of public education at the elementary and secondary levels is to teach good citizenship. This requires instilling faith in democracy, clarifying its meaning, appraising its achievements critically both on the positive and negative side. To do this fairly requires a belief in democracy in the first place, and a loyalty to its basic principles and institutions. It is not necessary to go to the length of proving that Communism represents a conspirational movement; it would be sufficient as far as qualification for teaching in the elementary and secondary grades to show that communist *belief* negates democratic *belief*. Professor Hook's admonition might be modified to read, Heresy, Yes! Disbelief, No!*

---

* I do not mean to justify the harassment to which teachers have been subjected in the wake of the Feinberg Law because of suspected affiliation with the Communist Party in years past. As administrated, the Feinberg Law has assumed the character of an *ex post facto* indictment. Nor, considering the circumstances, can the dismissal of teachers for use of the Fifth Amendment be regarded as a satisfactory solution—despite the fact that such use is rightly considered as incompatible with the teacher's obligation to be open and aboveboard. But we have caught the teachers on the hip and we ought not to judge them too harshly if they defend themselves by the means which legal counsel advises them is available to

In the sphere of higher education, however, a number of factors warrant a different position. Teaching in colleges and universities is to a large extent open to public view—to criticism by colleagues and to challenge by mature students. There is little chance for subversive propaganda to be introduced surreptitiously. Higher education, as well as elementary and secondary, has the obligation of supporting the democratic consititution under which it exercises the privileges of academic freedom, and the function also of advancing the universal values implicit in the national life. But the work of colleges and universities is not immediately directed toward, and certainly not confined to, the creation of good citizenship. Many of its professors are specialists in areas that have scant relationship to politics or to social philosophy. To be sure, personal associations and the organizational affiliations of teachers working in areas related to security problems—as for instance in atomic physics—cannot in this period of world conflict be disregarded.

Admitted Communist connection ought not of itself overbalance a record of competent service and a reputation for integrity. The burden of proof of subversive activity should rest on those who accuse, not on the accused, on the basis of tangible evidence and not on the assumption of association. Providing that the individual teachers' Communist commitment is open and aboveboard, the final decision should be left in institutions of higher learning to the uncoerced judgment of the faculty. This is essential if the spirit of academic freedom and professional ethics is to be preserved. On the other hand, it should be clear that the professor, as well as the teacher in the lower grades, has no unalienable *civil right* to his post. The future of academic freedom will depend on the courage, the fairness, and the discretion of university faculties in dealing with teachers of good character whose political and economic views are radical in the socialist and

them. For years, educational leaders have been preaching complete freedom of thought and affiliation and encouraging unqualified political criticism as a high virtue. Now we take advantage of those who have idealistically followed what authoritive leadership has defined as democracy. With reference to affiliation with the Communist Party *before the Feinberg Law was enacted*, I follow the "libertarian" view expounded by Justice Douglas. It goes without saying that teachers who have demonstrably violated the obligation of academic freedom in the classroom by carrying on propaganda or who have perjured themselves or engaged in subversive activities as proven by evidence that would stand up in the courts should be dismissed and should suffer the full penalties of the law.

Marxist sense or whose views differ from the majority on the matter of policy toward Communist powers, Communist plans for peace, and the like.

A service has been rendered by those who have labored to make clear that membership in the Communist Party is not to be taken lightly as a variant form of political affiliation comparable to membership in the democratic and republican parties. But, unavoidably in the context of the prevailing state of public opinion, the contribution thus made to the cause of academic freedom is questionable. The distinction between membership in the Communist Party and Marxist opinions which the intellectuals emphasize is not appreciated by the public or, for that matter, by all college authorities. The line between merely presenting and actually propounding Marxist teachings is likewise thin. And the distinction between Marxism and other forms of socialism, and between socialism and the New Deal, is of little concern to a large section of the anti-Communist wing who cry a plague on all these houses. In total effect, the anti-Communist agitation has cast a shadow of suspicion on deviating thought in the socioeconomic field.

Whether in a total summation there is less academic freedom than formerly is a complex question, particularly difficult to answer because there was so little genuine freedom of teaching before.[7] In some respects as in the religious area there is, no doubt, a greater latitude than a few generations ago. Big Business is less concerned than it was a generation ago about the economic theories of college professors. But against these advances we must reckon with the fact that the intrusion now comes from mass public opinion, from official state sources, from nationally organized efforts. Formerly, the intellectual world was united against encroachment; now the ranks of opposition have been broken. It cannot be denied that a damper has been placed on free discussion of political-economic questions which touch on socialism, communism, Marxism, and Russia. The situation described by Justice Douglas exists in a large area of the educational endeavor.

The remarks on the merits of the contending liberal positions on the Communist issue are incidental to the main point: at the root of the conflict among liberals on educational policy lies a deep-seated presupposition that complete neutrality on controversial social issues is desirable. This policy is a source of much equivocation. An educational institution should have a basic position on fundamental issues and state what degree of deviation it will permit in the various areas. If it has a quota of admission for various racial and religious groups, this should be avowed and defended as best it may. If it is not going to permit "leftists" to teach, this should be made known. The liberalist position which proclaims absolute freedom of thought is the more likely to decide that what was courageous heresy a few years ago is today treacherous conspiracy. There is an evil even worse than this that flows from the neutrality dogma—namely, the implication that there are no authoritative principles or standards of value. It is the doctrine of complete freedom of thought undirected by principles that has misled a generation of youth into perplexity and bewilderment. Absolutist experimentalism must share with "ritualist liberalism" the blame for the present confusion in educational theory.

4

Agreement on the ethical and political aspects of a democratic social philosophy would provide a positive basis for an educational policy. A consensus of working principles in harmony with American history and current trends of thought is in the making. However, a fully unified educational philosophy would need to go further: it would require a metaphysical orientation and thus trench upon religious doctrine. In this area, no general agreement can be expected. In the field of public education, strict neutrality in metaphysical position and in religious commitment must remain the rule. This is necessitated by the divergence of religious affiliations and is demanded by the accepted interpretation of the constitutional principle of the separation of church and state.

Read literally, the First Amendment which enjoins Congress from making any law respecting an establishment of religion does not of itself prescribe a strict "wall of separation" between church and state in the matter of education. This may have been intended by the chief sponsors of the inclusion in the fundamental American law of the Bill of Rights guaranteeing freedom of conscience. The First Amendment does not apply the principle of separation to the individual states, something that was achieved only by the Fourteenth Amendment of 1868, and even then only by inference. Also, the view that the First Amendment can be interpreted to mean "multiple establishment," that is, to permit state aid for denominational education provided that equal support is given to all sects, cannot be dismissed out of hand.[8]

In the early days of the Republic it was assumed that religious instruction was an indispensable part of education. Many of the state constitutions contain a clause favoring religion, and until the middle of the nineteenth century state support was frequently given to public educational bodies despite denominational affiliation. However, with the development of large urban centers and the increasing heterogeneity of the population, the threat to national unity inherent in religious education, necessarily denominational, became widely recognized by educators and statesmen. The growing secularism and religious liberalism attendant on industrialization and on the advance of science contributed to the movement of eliminating religious elements from state supported schools.[9]

As the American public school system became established throughout the country in the last quarter of the nineteenth century it assumed a predominantly secularist pattern. Vestiges of religious teaching remained, e.g., the recital of prayers, the singing of hymns, the public reading of the Bible, the celebration of Christmas and Easter as religious holidays. In some places, instruction in Christianity was retained as part of the regular program, the wearing of religious garb by public school teachers permitted, and the rental of church-owned buildings for public school purposes not infrequently practiced. In principle, however, the doctrine of the complete separation of church and state in education was almost universally accepted: by the end of the nineteenth century all but two of the states had laws or constitutional provisions prohibiting the teaching of religion in the public schools or the support of religious schools by public funds or both. At the beginning of our century, the present compromise arrangement with reference to the relation of the state to education was widely accepted. Parents may send their children to qualified religious schools in fulfillment of the compulsory education laws; but apart from the indirect subsidy through exemption from taxation such schools may not receive state aid; moreover, no religious instruction may be given under public school auspices or during the regular hours of public school attendance.

With varying interpretations as to the meaning of government aid and of religious instruction, these principles flowing from the doctrine of the separation of church and state have been sustained in the state and federal courts. In 1925, in the Oregon case, the United States Supreme Court confirmed the right of parents to send their children to private or parochial schools of their choice, at the same time asserting the right of the state to supervise such schools. Although challenged in the courts, Bible reading has been generally permitted without comment when state law does not prohibit it and no clear preference for the New as against the Old Testament is indicated. The Supreme Court of New Jersey, in defending the constitutionality of compulsory Bible reading, declared: "While it is necessary that there be a separation between church and state, it is not necessary that the state should be stripped of religious sentiment."

Both state and federal courts have ruled that public funds may be used at the discretion of each state to provide auxiliary services, e.g., textbooks and transportation to parochial schools and private schools on the same basis as to public schools. To support this decision, the "child benefit" theory was invoked—the principle that the state's obligation to serve the child should not be affected by the character of the school he attends. However, in the New Jersey Everson case (1947), in which the United States Supreme Court by a five to four decision held as constitutional the practice of using public funds to pay for bus transportation to Roman Catholic parochial schools, there was sharp dissent. Justice Rutledge in full analysis, voicing the opinion of the minority, denounced the decision as a clear violation of the First Amendment's prohibition of the establishment of religion in its original meaning as conceived by Jefferson and Madison and in its historical interpretation by the Supreme Court. "The prohibition broadly forbids state support, financial or other, of religion in any guise, form or degree. It outlaws all use of public funds for religious purposes."

A new issue is presented by the "release time" programs, of excusing pupils, usually for one hour a week, from their regular studies to receive religious instruction by denominational teachers, priest, minister, or rabbi. In the McCollum case (1948) which dealt with a release-time plan in Champaign, Illinois, where the religious instruction was carried on in the public school building, the State Supreme Court declared the practice unconstitutional despite the fact that Protestants, Catholics, and Jews were given equal consideration. The Court, by a nine-to-one decision, ruled that the compulsory school law and the tax-supported facilities of the public school were being exploited to promote sectarian education and that the principle of separation of church and state forbade utilizing its public school system "to aid any or all religious faiths or sects in the dissemination of their doctrines and ideals." This, the Court added, did not "manifest a governmental hostility to religion or religious teaching," which was a valid function of the church and home. But the public school as the most powerful agency for promoting national unity had to keep itself "free from entanglement in the strife of sects."

The majority of the Supreme Court took a different stand in the Zorach case in New York, where the release-time plan was instituted at the end of the school day and the instruction given off the school premises by each denomination in its own quarters. By a vote of six to three, the program was declared constitutional. Justice Douglas in delivering the majority opinion asserted: "We are a religious people whose institutions presuppose a Supreme Being. . . . When the state encourages religious instruction or cooperates with religious authorities by adjusting the schedules of public events to sectarian needs, it follows the best of our traditions. . . . Government may not finance religious groups nor undertake religious instruction or blend secular and sectarian education nor use secular institutions to force one or some religion on any persons. But we find no constitutional requirement which makes it necessary for government to be hostile to religion and to throw its weight against efforts to widen the effective scope of religious influence."

There was sharp retort on the part of the dissenting justices. Justice Black, writing the minority opinion, saw "no significant difference between the invalid Illinois system and that of New York here sustained." Both contained an element of coercion and incited sectarian distinctions. The assertion of the religious character of the American people implied a derogation of the nonreligious American, and the encouragement of cooperation with religious authorities represented an abandonment of traditional state neutrality as between believers and unbelievers. Justice Frankfurter, who strongly supported the dissenting opinion, suggested "dismissed time"—i.e., allowing all the children to be let out of school an hour earlier—as an expedient of avoiding discrimination between the religious and the nonreligious and eliminating the element of coercion and sectarian divisiveness.

5

The traditional conception of the relation of the state to religious education and the present legally sanctioned arrangements have the support of a large part of the community. Nevertheless, the situation represents an anomaly. Religion has entered into the very fabric of American civilization and in many ways still plays an important part in our culture. The majority of our people still associate their moral and spiritual values with religious sanctions and still adhere to some form of theism or deism. A large and leading part of the nation maintain an association with church or synagogue as communal agencies of charity and good works and as means of ethical as well as of religious development. Whatever element of the transcendental enters into common life comes largely through the ritual and conceptual resources provided by the religious institutions. On the other hand, the public school which preempts the instruction time of the child must exclude all religious teaching and in accord with the liberalist interpretation refuse to cooperate with the religious authorities in promoting religious education outside the school.

From this contradiction in the situation flow a number of serious difficulties. The retention of religious teaching often of a clearly denominational character contrary to the law has dubious moral consequences. It nourishes covert sectarian attitudes which work against American citizenship. In districts of mixed population with substantial minorities, a sense of alienation may be engendered which militates against full-fledged membership in a common community. The other extreme is an avoidance of dealing with religion, as far as this is possible, as if it were an object of taboo.[10] The exclusive concentration on secular studies tends to imply a depreciation of the attitudes and values represented by the religious allegiances. It may result in a dualistic intellectual standard amounting to a mental schism. Science and history are conceived as falling into the realm of truth, whereas to religion is rendered the acquiescence of uncritical faith. The youth grow up with immature views on religion acquired in childhood. General as well as religious education suffers from the duality of auspices, since the public school cannot develop its program on a consistent naturalist philosophy which the secular point of view implies.

In recent years, the question of the relation of the public schools to religion has again been opened up. The principle of the separation of church and state in education is no longer contested in principle but considerable difference of opinion persists as to its meaning in application. There is still some support for the introduction of a common core of religious instruction or of a form of prayer that might be acceptable to all denominations. This position assumes that moral and spiritual values require religious sanction. The view, nevertheless, meets with strong opposition from the religious as well as the secularist side. Religious groups oppose the common core and the general prayer as inadequate and as likely to suggest misleading connotations not in harmony with the denominational doctrinal commitments. Secularists view it as a serious breach in the principle of religious liberty, as an attempt to impose theistic views on persons who base their ethics on naturalistic and humanist philosophies. The attempt to inculcate faith in God by school regulation might properly be condemned by religious as well as secular opinion as opposed to genuine spiritual development, as more likely to induce insincerity than to secure belief.

The strongest opposition comes from those for whom "secularism" is a positive philosophy and not merely a negation of the traditional religious positions. According to this view the public school stands for an autonomous pattern of moral and spiritual values which, though rooted in Western religious and classical heritage, now represents a creative extension of its essential democratic doctrines of the dignity of the individual and the equality of all men. In the version expounded by John L. Childs, secularism is associated with the experimentalist conception of the morality of primary experience, continuous inquiry, and free communication. He believes that our secularist public school system is a genuine expression of the wishes of the American people, a response to the decline of sectarianism, supernaturalism, and of authoritarianism in morals as well as in doctrinal beliefs. To give religion any place in the public schools would be an invitation to clericalism and lead to a lowering rather than to a raising of the spiritual quality of American culture.[11]

Dr. Vivian T. Thayer, who maintains similar views as to the

positive significance of secularism, nevertheless regards it as compatible with diverse philosophic views and not of necessity bound to naturalism. He defines secularism as "an effort to carve out areas of common agreement and common action between people whose interests overlap and who disagree vigorously in matters they consider fundamental."[12] He recognizes the need of a sense of security on the part of the child with reference to his own religious and cultural background and the importance of encouraging an interest in the religious affiliations of his schoolmates. But Thayer as well as Childs would oppose any cooperation with the religious authorities, as in the matter of "release time."

American school administrators take a conciliatory position. With the secularists, they assert the significance of the public schools as promoters of moral and spiritual values which they identify with democratic ideals—respect for personality, tolerance of diversity, devotion to freedom of thought, and insistence on religious liberty.[13] Standing firmly on the principle of the separation of church and state, they oppose the introduction of religious instruction into the public schools in any form—either as a common core or in separate classes, for any denomination or for all denominations. They recognize the importance of religious faith in the development of the personality as a whole and in sustaining the common moral and spiritual values but maintain that such instruction must be left to the church and home. The public school can contribute by exercising care to avoid developing an anti-religious attitude, by inducing respect for religion, and by promoting tolerance of diversity of religious belief. Their major suggestion is that public schools should make provision for "factual study of religion" so as to develop an understanding of the role of religion in the development of civilization and of contemporary culture. As the Educational Policies Commission formulates it: "That religious beliefs are controversial is not an adequate reason for excluding teaching about religion from the public schools. Economic and social questions are taught and studied in the schools on the very sensible theory that students need to know the issues being faced and to get practice in forming sound judgments."[14]

This positive attitude toward religion marks an advance from the previous tendencies of indifference, avoidance, or depreciation. In an atmosphere of free inquiry much could be done by sympathetic teachers, themselves liberally educated, to further an understanding of the contribution of religion to Western thought and to convey an intimation of the possible significance of religious experience for personal development. But a truly objective treatment would require pointing up the negative as well as positive effects of religion, and it is doubtful whether such a critical analysis would be tolerated by those who are most insistent on the introduction of religious instruction in the public schools. Controversial issues in religion are obviously not analogous to conflicts of opinion in economic matters; the latter do not claim the authority of revelation. At best, knowledge *about* religion is a contribution to a rounded cultural development; it is not religious education in the sense used by its sponsors. The objective study of religion is as likely to lead to undermining the particular faith of the home and denomination to which the student belongs as to support it. The proposal made by the Educational Policies Commission does not touch the heart of the matter—the need of a better correlation between the education of family and church, on the one hand, and that of the public school, on the other.

To rely on the neutral public school for the major part of the child's education, leaving it to family and church to provide for the religious phase, does not yield a solution of the fundamental difficulty. The present arrangements do not allow the religious agencies fair opportunity for organizing supplementary instruction after school hours. The "release time" program has some value as a gesture of cooperation, but one period a week is insignificant as a contribution to religious knowledge and character. The plan of "dismissed time" suggested by Justice Frankfurter is better than released time, but it still leaves unresolved the problem of the conflict in basic philosophic orientation as between the public school and the church school. A consistent application of the secularist presuppositions implicit in much of the public school program involves a denial of the supernatural and theistic outlook. Before a genuine partnership between the two auspices can be achieved, they must come closer to each other in intellectual assumptions. This means that religion must, in its metaphysical foundations, move in the direction of a humanistic position; and that the public schools adopt a broader view of the nature of culture than implied in the usual scientific and secularist approach. Any genuine solution is difficult because the dualism between the religionist and the humanist philosophies represents a genuine conflict in Western civilization with deep historical roots.

As things stand, our public schools fall between two stools. They cannot develop their own programs on the thoroughly naturalistic basis congenial to their secularism. On the other hand, the major body of American educators look with disfavor on the parochial school and on the private school founded on definite systems of belief. The situation warrants a modification of the dominant view which regards the public school as the genuine American school and accords to other types only a none-too-friendly toleration. It is essential that the public school remain strong and that it retain its position as the main system. Since it is a state-maintained institution, there is little danger that it will lose its predominant place. But it should not have a monopoly on education. It is desirable that the public school move more consistently in the direction of a positive philosophy and serve more faithfully the needs of families whose moral and spiritual values are consciously rooted in humanistic and naturalistic presuppositions. But in the measure that it does so, educators must also grant to private schools the moral right to base their curricula on divergent patterns of social and ethical beliefs—religious as well as humanist.

Encouragement of minority schools within a broad framework of essentials is in the interest of a true freedom of thought. The experience of England indicates that a pluralistic system which includes denominational as well as non-denominational schools is compatible with the advance of liberal thought and with national unity. Today, when the encroachments come from the state and from mass opinion, private and religious institutions may offer greater protection for freedom of thought in political and economic questions than government maintained schools subject to local pressures.

The conflict between religion and science is not the central issue of our day. The battle has shifted to the arena of social problems. In the issues of racial equality, economic welfare, and international organization, the social-minded religionist and the liberal secularist have a common platform. From the point of view of the individual, a unified religious-intellectual-social outlook is requisite for the fully integrated personality. From the national point of view the major problem is to achieve a broad working unity of ethical-political-economic principles. To stress the importance of such a unity as a basis of educational policy has been the main purpose of this book.

NOTES

1. Howard Mumford Jones, editor, *Primer of Intellectual Freedom* (Harvard University Press, 1949), pp. 6-8.

2. New York *Times*, Sunday Magazine Section, March 27, 1949.

3. Arthur O. Lovejoy, "Academic Freedom," *Encyclopaedia of the Social Sciences* (The Macmillan Company, 1937).

4. Sidney Hook. *Heresy, Yes, Conspiracy, No* (John Day Company, 1953).

5. Arthur O. Lovejoy, "On a Supposed Resurgence of Vicious Intellectualism," *The Journal of Philosophy*, February 1952. Also, Sidney Hook, "Mindless Empiricism," in the same issue.

6. Howard Mumford Jones, editor, *op. cit.*, Introduction, p. xiii.

7. Milton R. Konvitz, "Are Teachers Afraid," also the comment by Sidney Hook in *The New Leader*, February 1956.

8. J. M. O'Neill, *Religion and Education Under the Constitution* (Harper & Brothers, 1949).

9. R. Freeman Butts, *The American Tradition in Religion and Education* (The Beacon Press, 1950).

10. Committee on Religion and Education, *The Function of the Public Schools in Dealing with Religion* (American Council on Education, 1953), pp. 12ff.

11. "Spiritual Values of the Secular Public School," in John S. Brubacker, editor, *The Public Schools and Spiritual Values* (Harper & Brothers, 1944), pp. 58ff.

12. "An Experimentalist Position," in F. Ernest Johnson, ed., *American Education and Religion* (Harper & Brothers, 1952).

13. Educational Policies Commission, *Moral and Spiritual Values in the Public School* (National Education Association, 1951).

14. *Ibid.*, p. 78.

PART FOUR

CONCLUSION: THE COMMUNITY AND
THE IDEAL

> Be loyal . . . So be loyal, that is, so seek,
> so accept, so serve your cause that thereby
> the loyalty of all your brethren throughout
> the world, through your example, through
> your influence, through your own love of
> loyalty wherever you find it, as well as
> through the sort of loyalty which you exem-
> plify in your deeds, shall be aided, furthered,
> increased so far as in you lies. . . . So be
> loyal to your own cause as thereby to serve
> the advancement of the cause of universal
> loyalty.
>
> —Josiah Royce
> *The Sources of Religious Insight*

16

CONCLUSION: THE COMMUNITY
AND THE IDEAL

IN THIS final chapter we may summarize the main line of thought and point up a number of applications to current issues in school policy.

THE COMMUNITY AND THE IDEAL

Education is at all times concerned with men-living-in-societies and its ends cannot be defined apart from a direct consideration of the character of the society into which the individual is to live. This approach stands at variance with the view that the purposes of education can be derived from metaphysics in the sense of an *a priori* conception of the nature of being. It is equally opposed to the contrary position that the aims of education are to be sought in biological process, in the natural history of man as a product of evolution. Some idea of man's relation to the cosmic order lies in the background of every educational philosophy; and the biological drives require attention in the analysis of the methods and objectives of education. But neither the former view of the nature and destiny of man which we may call the supernatural, or the latter, which we may term the subhuman, can be taken as the basis of major educational policy. Only a study of the history of man as creator and creature of civilization can give us a clue to man's distinctive nature, and provide us with the educational principles needed to bring about a progressive fulfilment of man's deepest and highest purposes and thus achieve self-realization.

Philosophy of education is an aspect of social philosophy. As such, it revolves around two opposing but complementary poles of reference. In classical parlance, we may designate the one as "ethics," the other as "politics." In the context of the present discussion, the former may be termed "the ideal," the latter, "the community." The one is reminiscent of the Platonist Idea of the Good—a unity of truth with a rational good that includes beauty. It points to a way of life consonant with man's highest nature, to a pattern of enduring universal values. The second refers to the Aristotelian proposition that man is a political animal, or civic creature. It draws attention to the fact that men *naturally* live in societies. A corollary is: men live not in society in general, but in definite communities, under specific types of government, institutional structures, and economic systems.

These two concepts—ideal and community—are distinct but not disparate. The ethical life can be lived only within a society and the communal life is impossible without a communion of ideas and values. In all societies—except the primitive perhaps—there is a distance between the ideally conceived way of life and the existing social order. In some instances the gap is so great that the idea of the good can be pursued only outside the political frame—in the monastery or in the Epicurean garden, in the ivory tower of contemplative philosophy or in the mystical communion with a transcendent reality. In the favorable situation—as in the democratic society—the opposition between the actual and the ideal creates a tension which impels toward the ever-greater embodiment of the ideal in the life of the individual and of the nation.

Every philosophy true to its Athenian origin will endeavor to see the individual in relation to his community and will strive for a harmony between the actual and the ideal. When something of the rational and ethical ardor that moved Plato invests a philosophy, the reconciliation it achieves will never be reduced to a practical and static compromise. It will direct the existing social order toward the ideally conceived republic. Chastened by historical experience, the social philosopher of today will not conceive the ideal in terms of utopian perfection. Impressed with the consciousness of the dimension of time, he will see it in continuity with history, emerging out of the existent.

NEITHER ABSOLUTISM NOR EXPERIMENTALISM

In its affirmation of the need of directing education by ideas, by universal principles and ends, the position here advanced is in accord with the perennialist outlook. In total conception, however, the educational philosophy expounded runs counter to the absolutist metaphysical premise which usually is brought in to support the concept of enduring values, namely, the assumption that the ground of universal ethical principles lies in a cosmic sphere outside the realm of human experience. The presupposition that man is essentially a social being implies a humanist interpretation. Education, it is maintained, must be based on ideas and beliefs, but ideas and beliefs must be warranted by human experience. Ideals transcend the experience of individuals and of particular societies, but they have no source or sanction except in the experience and visions of men living in distinctive communities. Although the concepts of justice and law, of freedom and equality, of individuality and fraternity represent enduring values, what these general ideas signify is inconceivable except in terms of social life and the content of their meaning varies with different societies and at different periods.

The educational philosophy proposed is in substance and outlook closer to the Deweyan view, which regards education as a social process and affirms democracy as its basis. But issue is taken with the metaphysics of continuous change with which the Dewey philosophy has become associated. The doctrine of the ever-changing leads to an underestimation of institutional stability as the foundation of continuity and progress. In the usual interpretation, experimentalism, confusing the definite idea with the fixed idea, deters from the clear expression of the principles and objectives of the good society. It induces an easy readiness to accept the new without setting forth the criteria of acceptance. It praises the method of cooperation without discriminating between the purposes for which we should cooperate and for which we should refuse to cooperate. Its conception of cooperation as interaction among individuals lacks a realistic consideration of the sociological mold in which interpersonal relations are carried on. As a result of its neglect to set forth clear aims and to describe structure, the definition of experimentalism becomes vague. In an era that requires decisiveness, it encourages an indecisive temper.

Despite its earnest social emphasis, the experimentalist interpretation of experience retains an individualistic bias. The reiteration of the principle that education must be based on experience—"which is always the actual life-experience of some individual"—introduces an element of ambiguity. Is this a methodological or a normative principle? That individual experience can properly and advantageously be

282 THE IDEAL AND THE COMMUNITY

used in the teaching procedures none will deny. That in some sense education represents a reconstruction of individual experience may perhaps, as a description of psychological process, be defended. But obviously enough, education's purpose is to substitute communally validated experience for the limited and inadequate experience of the individual. If the word "based" is to be used with any degree of accuracy, then we must say that education must be based not on individual experience but on accumulated and criticized social experience, on ascertained knowledge, and on warranted beliefs. Likewise the concept of critical intelligence as "thinking for oneself" is questionable. Critical thinking depends on full and accurate knowledge, on making proper assumptions, on following logical principles. The experimentalist conception of intelligence is too broad to be of real use in concrete cases. The method of effective thinking varies with the subject matter and with the area of activity.

Another element in the Deweyan philosophy which prevents a consistent application of the social principle is the overevaluation of the biological component in cultural formation. The experimentalist draws false inferences from the Darwinian evolutionary hypothesis. The demonstration of the descent of man from the lower species might be regarded as a confirmation of the traditional insight that man has an animal side to contend with, that the instinctual elements in the soul are in potential conflict with the rational tendencies. In exalting the "life process" as such, the naturalist view has tended to make the biological drives not only sources of vital energy nourishing the creative human achievements but guiding principles paramount in normative significance with the ideal ends of social life. Experimentalism overemphasizes the function of mind in its instrumentalist aspect as a means of survival and adaptation. It underrates indirectly the part that mind in its imaginative aspect plays in creating man's universe of art and literature, of religion and of philosophy. The Deweyan endeavor to achieve a biosocial synthesis turns out to be a *tour de force* which misses the main issue—the conflict between the natural-biological and the moral-cultural.

MAN AS CULTURAL, HISTORICAL, COMMUNAL

Experimentalism moved in the direction of an emphasis on the cultural; in his later writings Dewey referred to his view as "cultural naturalism." But it never crossed the bridge into the new territory. Its stress on naturalism with its Darwinian undertow represented in part an attack against supernaturalism with its connotation of an extra-mundane source of authority. It was this preoccupation with opposition to traditional religious conceptions and forms which diverted the experimentalist from a consistent following of the positive and social emphasis. The true antithesis to supernaturalism, it is suggested, is not naturalism but humanism. An unqualified cultural humanism is proposed as a substitute for the ambiguous cultural naturalism of the experimentalist.

Man is a creature of culture and not of nature. What man's original nature is can never be divined from a study of his biological constitution or from an inquiry into man's origin in the distant past of evolutionary development. Man's nature can be inferred only indirectly from a study of his achievements in civilized society. Man's unique character is revealed in two dimensions: through the institutions he has developed to fufil his biological needs in distinctive human ways; and in his aspirations for beauty, for truth, and for goodness, as expressed in literature and science, in music and art, in philosophy and religion.

As a creature of culture, man is also a "historical animal." To achieve full stature as men, we need to identify ourselves with the career of man in time. It is necessary to add that history is not only a recollection of events that are past and gone, but also a recovery of the prophets' vision of man's future destiny. Besides cultural and historical, a third term, namely "communal," is needed to give full-bodied meaning to the concept of man as a social being. Men live in communities—not merely in societies. Community implies "belonging" as well as associating; it involves a sense of common destiny and imposes an obligation of loyalty. Community implies common material interests and at the same time a bond of common ideas and aspirations.

The pivotal communities in our society are the family, the church, and the nation. Each represents a compound of material interests and ideal concerns, each supplements and checks the other. The loyalties which each community inspires and demands may become narrow and fanatical negating the humane ethics which it is their intent to embody. But if the purpose of drawing out our common human nature is not to evaporate into an empty intellectual abstraction and if the initiation into the great society of mankind is to be more than a sentimental hope, the individual must become involved in a plurality of communal loyalties. It is through identification with the communities of family, church, and nation, not through transcending them, that one becomes part of the historical and international world order.

The self cannot develop morally or spiritually in separation from the responsibilities and opportunities of community life. Neither the concept of self-realization through interpersonal relations nor the idea of self-transcendence through the identification with cosmic forces provides a basis for educational development.* Two roads are open to the growth and humanization of the self—one is through participation in the life of organized society, the other is through self-identification with the pattern of ideas correlated with the social organization. Both ways are indispensable. Through the struggle of the self to reconcile its several communal loyalties, and through the conflict between concern for the survival of the communities to which the individual belongs and commitment to their cultural, ethical and spiritual values, the individual achieves self-realization.

The self retains a consciousness of uniqueness never perhaps identifying itself completely with any single historical or social order. A residue of alienation may remain and the need of communion with the Source of Being may persist. The sense of unity with a transcendent reality may accompany our activities as with a sustaining obligato. But when, in the endeavor to attain spiritual perfection, the self becomes separated from the community, it must in the end fall back into the pit of self-annihilation, as in the meditative ecstasy of the

---

* In his high-minded book, *The Human Career* (Harper & Brothers, 1955), Robert Ulich presents "a philosophy of self-transcendence." He recognizes man's responsibility to himself and to his society. But he makes the identification of the self with cosmic forces the cornerstone of his educational fundamentals. Unwittingly, he shifts attention away from consideration of economic and political problems and places in the focus of attention "common participation in the world of mind."

It may be true, as Ulich says, that the lack of a metaphysical orientation may lead to a shallow "materially informed and busy society." But it would seem there is a greater danger—that the ethical impulse, divorced from central concern with social issues, will be dissolved in the stream of the transcendental consciousness and become no more than a self-indulgent moral tranquillizer with no genuine potency for advancing the life of the individual or of society.

Nirvana of Buddhism or, far worse, as in the despairing negations of contemporary existentialism.

EDUCATION AS ACCULTURATION AND IDEALIZATION

Education involves inducting the individual into the communities on which he depends for his material welfare, his cultural development, and his spiritual growth. The process of socialization includes two overlapping aspects which may be respectively designated "acculturation" and "idealization."

Acculturation signifies bringing up the individual to live on a satisfactory level of effectiveness and decency in the existing state of society. It includes the essentialist's purpose of the transmission of the social heritage, or looking at the matter from the point of view of the learner, as "the acquisition of the arts, the sciences, and the moral attitudes of civilization." It connotes the concept of adjustment to the existing society, to enable the individual "to get on in the world" and "to keep society as a going concern."[1] It involves the study of literature and music, of the civic and religious institutions. No definition of the purpose of education is adequate which does not include these fundamentals as a prerequisite purpose.

In the conservative versions of the definition of acculturation, the purpose of the school is limited to the "reproduction of the social type." The second term "idealization" is introduced to emphasize that the school has the purpose also of "growth beyond the type." As Jacques Maritain says: "If an accepted culture is permeated with errors, cruelty or slavery, the task of education is not to perpetuate it but to strive to change it."[2] To change society, means not only to correct errors—it implies reform in the light of the ideal implicit in its own cultural heritage. Idealization means transcending the conventional and the local. It requires seeing the present in its historical perspective; this means viewing it in relation not only to the past but also in relation to dynamic possibilities.

Both these conceptions, education as acculturation and education as idealization require relating education to a definite society and to a definite cultural pattern of values, not to society in general or to ideals in general. Only as we see the universal within the particular—the national ideal within the local, the international within the national, the enduring within the present, can we avoid meaningless generalities.

Every definition of education—transmission of the social heritage, education as social adjustment, or as personal growth, moral development, intellectual discipline—remains formal and empty of content unless the definition is related to a definite society, marked by a definite political system and economic order.

THE AMERICAN NATION AND THE UNIVERSAL DEMOCRATIC IDEAL

Applying the foregoing assumptions to the problem of education in the United States means relating the philosophy and the content of school work to the national life. Only as we view the task of education in terms of the practical and cultural, the social and spiritual needs of children and youth as potential members of American society in its various institutional and communal manifestations, is it possible to formulate the aims, the content, and the methods of education with any degree of clarity or definiteness. Only as we do so can we nurture the necessary moral commitments as well as develop the relevant knowledge, inspire loyalties as well as enlarge the outlook.

To make the nation the core of consideration implies neither a narrow patriotism nor a policy of isolation. America represents for its citizens an inclusive community of economic, political, and cultural interests which transcend the limitations of region, race, and denomination. Through the American heritage of history and literature, we become linked with the course of European thought and Western civilization. Through America's involvement in international affairs we are made part of the emerging world order. It is a function of education to promote a concern for the national security and well-being and to nourish a respect for its institutions and traditions. At the same time, it is imperative to guard against abetting any inclination toward chauvinism or sanctioning blind worship of the past. Education has a positive task to develop an understanding of how deeply-rooted American spiritual values are in the history of Western civilization and how closely bound is our destiny with that of the rest of the world.

Education for American life entails the affirmation of democracy as the unifying and directing principle. Democracy, as a social philosophy, represents the contemporary embodiment of the Western ethical and political tradition. Its twofold theme of the unique value of each person and of the unity of the human race may be traced to Biblical origins. Its high appreciation of the scientific attitude of inquiry is the modern version of the Hellenic devotion to the pursuit of truth through reason. Its conception of law as based on universal principles amenable in application to the will of the people in public assembly is likewise an outgrowth of classical conceptions. The democratic constitution represents the accumulated political wisdom of the ages. It is founded on the principle of inalienable human rights and it provides for the application of these principles to changing conditions of life and thought. It places responsibility for decisions in the hands of the majority, protects the minority in its elementary rights and in its place in government, and gives a basis for support of family and church communities. American democracy recognizes the importance of education for the maintenance of the constitution of the state, but allows the school a measure of autonomy; it protects the right of parents to bring up their children in harmony with their spiritual beliefs.

To instill faith in these principles is a primary responsibility of the school. In no smaller degree, is it the school's duty to subject the existing achievement to critical analysis—to point out failures as well as successes and to lead to an understanding of the problems involved in a better embodiment of democratic principles.

As we view the course of development of the democratic idea since its formulation in the opening paragraphs of the Declaration of Independence and in the Constitution we may assert with confidence that progress has been made in the implementation of the humane conceptions of these historic documents. But as we face the new era with its demand for equality, freedom, and well-being for all peoples, the gap between promise and fulfilment looms large. The principles of equality have been flagrantly violated in racial relations; discrimination against religious minorities, though less virulent than against colored peoples, remains a characteristic feature of American life in many sections of the country. Whatever advances have been made, have been forced by the pressure of "politics" and the need of survival rather than by regard for the principle of "a general equality of condition" as basic for true democracy. The social scene is still marred by class inequality and by a compulsive drive for financial success as a prerequisite for social position. Our support of measures designed to strengthen international comity has been halting and vacillating, comporting ill with the role of democratic world leadership which the course of history has assigned to us. As a result of compromise, expediency, and indecision, the influence of the idea of democracy as a moral force in the world has seriously weakened.

It is imperative in this age to go beyond the liberalism of the nineteen twenties which in the words of James Harvey Robinson, one of its outstanding exponents, had "no reforms to recommend, except the liberation of intelligence."* The following broad principles must be made directives:

1. Affirmation of the principles of the Constitution—subject to interpretation by the courts and to legislative enactments—as the framework of government.

2. Renewal of emphasis on the Bill of Rights, particularly on freedom of political and economic discussion in the public forum and in the academic hall.

3. Commitment to the unqualified application of the principle of equality for all races and nations in law, politics, economics, education, and social relations, at home and abroad.

4. Promotion of a welfare economy through extension of social security, public housing, health services, and educational facilities, and redirection of the free-enterprise system under government leadership toward an ever more satisfactory realization of equality of opportunity and of condition.

5. Support of the United Nations and of the Universal Declaration of Human Rights and encouragement of all other regional and international agencies devoted to the advancement of a world economic order, the maintenance of international law, and the strengthening of collective security.

Taken together, these principles represent a pattern of values and imply a program of action. They are not, of course, to be inculcated as abstract doctrines or interpreted in utopian terms. What each principle means in application is to be determined empirically with full consideration of technical advice; the strategy of implementation must have a regard for national public opinion. The school cannot of itself build a new social order. But there are already forces in the community—trends of thought and political activities—working toward a

---

* Quoted by Morton C. White, *Social Thought in America,* (p. 194) in the chapter "The Twenties" in which he subjects to spirited analysis the views of Dewey, Veblen, and Justice Holmes.

more consistent embodiment of the democratic promise. Cooperating with the liberal movements in the community—cultivating competent knowledge related to democratic purposes, upholding the national welfare against partisan and regional interests, relating the national good to international perspective—the school can aid greatly in transforming the climate of opinion and advancing the realization of avowed ideals. If, on the other hand, it remains beating about the bush in evasive neutralism, it becomes a negative force compounding the confusion and the disillusionment of the age.

LIBERAL EDUCATION FOR DEMOCRACY

In the elementary and secondary fields, there is a growing recognition that education as preparation for citizenship cannot be divorced from concern with contemporary political and economic issues, and that the acceptance of democracy as an underlying principle means the direction of education toward definite social ends. Higher education lags behind, still guided largely by individualistic purposes—on the one hand by the vocational aim of professional training, on the other hand by the idea of liberal education as the pursuit of culture in the pure. The former at least provides us with well-trained lawyers, physicians, engineers, and scientists in many fields. Liberal education, as conceived by some of its ardent advocates, is calculated to produce a caste of Brahmins indifferent to social welfare.

The modern humanistic view of a liberal education is a far cry from its original classic conception. In Athens, where it had its beginnings, education was conceived in terms of a balanced development of body and mind, the development of mind being conceived as the harmonious cultivation of the intellectual, aesthetic, and moral aspects of personality. The conception was never an individualistic one; its ethical ideal was always related to the political life. The concept of liberal education as propounded by Cicero and Quintilian meant a broad education not in the sense of a general education without purpose, but a broad education of the "orator" as a man of public affairs. Despite its mainly practical aim, the Roman conception of liberal education emphasized the obligation of the educated class to be concerned with the welfare of the state. In the period of the Renaissance, when the idea of a liberal education was revived, the "education of the gentleman" was not conceived as an education for leisure, but as the all-round education of the man of affairs.

Liberal education today has largely lost its earlier central reference to social life and politics. As expounded by typical representatives, its interests are literary and humanistic rather than socially humane. It reflects an upper class orientation toward life which characterizes an interest in social betterment as "damp humanitarianism."[3] It is not friendly to democracy as a social philosophy. Its conservatism expresses itself in the doctrine of noninvolvement in controversial issues. Its emphasis on abstract intellectual discipline too easily becomes a means of drawing thought away from its application to current affairs.

The traditional purpose of liberal education to secure for the individual and for the community a high level of cultural life remains indispensable in educational philosophy. Liberal education is properly conceived as a balanced program of studies in the humanities, the natural sciences, and the social studies. The distinction between education and professional training, the emphasis on basic principles as against factual instruction, the insistence on recourse to classics—these and similar principles urged by the proponents of liberal education are welcome. But these invaluable elements in the program of liberal education are bowdlerized when it is divorced from concern with present-day economic and political problems. Liberal education implies a pursuit of knowledge and truth in the spirit of objective understanding and aesthetic appreciation. But it entails more than passive absorption; it means grasping the significance of the great ideas in science, in philosophy, and in religion for the enhancement of the quality of life. It means building ideas firmly into character so that they become directives for the guidance of personal life and for the improvement of the life of society.

Liberal education misses its goal if it fails to make central the ethical-political theme of Western civilization. As Professor E. L. Woodward rightly says: "The Western tradition so strong and yet so intangible, so full of paradoxes, as one might say, so given to heresy—this Western tradition has one constant feature about it; it is concerned above all with men and society. Western thought in its main lines of development is neither defeatist nor quietist in regard to politics."[4] The great European thinkers—Plato, Aristotle and Aquinas, Locke, Mill and Rousseau—have been studied to little purpose, if this central point has not been grasped.

Three aspects of study are particularly significant for an education that will be liberal in the broad political and humanist sense. One is the history of political theory, the philosophy and practice of government. The second is the study of the growth of Western law from its origin in classic times and in its development through American constitutional law. It is in law that we find embodied ethical conceptions as they arise out of, and are refracted by, economic interests and political organization. The third is education which endeavors to realize the envisioned ethical ideal ever more fully in the lives of persons and of societies. A course in the history and problems of education viewed in the light of philosophical conceptions and cultural forces offers a broad foundation for an integrated liberal program of studies.

Liberal education, it should be clear, is not concerned with a preservation of the past as such but with the enrichment of the present and the advance toward the future. As Whitehead has said: "The present is all there is. It is holy ground; for it is the past; and it is the future."[5] A liberal education will include a study of contemporary literature, of present-day religious tendencies, and of the current social philosophies including communism and fascism. In the study of contemporary affairs, there will be, as in the study of the ideas of earlier periods, an element of factual observation and detached description. But the requirement of a liberal education will not be fulfilled by an ethical and political neutralism. In all true liberal education there is implicit a standard of judgment—the degree to which any system of ideas advances the spiritual insights and growing democratic ideal of Western civilization.

REORIENTATION IN TEACHER EDUCATION

The teacher whatever his individual attainments and however humble his position formerly represented in his person a cultural tradition and a community purpose. When education was still associated with religion, the teacher, whatever his private views and however provincial the attitudes of the region in which he taught, stood as the symbol of universal enduring values. As long as the classic studies had an important place in the curriculum, the pedagogue embodied a respect for scholarship, however deficient in learning he might himself have been. Traditionally, the image of the teacher in the ideal at least called to mind the highest moral and cultural aims of the civilization of which he was a part.

Under the pressure of modern forces—the growing complexity of knowledge, the decline of the classical-religious pattern, the development of mass education at the high school as well as at the elementary level—the figure of the teacher has changed. At the college level, he is likely to be a specialist appreciated for his contributions to research rather than for his breadth of cultural background. He tends to be isolated not only from teachers in other departments but also, not seldom, from the religious and civic activities of the community. At the elementary levels, the teacher is valued as a skillful pedagogue and guardian *in loco parentis*. The conception of the high school teacher is, at present, confused, a blur between specialist in a branch of subject-matter and of expert in guidance counselling.

Professional training has had an enormous influence for good in the improvement of teaching at the elementary and, in some aspects, at the junior high school, levels. Academic critics of the concentration on psychology and pedagogy in schools for the training of teachers frequently exhibit a lack of understanding of the extraordinarily difficult problems involved in the great democratic endeavor to educate all the people, of different cultural backgrounds, for the variety of vocations in life. Too often, also, they reveal not only a lack of sympathy with the burdens of the teacher but also an absence of concern with the needs and difficulties of the main body of children and youth who attend our public schools. But it is not to be denied that something essential has been lost in the contemporary concepts of the teacher as pedagogue and custodian to the neglect of his character as a representative of a cultural tradition and as an agent of a community ideal.

Under the influence of the psychological guidance trend and of the progressivist emphasis on present-day living, the history of education has been eliminated in many institutions from the requirements for the certification of teachers. In many teacher-training courses, formerly, the history of education was the main—sometimes the only— subject which gave opportunity for the discussion of fundamental educational ideas in the light of philosophic principles and social forces. The study of the history of education gave a sense of the continuity of Western thought; it liberated from indoctrination in one-sided views of current educational cultists. Nor has the elimination of the history of education been compensated by the introduction of courses in contemporary educational thought. The study of ideas is sacrificed to the study of method.

The program of teacher-training requires reorientation to restore the image of the teacher as a bearer of the cultural heritage and as representative of the moral aims of the community. Professional training in pedagogy and psychology is necessary—desirable for the college instructor as well as indispensable for the earlier stages of teaching. But professional training should not be at the expense of the broad education of the teacher as cultivated person. This means that the training of the teacher should have as basis a general liberal education —a reformed liberal education which will embrace the humanities, the general principles of natural science, and give a central place to the study of contemporary social issues. It implies, moreover, that the social studies—to include economics, politics, and constitutional law —are to be carried on not in the Olympian spirit of academic neutrality and unconcern but in the humane, though dispassionate, spirit that has characterized Western philosophy—which at its best has aimed for a reconciliation of the ethical and the political.

The teacher should be led to see himself in the perspective of history as a carrier of enduring values—more, as an active co-worker with the religious leader and with the statesman in the age-long endeavor to bring about an ever more satisfactory realization of the ideal, in the life of the individual, of the nation, and of the world community.

NOTES

1. Herbert C. Morrison, *The Curriculum of the Common School* (University of Chicago Press, 1940), p. 1.
2. Jacques Maritain, *Education at the Crossroads* (Yale University Press, 1943), p. 99.
3. Gordon Keith Chalmers, *The Republic and the Person* (Henry Regnery and Co., 1952).
4. E. L. Woodward, "Liberty and Democracy," in *The Western Tradition* (The Beacon Press, 1951).
5. Quoted by Sidney Hook, *Education for Modern Man* (The Dial Press, 1946), p. 71.

Index

Set in Linotype Electra
Format by Marguerite Swanton
Manufactured by The Haddon Craftsmen, Inc.
Published by HARPER & BROTHERS, New York